ATRAVESADOS

Children's Literature Association Series

ATRAVESADOS
Essays on Queer Latinx Young Adult Literature

Edited by Trevor Boffone and Cristina Herrera
Afterword by Frederick Luis Aldama

University Press of Mississippi / Jackson

The University Press of Mississippi is the scholarly publishing agency of
the Mississippi Institutions of Higher Learning: Alcorn State University,
Delta State University, Jackson State University, Mississippi State University,
Mississippi University for Women, Mississippi Valley State University,
University of Mississippi, and University of Southern Mississippi.

www.upress.state.ms.us

Chapter Two, "When Bisexuality Is Spoken: Normalizing Bi Latino Boys in Adam Silvera's *They Both Die at the End*," was first published in
Research on Diversity in Youth Literature 4, no. 2 (2022).

Chapter Thirteen, "Imagining the Future: The (Im)Possibilities of Queerness in Two Latinx Speculative Young Adult Novels," was first published in
Label Me Latina/o 11 (2021).

Any discriminatory or derogatory language or hate speech regarding race, ethnicity, religion, sex, gender, class, national origin, age, or disability that has been retained or appears in elided form is in no way an endorsement of the use of
such language outside a scholarly context.

The University Press of Mississippi is a member
of the Association of University Presses.

Copyright © 2025 by University Press of Mississippi
All rights reserved
Manufactured in the United States of America
∞

Library of Congress Cataloging-in-Publication Data

Names: Boffone, Trevor, editor. | Herrera, Cristina, editor. |
Aldama, Frederick Luis, 1969– writer of afterword.
Title: Atravesados : essays on queer Latinx young adult literature /
edited by Trevor Boffone and Cristina Herrera ; afterword by Frederick Luis Aldama.
Description: Jackson : University Press of Mississippi, 2025. |
Series: Children's literature association series |
Includes bibliographical references and index.
Identifiers: LCCN 2024043044 (print) | LCCN 2024043045 (ebook) |
ISBN 9781496854483 (hardback) | ISBN 9781496854490 (trade paperback) |
ISBN 9781496854506 (epub) | ISBN 9781496854513 (epub) |
ISBN 9781496854520 (pdf) | ISBN 9781496854537 (pdf)
Subjects: LCSH: Young adult fiction, American—History and criticism. |
American fiction—Hispanic American authors—History and criticism. |
Hispanic Americans in literature. | Sexual minorities in literature. |
Teenagers in literature. | LCGFT: Literary criticism. | Essays.
Classification: LCC PS374.Y57 A87 2025 (print) | LCC PS374.Y57 (ebook) |
DDC 813/.60935266—dc23/eng/20241107
LC record available at https://lccn.loc.gov/2024043044
LC ebook record available at https://lccn.loc.gov/2024043045

British Library Cataloging-in-Publication Data available

Dedication

To all the queer Latinx teens

Contents

Acknowledgments xi

Introduction: Ni de aquí ni de allá: Queering Latinidad, Latinicizing Young Adult Literature 3
Trevor Boffone and Cristina Herrera

Section One: Articulating the Spectrum of Queer Latinidad

Chapter One. "He Could Still Hear Muffled Voices": Materializing Queer Latinidad in Aiden Thomas's *Cemetery Boys* 25
Alexander Lalama

Chapter Two. When Bisexuality Is Spoken: Normalizing Bi Latino Boys in Adam Silvera's *They Both Die at the End* 41
Trevor Boffone

Chapter Three. Latinx Queer Worldmaking: Boys Loving Boys in Latinx Children's and Young Adult Literature and Film Adaptations 56
T. Jackie Cuevas

Chapter Four. "Everyone Is Gay": Queer Latina Identity in Isabel Millán's *Chabelita's Heart* and Gabby Rivera's *Juliet Takes a Breath* 69
Sonia Alejandra Rodríguez

Section Two: Queerness and Bodies in Transformation

Chapter Five. Transformation and the Queer Latinx Body in the Collected Works of Anna-Marie McLemore 85
Cristina Rhodes

Chapter Six. "We Are Something New": Disability and Latinx Adolescence in Mia García's *The Resolutions* 99
   Cristina Herrera

Chapter Seven. "Breathing Room": Sustaining Queer Brown Socialities in the Latinx Bildungsroman 116
   Joseph Isaac Miranda

Section Three: (Alternative) Spaces of Queer Latinidades

Chapter Eight. Queering TikTok: Gen Z's Latinx BookTok and Adam Silvera's *They Both Die at the End* 133
   Trevor Boffone

Chapter Nine. Sideways Latinx Queerness in Young Adult Video Games: *Life Is Strange 2* and *Gone Home* 148
   Regina Marie Mills

Chapter Ten. Atravesando Nepantla: Queer Familia in Chicanx and Mexican Young Adult Novels 163
   Jesus Montaño and Regan Postma-Montaño

Section Four: Queer Futurities

Chapter Eleven. Roses and Remedios: La Llorona's Queer Children in *When the Moon Was Ours* 180
   Domino Renee Pérez

Chapter Twelve. "Silence, at Least Right Now, Equals My Survival": The Absence of AIDS in the *Aristotle and Dante* Series 195
   Angel Daniel Matos

Chapter Thirteen. Imagining the Future: The (Im)Possibilities of Queerness in Two Latinx Speculative Young Adult Novels 209
   Cristina Rhodes

Afterword: Daydreams Made Real: New Narrative Maps of Resplendent Queer Latinx Futurities 222
   Frederick Luis Aldama

About the Contributors 229

Index 233

Acknowledgments

We wish to thank the entire staff at the University Press of Mississippi, especially Katie Keene and Katie Turner, for a wonderful second experience publishing with them. Thank you to the anonymous peer reviewers for helping us improve the quality of this book. We thank our contributors for lending their time and expertise to this collection. As always, Frederick Luis Aldama has been a tremendous source of inspiration and support, and we appreciate all he's done for us and the field. Additional thanks to Portland State University for research support. Thank you to the editors of *Label Me Latina/o* and *Research on Diversity in Youth Literature* for giving us permission to reprint selected chapters.

This work would not be possible without the unwavering support we both receive at home. To Kris and Kayla, thank you for your love and especially your patience throughout this project.

Of course, it takes a village, and our village is filled with furry ones. To Cindy, Cleo, Teddy, and Pickles, thank you for the warm snuggles, purrs, and allowing us to give you belly rubs.

ATRAVESADOS

Introduction

Ni de aquí ni de allá

Queering Latinidad, Latinicizing Young Adult Literature

Trevor Boffone and Cristina Herrera

In addressing the future of queer young adult (YA) literature in their foundational volume, *The Heart Has Its Reasons: Young Adult Literature with Gay/Lesbian/Queer Content, 1969–2004* (2006), Michael Cart and Christine Jenkins pose the following questions to scholars, students, and readers to evaluate realistic and relatable queer texts for youth: "Does it have not only an authentic but an original voice? Does it offer fresh insights into the lives of GLBTQ people? Does it offer other innovations in terms of narrative strategy, structure, theme? Or is it the same old story, told in the same old way that readers have encountered countless times in the past?" (166). Their provocative questions call on YA writers to reject the common early storylines in this genre's emergence that far too often relied on plot tropes of suicide, gay-bashing, homophobia, or eventual straightness that needed to be coaxed out from the "phase" of queerness. Indeed, in the almost two decades after their publication, it is safe to say that the concerns raised by Cart and Jenkins have largely been answered by Latinx YA writers who engage with queer content, themes, and characters. What *has not* changed so much, unfortunately, is another version of the "same old story," the overall paucity of literary scholarship on queer Latinx YA literature.

In the spirit of Cart and Jenkins's collection and others, which we will discuss throughout this collection, *Atravesados: Essays on Queer Latinx Young Adult Literature* shows how Latinx queer YA writers discard the "same old story," offering critical representations of queerness that broaden the vibrant field of YA writing to insist on the presence of queer teens of color. Our title draws on foundational Chicana queer theorist Gloria Anzaldúa's notion of "atravesados" to speak to the spectrum of queer youth Latinidades as they materialize in YA literature. Los atravesados, according to Anzaldúa, are "The squint-eyed, the perverse, the queer, the troublesome, the mongrel, the mulato, the half-breed, the half dead; in short, those who cross over, pass over, or through the confines of the 'normal'" (*Borderlands* 3). Los atravesados reside in the borderlands space of ni de aquí ni de allá, neither here nor there, present yet liminal, their queerness the very source of both frustration and empowerment, a paradox of joy and tragedy. Although written in 1987, Anzaldúa's theory speaks to the realities of queer Latinx teens that fill the pages of YA literature well into the twenty-first century. Characters such as Juliet from Gabby Rivera's *Juliet Takes a Breath* (2016), Aaron from Adam Silvera's *More Happy Than Not* (2015), or the titular Chulito from Charles Rice-González's novel (2011) encompass the highs, lows, and everything in-betweenness of queer Latinx teen lived experiences. This collection tells their stories.

This text, the first critical volume of essays that examines queer Latinx YA literature, offers scholars and students in the fields of young adult literary studies, Latinx studies, and youth studies a foundation in which to engage with this rich body of work that powerfully imagines what it means to be a queer Latinx teen in the twenty-first century. While queer YA scholarship has emerged as a major field within youth studies, with foundational texts like the aforementioned *The Heart Has Its Reasons*, or other titles like *Over the Rainbow: Queer Children's and Young Adult Literature* (2011) and *Representing the Rainbow in Young Adult Literature* (2018), seldom have these volumes thoroughly engaged with a discussion of the wide range of queer Latinx YA texts. Expanding upon the important work of these benchmark texts, *Atravesados: Essays on Queer Latinx Young Adult Literature* calls for a lively, critical discussion not only on representations of queerness in Latinx YA literature but how queerness should be a central component of how we understand Latinx YA literature as a field. Despite the achievements of award-winning authors, such as Anna-Marie McLemore, Charles Rice-González, Gabby Rivera, Benjamin Alire Sáenz, Alex Sanchez, and others, scholarship on queer Latinx literature has overwhelmingly ignored texts written for younger audiences.

In many respects, *Atravesados* expands upon our 2020 volume, *Nerds, Goths, Geeks, and Freaks: Outsiders in Chicanx and Latinx Young Adult Literature* (University Press of Mississippi), where we posited that themes of outsiderness necessarily intersect with questions of queer identities. We offered the invitation to scholars in young adult literary studies to centralize the study of Latinx YA works through the lens of the outsider, the misfit, weirdo, and queer young person. As we contended both then and now, privileging "odd," queer, Latinx youth offers a robust entrance into critical discussions of white supremacy, neocolonialism, race, violence, gender, bordered notions of citizenship, language, and belonging. Here, we provide a brief panoramic overview of seminal works in queer Latinx young adult literature (hereafter QLYA), highlighting that these fictional works have long existed. After that, we situate this field's rather limited scholarship within the at-times fraught relationship between young adult literary studies and Latinx studies, two disciplines that have seldom examined the works explored in this collection. With the exceptions of Benjamin Alire Sáenz and Alex Sanchez, whose works are widely celebrated and studied even by scholars outside Latinx studies, seldom have other QLYA writers received anywhere near this much visibility. Thus, this volume bridges the fields of young adult literary studies and Latinx studies to trouble these disciplinary tendencies that have not adequately explored literature marketed to young adults authored by queer Latinx writers.

The essays in this volume pose critical questions, namely: how do twenty-first century QLYA texts respond to or expand queer Latinx theories that have not fully engaged with youth as a significant identity category? How does QLYA literature trouble queer theory that negates issues of race, class, citizenship, language, and culture? More than simply pointing to the obvious gap in scholarship on QLYA, the essays in this volume assert that Latinx queer theories must attend to youth identities that complicate our understandings of queer Latinidad, race, ethnicity, gender, and belonging.

QUEER LATINX YOUNG ADULT LITERATURE

Queer Latinx literature is not a new phenomenon. Throughout the 1980s, writers like Arturo Islas, Sheila Ortiz Taylor, Cherríe Moraga, Ana Castillo, and Gloria Anzaldúa, to name only a few, published groundbreaking works that are now routinely taught in college classrooms throughout the globe. Landmark texts such as *Loving in the War Years* (1983), *The Rain God* (1984), *The Mixquiahuala Letters* (1986), and *Borderlands/La Frontera* (1987) troubled the heteronormativity of Chicano nationalism that had come to dominate Latino literary studies in the 1960s and '70s.[1] However, while major publishing houses rarely took a chance on Latinx writers who wrote for "adult" audiences, even fewer publishers showed much interest in literature marketed to teen readers. Smaller presses like Arte Público and Aunt Lute were instrumental in promoting queer Latinx voices during a time in which few texts reached widespread circulation. Even decades later, as Chicanx-literature scholar Carolina Alonso claims, "there still remains a lack of Chicanx publications that center queer coming-of-age issues," a fact which, set against the background of the United States' racism towards the Latinx community and ever-present threats of homophobia, is magnified (175).

It was not until the 1990s that publishing houses began circulating young adult novels that tackled adolescent queerness, an act that was revolutionary at a time when the AIDS pandemic was still ravaging queer communities and gay men especially were vilified because of it. In mainstream US culture, queerness was still seen as taboo, with notable roadblocks such as President Bill Clinton's "Don't Ask, Don't Tell" coming into law in 1994, preventing queer people from being out while serving in the military. Moreover, queer representation in film and television continued to rely on tired stereotypes. Even groundbreaking television shows such as *Will & Grace* (1998–2006) still relied on portraying gay men as flamboyant sidekicks and showed whiteness as the norm. While this hostility and uneasiness with the LGBTQ+ community was pervasive, it is precisely the context in which the first queer Latinx YA novel emerged: *Tommy Stands Alone* by Gloria Velásquez. Published in 1995 by Arte Público Press as the third installment in Velásquez's Roosevelt High School series, *Tommy Stands Alone* tackles Tommy's journey coming to terms with his queerness, something that seems at odds with his family's traditional Latinx expectations and cultural norms. Nearly two decades later, Velásquez continued Tommy's story with *Tommy Stands Tall* (2013). Now a senior at Roosevelt High, Tommy forms a Gay/Straight Alliance at school to help other queer kids go through the same struggles that he has gone through. While Tommy may have once been desperate to cope with being gay, he can now stand tall (in 2013), knowing that his queerness is what makes him who he is, and there is no reason to be ashamed of it. He's perfect just as he is—a gay Latino.

Despite the success of *Tommy Stands Alone*, neither Latinx literature nor young adult literature saw a marked increase in stories about adolescent queer Latinxs. The lack of titles in the years following *Tommy Stands Alone*'s publication reinforces how pathbreaking Velásquez's novel truly is. Curiously, the lack of QLYA titles in the late 1990s does not reflect larger trends in Latinx literature at large. Texts such as *Gulf Dreams* (1996) by Emma Pérez, *Faults* (1999) by Terri de la Peña, *We Came All the Way from Cuba So You Could Dress Like This?* (1999) by Achy Obejas, and Michael Nava's Henry Ríos mystery book series, for example, reveal how Latinx literature was beginning to shift towards more queer inclusive content, and more importantly, this queer content had been available even prior to this decade. Yet, it is no secret that adolescent Latinxs were largely excluded from this conversation, reiterating how queerness has not always been a viable identity for Latinx teens.

The next big push in QLYA came in 2001 with the publication of *Rainbow Boys* by Alex Sanchez. Published by the powerhouse press Simon & Schuster, *Rainbow Boys* focuses on three queer high school seniors as they confront what it means to come of age as queer boys. Having spawned a series with titles such as *Rainbow High* (2003) and *Rainbow Road* (2005), *Rainbow Boys* is now considered to be "canonical" and the text most cited in general YA scholarship, a feat that other Latinx YA writers, with the exception of Benjamin Alire Sáenz, are still waiting to enjoy. Unlike the Rainbow Boys series by Alex Sanchez, which has achieved mainstream visibility and scholarship even as the texts reinforce stereotypes concerning gay male sexuality,[2] Rigoberto González's Mariposa Club (2009) series offers a striking counter to Sanchez's series. Like *Rainbow Boys*, *The Mariposa Club* traces the friendship of queer teens in their final year of high school, but the similarities end there. "The Fierce Foursome" (Maui, Trini, Liberace, and Isaac) live in the fictional town of Caliente, California, within the Coachella Valley region of González's birth. Small town Caliente serves as the backdrop to the teens' coming of age, where homophobia and transphobia are common, where creating an LGBTQ club at their high school causes outrage and anger by the residents whose fragile heterosexuality is on display.[3] *The Mariposa Gown* (2008) and *Mariposa U* (2014) make up the rest of the series, where González addresses violent transphobia, even rape, in an unflinching manner to display the real life challenges that young, queer Latinx teens face, while simultaneously representing loving family units that protect their queer kin.

Sanchez's and González's novels inarguably did heavy lifting for stories of queer Latinx adolescence, forging valuable spaces to discuss the lived realities of queer teens during a time in which cultural attitudes towards the LGBTQ+ community in the US began to shift. By the beginning of President Barack Obama's administration in January 2009, the country began to see policy changes that reflected these shifting cultural mores that saw equality for LGBTQ+ communities as a gold standard. For example, the Matthew Shepard and James Byrd Jr. Hate Crimes Prevention Act became law in October 2009, officially including legislative language that defines violent acts against queer people as hate crimes. Don't Ask, Don't Tell was repealed in September 2011, allowing queer people to openly serve in the US military. And, of course, the Supreme Court overturned the Defense of Marriage Act in June 2015, making marriage equality the law of the land. And, most notable to the present collection, queer Latinx YA literature was ready to become a necessary literature, filling important gaps and allowing Latinx teens to see their identities and experiences legitimized by mainstream publishing.[4]

But even as we celebrate these milestones, this same period, the early 2000s, witnessed the brutal murder of a Latina transgender teenager named Gwen Araujo. In 2002, seventeen-year-old Gwen was murdered by men she assumed were her friends when they discovered she was trans. In one of the few academic articles to center Gwen Araujo's story, historian L. Heidenreich addresses the marked disparity between media coverage of Matthew Shepard's murder and Gwen's, pointedly stating, "Gay and 'just like you' and transgender and 'could not pass for you if my life depended on it' remain at two very distinct ends of the queer spectrum" (52). Heidenreich's chilling, crucial words reveal how certain bodies, in this case, trans Latina bodies, are rarely, if ever, afforded the human concern we witness when victims are white, middle-class, or cisgender. While Matthew Shepard became almost a household name, few people know Gwen Araujo's story. On one hand, mainstream markers of cultural citizenship, such as marriage equality and military service, signal a supposed tacit acceptance of queerness. On the other hand, transgender, queer, and nonnormative bodies of color remain vilified, hunted down, and brutalized within a white supremacist system that erases their humanity and right to live with dignity and safety.[5] QLYA, thus, we contend, must be studied within the context of these markedly different systemic realities.

This context shapes, for example, the overwhelming critical success of writers like Sáenz and Sanchez. Perhaps no QLYA text has better represented the mainstream's growing interest in stories about queer Latinxs than *Aristotle and Dante Discover the Secrets of the Universe*, Benjamin Alire Sáenz's 2012 novel that tells the story of two queer Mexican American boys who come of age between 1987 and 1988. While not the first QLYA text, as we have documented already, this novel became foundational for deftly addressing internalized shame and homophobia, particularly violence against queer young men in an unflinching, raw manner. Another element that makes this work unique is the fascinating story behind Sáenz's own coming out journey, a dramatic departure from other QLYA authors, or even his protagonists, Ari and Dante, who acknowledge their queerness in their youth. Sáenz famously did not come out until past middle age, and as Angel Daniel Matos explains, Sáenz "envisioned *Aristotle and Dante* as a text that was designed to heal both himself and his readership" (33). Unlike earlier texts by Velásquez or Sanchez, *Aristotle and Dante* represented fully accepting, loving Chicanx families, a marked shift from the commonly held trope of rigid, "traditional," or even abusive family units that reject their queer kin. Bolstered by *Aristotle and Dante*'s sustained commercial success, Sáenz continued Ari and Dante's story, publishing *Aristotle and Dante Dive into the Waters of the World* in 2021. The sequel picks up right where the original story left off. Although the first novel notoriously painted an almost utopian picture of adolescent queer Latinidad in the late 1980s,[6] even going so far as to completely disregard the AIDS pandemic, *Waters of the World* acts as a corrective with both boys dealing with the reality of growing up gay in 1988 El Paso amidst the AIDS pandemic, which casts a dark cloud over this coming-of-age story.[7] *Aristotle and Dante*'s sustained success reveals how large the audience is for QLYA.

It should not be lost on bookworms that many of the aforementioned titles focus on one type of queer Latinx. That is, novels such as *Tommy Stands Alone*, *Rainbow Boys*, and *Aristotle and Dante* privilege gay and (sometimes) bisexual Latino *boys*. Undoubtedly, these novels provide important outlets for queer representation. Not to mention, the publication of these novels feels incredibly progressive given the norms in YA publishing during the time period. Even so, we would be remiss not to acknowledge that YA publishing has systemically excluded certain Latinx identities—namely queer girls, nonbinary teens, and trans Latinxs. When we consider other identity factors such as race, ethnicity, disability, and language, for example, it is clear that, despite how far QLYA has come, there still remains critical work to fill gaps and allow teen readers of all identities the opportunity to see themselves reflected on the page. What is more, nuanced and far-reaching depictions of adolescent Latinidades hold the potential to educate non-Latinx readers, teach young people about difference, and build bridges that can shift cultural norms in the US.

Since the late 2010s, nonbinary writer Anna-Marie McLemore, for example, has corrected and updated the narrative, writing almost exclusively about nonbinary, queer, and trans characters in their works, imbuing these storylines with elements of fantasy and myth.[8] McLemore's 2016 *When the Moon Was Ours* features Miel, who grows roses from her wrists and must combat a group of suspected witches who are convinced that the scent from Miel's roses can make anyone fall in love. Their 2022 novel, *Lakelore*, introduces readers to Bastián Silvano and Lore Garcia, two nonbinary teens who are forced to negotiate between a newfound magical world under a lake and their lives above water.[9] In a similar vein, gay Puerto Rican writer Adam Silvera's YA work frequently delves into speculative fiction and fantasy in his work. Titles such as *More Happy Than Not* (2015), *They Both Die at the End* (2017), *Infinity Son* (2020), and *Infinity Reaper* (2021) ask readers to draw parallels between real life and alternative realities in which queer Latinxs deal with age-old concerns of queer teens such as coming out and dating while also tackling speculative issues like having super powers (Inifinity Son series) and being notified by a government agency about the day you're going to die *(They Both Die at the End)*. Or take, for example, his best-selling debut *More Happy Than Not*, in which Silvera introduces readers to Aaron, a gay Latino teen who "seeks to erase memories of his queerness, via the Leteo procedure, a memory alteration surgery" (Rhodes 1). Ecuadorian American writer Zoraida Córdova's personal website vibrantly subtitles the author's name with the words: "magic & mayhem." And this is precisely what bookworms will find in Córdova's Brooklyn Bruja series: *Labyrinth Lost* (2016), *Bruja Born* (2018), and *Wayward Witch* (2019). The queer-infused fantasy trilogy introduces readers to Alex, Lula, and Rose, three sisters—and brujas, or witches. The trio develops their powers and battles magic in their everyday lives and in magical worlds unknown, reflecting what Domino Pérez describes as a "vision of heroism that we do not see nearly enough" in mainstream YA or popular culture (84).

As the commercial and artistic successes of McLemore, Silvera, and Córdova convey, speculative fiction and fantasy have undoubtedly been a home for the growing literary landscape of QLYA. But even so, other queer Latinx writers have leaned into depictions of the intersections of adolescence, Latinidad, and queerness that privilege hyperrealism. One such writer is Gabby Rivera, whose 2016 YA novel *Juliet Takes a Breath* has quickly become a fundamental part of the QLYA canon for its deft portrayal of one Nuyorican so-called baby dyke nerdburger's coming of age set against the supposedly liberal—and supposedly more inclusive—haven of Portland, Oregon. As the titular character "struggles to vocalize and proclaim her queer Puerto Ricanness amid pressures to be straight (her mother), 'less gringa' (her hood), and 'less brown' (her white girlfriend)," she casts off the haters to achieve self-love, "a radical act of queer Latina feminism" (Boffone and Herrera, *Latinx Teens* 71).[10] Although queer nonbinary Latinx author and activist Mark Oshiro's young adult works are expansive in theme and approach, their critically acclaimed novel *Anger Is a Gift* (2018) uses realism to tell the story of gay teen Moss Jeffries, who must confront the very real and very ugly side of racism in Oakland, California.[11] In many ways a companion piece to best-selling novels *The Hate U Give* (2017) by Angie Thomas, *Dear Martin* by Nic Stone (2017), and *Tyler Johnson Was Here* by Jay Coles (2018), *Anger Is a Gift* doesn't sugarcoat the effects of racism, mental health, race, and queerness. Much like real-life queer teens such as Emma González and Sage Grace Dolan-Sandrino,[12] Moss learns how to harness his intersecting identities to become a leader in his community.

A *New York Times* Best Seller about trans Latinx teens would have been unthinkable even ten years ago, but that's precisely where Aiden Thomas's debut novel *Cemetery Boys* landed in 2020. *Cemetery Boys* is a paranormal novel about Yadriel, a trans boy who is determined to become a real brujo despite his family's adherence to traditional gender roles. The novel is one of the few YA novels that tackles themes relevant to trans Latinidad such as transphobia, misgendering, and gender dysphoria, in addition to other pressing themes such as parental death, deportation, and grief. Perhaps signaling a shift in the open-mindedness of teen readers, *Cemetery Boys* was quickly adopted by readers on TikTok, becoming a trending title on BookTok, the community of TikTok dedicated to bookworms (Boffone and Jerasa 10). As queer Latinx YA moves well into the third decade of the twenty-first century, novels like *Cemetery Boys* remain at the forefront of the type of stories being told. That is, QLYA is invested in expanding the spectrum of queer Latinidad. What once may have been a land of gay and lesbian characters, with the occasional bisexual Latinx thrown in, is now a space where trans, nonbinary, and asexual teens, for example, can see their identities and stories represented.

It's no secret that the field of YA publishing has now begun to recognize the value of queer Latinx stories told *by* queer Latinx writers. Bolstered by the commercial and critical successes of the aforementioned titles, there is no denying that stories about queer Latinx teens coming of age not only are marketable, but that these stories can turn a profit. Following Jonny Garza Villa's 2021 debut *Fifteen Hundred Miles from the Sun*, 2022 became a banner year for QLYA with a veritable explosion of new titles running the full spectrum of queer Latinidad: *The Lesbiana's Guide to Catholic School* by Sonora Reyes; *Ophelia After All* by Racquel Marie; *Café con Lychee* by Emery Lee; *This Is Why They Hate Us* by Aaron H. Aceves; *Just Your Local Bisexual Disaster* by Andrea Mosqueda; *Boys of the Beast* by Monica Zepeda; *The Turning Pointe* by Vanessa L. Torres; *Lakelore* by Anna-Marie McLemore; and *It Sounds Like This* by Anna Meriano. As we move into the third decade of the twenty-first century, QLYA has moved from beyond the fringes of publishing and is now firmly centered in the mainstream. As the Latinx teen population continues to grow and younger generations are more open to a diversity of stories, there is a need for literature that holds a mirror up to society while also teaching others about narratives that encompass queer Latinx adolescence. Scholar and executive editor of Arte Público Press, Gabriela Baeza Ventura, recognizes,

> If as scholars, readers, parents, educators, citizens, and more importantly, as Latinas/os, we do not demand that the generations to come find themselves in what they read, we will continue to foster unjustified hierarchies that categorically place Latinas/os below white,

monolingual, and minimally diversified cultures and thus foment second-class citizenship and discrimination. (246)

QLYA holds the potential to address issues of racism, xenophobia, homophobia, transphobia, mental health, complex family/peer relationships, and the fraught dynamics of space and belonging. With new, cutting-edge titles being published seemingly every month, all that's left to do is find a new book, curl up on the sofa with your favorite reading beverage (coffee for Trevor, chocolate Mexicano for Cristina), and let the queer Latinx teens who fill these pages show us the way.

ATRAVESADOS: TOWARDS A THEORY OF QUEER LATINX YOUTH

In the previous section, we provided a panoramic overview of the rich corpus of QLYA writing, connecting this body of work within the landscape of queer Latinx writing that is now routinely explored by scholars throughout the globe. However, as we contended earlier in this introduction, with the exception of canonical writers like Alex Sanchez and Benjamin Alire Sáenz, who have gained mainstream visibility, QLYA remains a vastly understudied field. Whether in mainstream youth literary studies or Latinx studies, scholars within these disciplines have rarely examined QLYA by writers whose last names are not Sanchez or Sáenz. While these works have been widely celebrated by scholars and critics, they are all too often treated as representative examples of the QLYA corpus, which overlooks other equally important, pathbreaking texts that portray queer Latinx teens in refreshing and original ways.[13] Few foundational texts in queer Latinx studies focus on youth identities and experiences, resulting in a theoretical gap that omits youth as another critical component of identity that influences expressions of gender, queerness, the body, belonging, race, and citizenship. This book asserts Latinx youth studies as a robust field, one in which queerness is central and offers a critical lens to "typical" themes scholars take up in Latinx letters overall, including but not limited to colonialism, race, borders of space, gender, and ethnicity, family, trauma, and identity. As we explore here, a critical queer lens is now and has been routinely examined in children's and YA literary scholarship, where scholars have convincingly argued that literature for youth is a necessary landscape on which to explore diverse gender expressions and sexualities.

For example, in the introduction to Michelle Ann Abate and Kenneth Kidd's foundational volume, *Over the Rainbow: Queer Children's and Young*

Adult Literature (2011), the editors offer a discussion of queerness, which "has long meant 'strange,' 'unusual,' and 'out of alignment,' even as it has been linked to non-heteronormative sexuality since around the turn of the twentieth century" (3). In this sense, queerness has an expansive history in English language and literature, but Abate and Kidd correctly point out the notable absence of much inquiry that bridges queer theories and children's literature (8). In a fascinating turn, Derritt Mason does not define queer YA as literature that necessarily follows marketing tactics or generic boundaries but rather as a "set of affects and effects" (16) that reflects anxieties about what YA writing is, what queerness is, and who adolescents are (or should be). Notions of how adolescents should act proliferate in much YA publishing, particularly in the genre's early emergence, and sexuality especially is a concern. To that end, Lydia Kokkola convincingly argues that "*all* adolescent sexual desire can be regarded as a queer desire" (98, emphasis in original) because of prevailing ideologies that punish or prevent teens from acting out their sexuality. Noticeably absent from these discussions, though, is how ideologies surrounding categories of adolescence presume whiteness, and as we elaborate further, even early foundations of queer theories erase BIPOC experiences, histories, and realities. As Jon M. Wargo pointedly argues, "For queers of color, however, queer is not a unitary or isolated identity category, but rather a 'yes-and' identity marker. When layered with race and ethnicity, queer is seen and felt, relegating the individual to an even more subordinate position on the hierarchy of identities of difference" (176). The complexity of youth Latinx queerness (the "yes-and" of which Wargo speaks) means that even in texts where queerness is central to the protagonists' realities, this perspective does not negate deep concerns around community, violence, immigration, white supremacy, and schooling, for example, themes that are ever-present in Latinx literature overall.

Like Abate and Kidd, we are optimistic about the work yet to be done; but even as these scholars and others lament the tendency to overlook children's or YA literature as a site for queer theoretical interventions, we also assert that scholars in children's and YA literature have overwhelmingly ignored the large corpus of queer writings by Latinx YA authors. As Kidd comments, YA literature as a tradition is, not surprisingly, "extraordinarily receptive to lesbian/gay themes, largely because coming out is often described in the idiom of adolescence as an intense period of sexual attraction, social rebellion, and personal growth" (114). But lest we presume that this reception signals *acceptance* of queer lived realities, scholars like Roberta Seelinger Trites argue that gay YA literature between the 1960s and 1990s "parallels the cultural traditions of repression that have long stigmatized homosexuality" (149). In this foundational essay, "Queer Discourse and the Young Adult Novel," Trites cautions against an overly optimistic interpretation of YA literature as a genre that by default openly represents sexual encounters between queer teens, much less celebrates a wide range of sexual and gender expressions. In a similar vein, Thomas Crisp troubles the popularity of Sanchez's highly regarded Rainbow Boys series, arguing that the novels offer problematic representations of young gay males, reinforcing the very stereotypes the books purportedly disrupt (216). As these scholars of YA literature maintain, queer YA texts, while widely available to adult and teen readers alike, have more often than not served as cautionary tales of queerness, seldom representing queer teen characters whose lived realities balance hardship, pain, and complexities.

In their updated volume, *Representing the Rainbow in Young Adult Literature*, Jenkins and Cart state, however, that queer YA published in the first two decades of the twenty-first century has vastly corrected the early literature. For example, they note that post-2010 literature has witnessed "the increasing appearance of people of color in a literature that historically has been almost exclusively white and middle class" (128), a point that Derritt Mason supports in his study *Queer Anxieties of Young Adult Literature and Culture* (5).[14] To be sure, we have claimed throughout this introduction that Latinx literature has a rich queer tradition, even in texts not marketed for a younger readership. However, even as Jenkins and Cart rightfully celebrate the robust body of queer YA texts by nonwhite authors, their extensive overview nevertheless omits sustained discussion of Latinx writers.

While these important studies document the long tradition of queer YA literature, these works use Anglo/European children's literary cultures to engage in queer theoretical scholarship, a tradition that cannot fully account for a genre of literature, QLYA, that often takes to task white supremacy and colonial histories and legacies that erase, marginalize, and traumatize Latinx peoples. Although not explicitly addressing QLYA, scholar Marilisa Jiménez García argues that "when it comes to fundamental questions within the overall field of children's literature ... scholars have mainly drawn on a heritage of Anglo literature to create theory" (114–15). In volumes like *Over the Rainbow: Queer Children's and Young Adult Literature*, edited by Michelle Ann Abate and Kenneth Kidd (2011), only one chapter examines a text by a queer Latinx writer, Alex Sanchez. Similarly, the edited volume, *Beyond Borders: Queer Eros and Ethos (Ethics) in LGBTQ Young Adult Literature* (2016), features only one chapter on QLYA, not surprisingly, that addresses *Aristotle and Dante Discover the Secrets of the Universe* and *Rainbow Boys*. Moreover, while *Representing the Rainbow* provides a much-needed update on queer YA published since the 2010s, there is scant attention paid to Latinx texts besides *Rainbow Boys*, and very recent studies, such as Mason's *Queer Anxieties* and Moruzi and Venzo's *Sexuality in Literature for Children and Young Adults* (2021), do not consider Latinx queers at all. Our work here, thus, asks a complex but straightforward question: what does queer YA literary studies look like when we draw from a tradition of queer Latinx theories and the rich history of QLYA? This book is indebted to pathbreaking queer Latinx theorists that provide a language to document desire, sexuality, and gender in queer Latinx lives. Richard T. Rodríguez, Daniel Enrique Pérez, José Esteban Muñoz, María Lugones, Catrióna Rueda Esquibel, and others have charted what we can refer to as queer Latinx theory, centering sexuality and desire in our understanding of Latinx communities.

Originally published in 1991, Carla Trujillo's edited volume, *Chicana Lesbians: The Girls Our Mothers Warned Us About*, was pathbreaking for how it charted Chicana lesbian desire on the page, visible in essays, poetry, and short stories, the first such compilation. Undoubtedly inspired by Chicana lesbian theorists like Gloria Anzaldúa and Cherríe Moraga, whose individual works and collaborative volume, *This Bridge Called My Back* (1981), ushered in an era of queer of color voices, Trujillo's book specifically addressed the heteropatriarchy of Chicano Nationalism and family dynamics that construct Chicana lesbians as threats to la familia.[15] The 1980s also witnessed foundational anthologies like *Compañeras* (1987), and like Trujillo, whose volume privileged Chicana lesbian identity to confront their erasure within Chicano heteropatriarchal traditions, Catrióna Rueda's Esquibel's important study, *With Her Machete in Her Hand: Reading Chicana Lesbians* (2006), maintained that even those texts we presume to be heteronormative can be read as inherently lesbian for the ways they center desire between Chicana subjects.

In the following years, Latinx studies saw a more marked publishing regime centered around queerness. Notable publications include titles such as *The Chicana/o Cultural Studies Reader* (2006) edited by Angie Chabram-Dernersesian; *Gay Latino Studies* (2011), edited by Michael Hames-García and Ernesto Javier Martínez; *Queer in Aztlán: Chicano Male Recollections of Consciousness and Coming Out* (2015), edited by Adelaida R. Del Castillo and Gibran Güido; *Decolonizing Latinx Masculinities* (2020) edited by Arturo J. Aldama and Frederick Luis Aldama; and *Transmovimientos: Latinx Queer Migrations, Bodies, and Spaces* (2021), edited by Ellie D. Hernández, Eddy Alvarez, and Magda García; not to mention solo authored books such as *Queer Latinidad: Identity Practices, Discursive Spaces* (2003) and *Sexual Futures, Queer Gestures, and Other Latina Longings* (2014) by Juana María Rodríguez; *Homecoming Queers: Desire and Difference in Chicana Latina Cultural Production* (2009) by Marivel Danielson; *Reading Chican@ Like a*

Queer: The De-Mastery of Desire (2010) by Sandra K. Soto; *Performing Queer Latinidad: Dance, Sexuality, Politics* (2012) by Ramón H. Rivera-Servera; *Brown Trans Figurations: Rethinking Race, Gender, and Sexuality in Chicanx/ Latinx Studies* (2021) by Francisco J. Galarte; and *Translocas: The Politics of Puerto Rican Drag and Trans Performance* (2021) by Lawrence La Fountain-Stokes. These works and others not listed here form the body of work we call Latinx queer theory. While this is not an exhaustive list by any means, we reference these titles to illuminate the vast oeuvre of queer Latinx theory that has undoubtedly inspired and impacted the writers and works explored in this volume and to assert that queer Latinx theories have been productive sites of knowledge and world building, even when erased by dominant discourses.

In his foundational essay "Queer Theory Revisited," Michael Hames-García addresses some of the crucial ways that early queer theory neglected to fully account for race, capitalism, and even citizenship. In oft-cited "foundational" queer theoretical texts, according to Hames-García, "none ... tells me how to understand the connections between white homosexuality and white supremacy ... between the experience of class and that of race for a queer subject, or between the racialized misogyny faced (differently) by all straight women and the racialized homophobia faced (differently) by all gay men and lesbians" (20). In response to this erasure of the raced and classed elements of queer theory, Hames-García proposes a queer genealogy that centers the knowledges of queers of color. In so doing, he takes to task the ways white queer theorists have buried the important works of queers of color, or how queer of color thought has rarely been considered theory at all.

Similarly, Cherríe Moraga critiques the white queer movements that, at their core, are assimilationist. In her pointed question, "What do our families really look like and is that model deficient or might it not proffer less privatized, more interdependent alternatives to sustaining community?" (*A Xicana Codex* 179), Moraga insists on creating theory that speaks to Chicanx queer lived experiences and knowledges, a more radical reenvisioning of familia and community. Like José Esteban Muñoz's notion of disidentification, which asserts that Latinxs neither identify with nor completely disavow stereotypes but construct themselves in a fashion to disrupt white hegemony, Moraga's query confronts assimilationist rhetoric that undermines queer Chicanx liberationist politics. In this regard, Luz Calvo's and Catrióna Rueda Esquibel's essay from *Gay Latino Studies* is apt: "Queer identification creates and imagines a 'we' that includes men, women, and gender queers" (110), a politic borne out of survival, struggle, and erasure. Rejecting the binary of gay/lesbian, queer denotes the disruption of this; but we take queer, specifically *queer Latinx*, to mean a worldview that (re)imagines community, even a future, to which young queers of color have access to, on their own terms, one in which the nonnormative, los atravesados, reside. Queer Latinx acknowledges, grapples with, confronts, questions, challenges, and resists the many structures, past and present, that threaten queer lives. Matos and Wargo are correct to point out the fraught nature of futurity, stating, "Simply put, many queer, non-white, gender nonconforming, Indigenous, disabled, and lowerclass youth simply do not have access to the material, aesthetic, practical, and ideological means to exist and thrive in the present—much less to envision realities different from the ones in which they currently live" (6).

The texts imagined in this volume also caution us against the optimistic worldview we tend to see in children's and YA literature that fails to consider how queer BIPOC communities must navigate the brutalities of white supremacist structures from the past, present, and surely into the future. QLYA, influenced by a tradition of queer Latinx theory, however, dares to shape communities in which queer young people possess the language to speak of their realities, including the tensions, tragedies, and challenges they must confront every day. QLYA does not negate the real-world issues of racialized capitalism, xenophobia, or white supremacy. But in representing queer Latinxs who navigate these hostilities, we theorize QLYA as a space of liberation, validation, even empowerment. In this lens, we are indebted to Juana María Rodríguez's theorizing of those whom she calls "divas," "atrevidas," and "entendidas." As she explains, "In Spanish, there is no direct translation for "queer." These words speak to something that is both the same as and different from "queer": attitude, defiance, knowledge, the excesses of categories" (24). Both playful and resistant, as Rodríguez sees it, *queer* demands of us an embrace of the messiness, the bold, the ever-shifting and growing identities and landscapes of desire, language, sexuality, and gender. QLYA embodies this attitude, offering crucial glimpses into ways of knowing and moving in a world where queer youth of color are always potential targets of violence.

In closing this section, we return to the title of our book, *Atravesados*, Gloria Anzaldúa's name for those maligned beings who are shunned, harmed, and rendered broken by normative cultures. Much as José Esteban Muñoz envisioned "queerness as horizon [which] rescues and emboldens concepts such as freedom that have been withered by the touch of neoliberal thought and gay assimilationist politics" (32), Anzaldúa saw queers like herself as being "the people that don't belong anywhere, not in the dominant world nor completely within our own respective cultures" ("La Prieta" 50). This in-betweenness informs queer Latinidad, a politic that, as Muñoz posited, flees the confines of assimilation, a way of existing and being in a world that more often than not poisons, maims, and assaults queer lives. For Anzaldúa, these atravesados, thus, must create their own worlds, communities, and stories that fully capture the life of the queer Latinx young person: the good, the bad, the ugly, the horror, joy, tragedy, and pleasure that intersect, mesh, blend, and crash into each other.

YA fiction builds worlds in which readers can envision an alternate way of being, one that just might be inclusive to those marginalized in the world we already live in. As such, the field can help shape our experiences and viewpoints toward the cultures and aesthetics that we find ourselves navigating. Children's literature scholar Kimberley Reynolds proposes that the stories we share with young people "are blueprints for living in a culture as it exists, but they are also where *alternative* ways of living are often piloted in recognition of the fact that children will not just inherit the future, but need to participate in it" (14). The essays in this volume respond to Reynolds's crucial argument, addressing the ways that QLYA imagines, represents, and—we hope—dreams into existence a world for atravesados to dwell and thrive in.

CHAPTER OVERVIEW

The book's first section, "Articulating the Spectrum of Queer Latinidad," unpacks the nuanced identities that make up the LGBTQ+ community, paying close attention to how youth cultures are potent sites through which to explore the intersections of queerness and Latinx identity. As these chapters reveal, queerness is twin skin to Latinidad. In chapter one, "He Could Still Hear Muffled Voices": Materializing Queer Latinidad in Aiden Thomas's *Cemetery Boys*," Alexander Lalama introduces the term "Barrio Gothic" to theorize how queer inner-city Latinx communities' voices are muffled by dominant culture to resist erasure and confront issues that entrap Brown communities such as police brutality, deportation, and forced assimilation. The following chapter by Trevor Boffone, "When Bisexuality Is Spoken: Normalizing Bi Latino Boys in Adam Silvera's *They Both Die at the End*," questions the scarce representation of bisexual Latino boys in the canon of Latinx YA literature, paying close attention to how *They Both Die at the End* updates the narrative by making Rufus's bisexuality front and center. In chapter three, "Latinx Boys Loving Boys: Centering Queerness in Latinx Film Adaptations," T. Jackie Cuevas focuses on how the short films *We the Animals* and *La Serenata* strategically mobilize the filmic medium to visually convey the challenges as well as beauty of queer Latinx young lives, especially young Latino boys who love other boys. In the section's final chapter, "Everyone Is Gay": Queer Latina Identity in Isabel Millán's *Chabelita's*

Heart and Gabby Rivera's *Juliet Takes a Breath*," Sonia Alejandra Rodríguez examines Isabel Millán's picture book *Chabelita's Heart* and Gabby Rivera's *Juliet Takes a Breath* to analyze how the Latinx family unit can shift from an exclusively oppressive space for queer Latinx youth to a type of Latinx family that encourages and embraces messy changes. Collectively, these chapters reveal how Latinx youth cultures are forging new pathways for queer Latinx identities to not only emerge but thrive.

Section two, "Queerness and Bodies in Transformation," examines how Latinx YA writers represent Latinx queerness through new understandings of transformation, power, and subjectivity. In chapter five, "Transformation and the Queer Latinx Body in the Collected Works of Anna-Marie McLemore," Cristina Rhodes contends that the award-winning author "utilizes metamorphosis to facilitate positive and ameliorative queer realities," using fantasy and Latinx reimaginings of fairy tales to explore transformation and power. Following this, Cristina Herrera analyzes the relationship between disability and queerness in chapter six, "'We Are Something New': Disability and Latinx Adolescence in Mia García's *The Resolutions*," to investigate a group seldom considered in queer YA studies and disability studies: Latinx teens. Closing the section is chapter seven by Joseph Isaac Miranda, "Breathing Room: Sustaining Queer Brown Socialities in the Latinx Bildungsroman," which explores Gabby Rivera's immensely popular text *Juliet Takes a Breath* to unpack the ways the protagonist disrupts the limiting constraints of the bildungsroman genre through an analysis of the text's concern with breathing, the body, and Juliet's real struggles with asthma. With their explorations of change, transformation, and empowerment, the chapters in section three engage with timely debates that expand dialogues in Latinx studies, disability studies, and queer theory.

The book's third section, "(Alternative) Spaces of Queer Latinidades," questions where Latinx youth cultures live. These chapters explore underrepresented spaces—social media, video games, and the geographical US-Mexico border—to convey how Latinx culture-makers trouble the notion of young adult literature as being a static genre that exclusively lives on the page. In chapter eight, "Queering TikTok: Gen Z's Latinx BookTok and Adam Silvera's *They Both Die at the End*," Trevor Boffone looks at how queer teens use BookTok to critically engage with *They Both Die at the End*, something that made the book go viral and top the *New York Times* Young Adult Paperback Best Seller list four years after the book's debut. In the following chapter, "Sideways Latinx Queerness in Young Adult Video Games: *Life Is Strange 2* and *Gone Home*," Regina Marie Mills uses the video games *Life Is Strange 2* and *Gone Home* to illustrate "sideways Latinx queerness" by means of the games' walking simulator structure—winding, exploratory, encouraging dead ends and backwards movement—which provides a queer Latinx critique of the American Dream. In chapter ten, "Atravesando Nepantla: Queer Familia in Chicanx and Mexican Young Adult Novels," Jesus Montaño and Regan Postma-Montaño use a transnational approach to examine Latinx and Mexican YA novels, thus teasing out the possibilities of resistance and solidarity across transborder crossings. As these chapters convey, to better understand the role of Latinx youth culture in the United States and abroad, we must also explore how Latinx youth identities live in spaces beyond print literature.

Section four, "Queer Futurities," offers robust discussions and debates surrounding the relationship between queerness and the (im)possibility of futurity. In chapter eleven, "Roses and Remedios: La Llorona's Queer Children in *When the Moon Was Ours*," Domino Renee Pérez investigates how Anna-Marie McLemore's fantastical, queer reimagining of the Mexican folkloric figure La Llorona grants queer characters agency, history, and the possibility of a future. Following that is chapter twelve by Angel Daniel Matos, "Silence, at Least Right Now, Equals My Survival": The Absence of AIDS in the *Aristotle and Dante Series*," which unravels Benjamin Alire Saénz's two-part series and its original omission of AIDS in the first text; according to Matos, Saénz's sequel critiques the overall silences and erasures of queer Latinidad within utopic and reparative readings of the series. Cristina Rhodes concludes section four with the chapter, "Imagining the Future: The (Im)Possibilities of Queerness in Two Latinx Speculative Young Adult Novels," which tackles the genre of speculative fiction to account for the critical ways Latinx YA novels must be read as a "call to action" to imagine a more just, queer future for Latinx youth. Ultimately, the chapters in this section confront the complicated, unique ways Latinx YA authors (re) imagine, explore, and contend with past, present, and future queer lives.

The book concludes with an afterword by Frederick Luis Aldama that places the book's themes within the rich tradition of Latinx comics and graphic novels.

NOTES

1. Here we intentionally use the masculine Chicano and Latino to reflect the patriarchal forces at play in the early years of the Chicano Movement.
2. See Thomas Crisp, for example.
3. See Sonia Alejandra Rodríguez, for example.
4. There has also been a groundswell of nonqueer Latinx writers who frequently include queer characters in their work. These writers, such as Elizabeth Acevedo and Daniel José

Older, also update the narrative around Latinx queerness. Although they may not write from first-hand experiences, their characters are sensitive to the realities of queerness and offer blueprints for how Latinx YA writers at large may collectively work to center queerness within Latinx youth studies. This shows that queerness and queer characters are not "add-ons" but central to Latinx YA writing.

5. Black trans people have particularly been victims of transphobic violence and murder, and rarely do these stories reach mainstream media attention. See Rummler and Sosin, "2021 Is Now the Deadliest Year on Record for Transgender People."

6. This is not to say that *Aristotle and Dante Discover the Secrets of the Universe* does not tackle homophobia, both from outside and within. But both boys experience immediate acceptance from their families upon coming out. Even so, the novel does detail transphobia in the time period and in the Latinx community, an act that situates queerness at large outside of the scope of normative Latinx identities in the late eighties. As another sign of its mainstream success, it was reported in late 2021 that *Aristotle and Dante* was being produced into a film.

7. See Angel Daniel Matos's chapter in this volume.

8. See chapters by Domino Renee Pérez and Cristina Rhodes in this volume.

9. Other notable titles by McLemore include *Dark and Deepest Red* (2020) and *Miss Meteor* (2020, with Tehlor Kay Mejia).

10. See also chapters by Joseph Isaac Miranda and Sonia Alejandra Rodríguez in this volume.

11. While *Anger Is a Gift* is grounded in realism, Oshiro's *Each of Us a Desert* (2020) is a fantasy coming-of-age novel about two young Latinas who find they are kindred spirits.

12. For more on Latinx teen activists such as Emma González and Sage Grace Dolan-Sandrino, see Boffone and Herrera, *Latinx Teens: US Popular Culture on the Page, Stage, and Screen* (2022).

13. Notable exceptions to this pattern of uncritical celebration are insightful essays by Thomas Crisp and Angel Daniel Matos, who provide interventions into traditional readings of *Rainbow Boys* and *Aristotle and Dante*. While these scholars address the importance of these canonical texts, they also pose critical questions related to temporality, the omission of AIDS in *Aristotle and Dante*, and stereotypes of gay males, for example.

14. In fact, Laura M. Jiménez's 2015 study found that between the years 2000 and 2013, winners of the prestigious Stonewall and Lambda Awards were mainly white males, despite the publication of a number of queer texts by BIPOC writers.

15. For an in-depth exploration of the family as a symbol of Chicano cultural politics, see Richard T. Rodríguez's book *Next of Kin*.

WORKS CITED

Alonso, Carolina. "The Coming-of-Age Experience in Chicanx Queer Novels *What Night Brings* and *Aristotle and Dante Discover the Secrets of the Universe*." In *Nerds, Goths, Geeks, and Freaks: Outsiders in Chicanx and Latinx Young Adult Fiction*, edited by Trevor Boffone and Cristina Herrera. University Press of Mississippi, 2020, 175–89.

Anzaldúa, Gloria. *Borderlands/La Frontera: The New Mestiza*. Aunt Lute, 1987.
Anzaldúa, Gloria. "La Prieta." *This Bridge Called My Back: Writings by Radical Women of Color*, edited by Cherríe Moraga and Gloria Anzaldúa. Third Woman Press, 2002, 220–33.
Baeza Ventura, Gabriela. "Latino Literature for Children and the Lack of Diversity," in *(Re)Mapping the Latina/o Literary Landscape*, edited by Cristina Herrera and Larissa Mercado-Lopez. Palgrave Macmillan, 2016, 241–54.
Boffone, Trevor, and Cristina Herrera. *Latinx Teens: US Popular Culture on the Page, Stage, and Screen*. University of Arizona Press, 2022.
Boffone, Trevor, and Cristina Herrera, eds. *Nerds, Goths, Geeks, and Freaks: Outsiders in Chicanx and Latinx Young Adult Literature*. University Press of Mississippi, 2020.
Boffone, Trevor, and Sarah Jerasa. "Toward a (Queer) Reading Community: BookTok, Teen Readers, and the Rise of TikTok Literacies." *Talking Points* 33, no. 1 (2021): 10–16.
Calvo, Luz, and Catrióna Rueda Esquibel. "Our Queer Kin." *Gay Latino Studies: A Critical Reader*, edited by Michael Hames-García and Ernesto Javier Martínez. Duke University Press, 2011, 105–12.
Hames-García, Michael. "Queer Theory Revisited." *Gay Latino Studies: A Critical Reader*, edited by Michael Hames-García and Ernesto Javier Martínez. Duke University Press, 2011, 19–45.
Jiménez, Laura M. "Representations in Award-Winning LGBTQ Young Adult Literature from 2000–2013." *Journal of Lesbian Studies* 19, no. 4 (2015): 406–22.
Jiménez García, Marilisa. "Side-by-Side: At the Intersections of Latinx Studies and ChYALit." *The Lion and the Unicorn* 41, no. 1 (2017): 113–22.
Kidd, Kenneth. "Introduction: Lesbian/Gay Literature for Children and Young Adults." *Children's Literature Association Quarterly* 23, no. 3 (1998): 114–19.
Kokkola, Lydia. *Fictions of Adolescent Carnality: Sexy Sinners and Delinquent Deviants*. John Benjamins Publishing Company, 2013.
Matos, Angel Daniel. "A Narrative of a Future Past: Historical Authenticity, Ethics, and Queer Latinx Futurity in *Aristotle and Dante Discover the Secrets of the Universe*." *Children's Literature* 47, no. 1 (2019): 30–56.
Matos, Angel Daniel, and Jon Michael Wargo. "Editors' Introduction: Queer Futurities in Youth Literature, Media, and Culture." *Research on Diversity in Youth Literature* 2, no. 1 (2019): 1–16.
Moraga, Cherríe. *A Xicana Codex of Changing Consciousness: Writings, 2000–2010*. Duke University Press, 2011.
Moruzi, Kristine, and Paul Venzo, eds. *Sexuality in Literature for Children and Young Adults*. Routledge, 2021.
Muñoz, José Esteban. *Cruising Utopia: The Then and There of Queer Futurity*. New York University Press, 2009.
Pérez, Domino. "Afuerxs and Cultural Practice in *Shadowshaper* and Labyrinth Lost." *Nerds, Goths, Geeks, and Freaks: Outsiders in Chicanx and Latinx Young Adult Literature*, edited by Trevor Boffone and Cristina Herrera. University Press of Mississippi, 2020, 74–87.
Reynolds, Kimberly. *Radical Children's Literature: Future Visions and Aesthetic Transformations in Juvenile Fiction*. Palgrave Macmillan, 2007.

Rodríguez, Juana María. *Queer Latinidad: Identity Practices, Discursive Spaces*. New York University Press, 2003.

Rodríguez, Richard T. *Next of Kin: The Family in Chicano/a Cultural Politics*. Duke University Press, 2009.

Rodríguez, Sonia Alejandra. "'Fierce and Fearless': Dress and Identity in Rigoberto González's *The Mariposa Club*." *MeXicana Fashions: Politics, Self-Adornment, and Identity Construction*, edited by Aída Hurtado and Norma E. Cantú. University of Texas Press, 2020, 216–34.

Rhodes, Cristina. "Imagining the Future: The (Im)Possibilities of Queerness in Two Latinx Speculative Young Adult Novels," *Label Me Latino* XI, Special Issue: YA Latinx Literature (2021).

Rummler, Orion, and Kate Sosin. "2021 Is Now the Deadliest Year on Record for Transgender People." *The 19th*, 9 November 2021. https://19thnews.org/2021/11/2021-deadliest-year-record-transgender-people/

Wargo, Jon M. "At the Risk of 'Feeling Brown' in Gay YA: Machismo, Mariposas, and the Drag of Identity." *Affect, Emotion, and Children's Literature: Representations and Socialisations in Texts for Children and Young Adults*, edited by Kristine Moruzi, Michelle Smith, and Elizabeth Bullen. Routledge, 2017, 175–91.

Section One

Articulating the Spectrum of Queer Latinidad

Chapter One

"HE COULD STILL HEAR MUFFLED VOICES"

Materializing Queer Latinidad in
Aiden Thomas's *Cemetery Boys*

Alexander Lalama

Aiden Thomas's Young Adult novel *Cemetery Boys* (2020) reveals a replicating pattern of marginalization. Latinxs have historically been pushed to the margins of US culture through narratives that either criminalize and demonize them or erase them completely from the dominant narrative of American history. Yet, Latinx literature and culture is also guilty of pushing away those who challenge heteronormative constructs of Latinidad further into the shadows. This is also evident within the study of young adult (YA) literature, and Latinx YA literature in particular. Marilisa Jiménez García notes "a history of curricular policies that specifically 'invisibilize' Latinx youth and texts" (20). And while this concealment of narratives of Latinx youth is far from being resolved, there has been "an explosion of Chicanx/Latinx Young Adult (YA) Literature" (Santos 45) in the past decade, with the publication of germinal and lauded texts such as Benjamin Alire Sáenz's *Aristotle and Dante Discover the Secrets of the Universe* (2012) and Elizabeth Acevedo's *The Poet X* (2018). These texts have been a boon for amplifying Latinx youth narratives; yet some Latinx voices continue to remain inconspicuous. Narratives of trans Latinx youth continue to be buried, despite the growing demand and visibility of the Latinx YA genre. *Cemetery Boys* disinters the lives of LGBTQ Latinxs, allowing them to fully materialize not just to demonstrate that they exist, but also to construct a community committed to challenging a dominant, hegemonic, heterosexist Latinidad, forcing Latinxs to see how they, too, have contributed to the destruction of members of their own community.

Cemetery Boys centers on Yadriel, a trans brujo living in East Los Angeles. Despite coming out to his family, Yadriel receives less than enthusiastic support from his father. He lives in a community of brujx,[1] and initiation into the order comes through performance of particular rites that fall within gendered lines. Yadriel seeks to assert his masculine identity through conjuring a spirit, which serves as proof that he has the powers of a brujo. Yet, the ghost he conjures is Julian, a troubled urban Latinx youth. Enlisting the help of Santa Muerte's benediction, Yadriel's trans identity is validated not from Enrique, Yadriel's father, but the ghosts of other queer and trans Latinxs. While Julian is disembodied, only visible to brujx like Yadriel, he exercises spectral power, moving objects to dispute rumors, such as him being a gang member. Julian, although a ghost, forces confrontation, to challenge the interpellation of his "gang" of other LGBTQ youth, who are cast aside from Latinx culture due to their non-normative gender and sexuality. In what I term the Barrio Gothic, which borrows elements from the American Gothic, ghosts within inner city Latinx communities voice experiences muffled by dominant culture to resist erasure and confront issues that entrap Brown communities such as police brutality, deportation, and forced assimilation. I look specifically at *Cemetery Boys* as a queer Barrio Gothic novel, one that turns the lens back on the Latinx community that has rendered queer Latinidad ghostly, and how Yadriel and Julian use their supernatural powers as evidence of a queer Latinx past, present, and future.

Cemetery Boys both stands within and expands the Barrio Gothic, where the threat within this magical barrio community is not just the fears of outside, hostile forces, but queer, trans, Latinx identity. Vernon Rosario discusses that queer, trans, and other non-gender-conforming Latinxs are often found "contending with tremendous deprivations and traumas as well as familial, religious, and cultural strictures that often are hostile to their gender and sexual diversity" (64–65). Yadriel and Julian challenge hegemonic, heteronormative notions of Latinidad by showing the ways the Latinx community replicates patterns of violence and systematic marginalization of LGBTQ folks seen in dominant, white US culture. Yet, these two teenagers also lift the curtain of a past by revealing the subjugated knowledge of queer, Latinx history.

THE BARRIO GOTHIC

Cemetery Boys represents a particular iteration of a Latinx Gothic that exists within the urban city center: the Barrio Gothic. The barrio is the "spatial concentration of Latinx culture and life in US cities" (Lodoño 3). But, more than just enclaves of a Latinx population, Gina M. Pérez notes their importance extends just beyond population density:

> They are places born out of histories of segregation, uneven development, conflict, and marginalization; but they are also the precious spaces that affirm cultural identities, nurture popular cultural production, and provide sanctuary for people with long histories of displacement, land loss, repression, and collective struggle. (18)

The Barrio Gothic looks at the hauntings associated with living in the barrio. These enclaves rise up from the forced isolation of Latinxs through segregation, in their geographical location but also from equal access to public services such as education and high-paying labor-market sectors. Authors who write in the Barrio Gothic mode look at how this isolation that results from modern-day colonialism leads to fears, superstitions, and hauntings amongst Latinx folks who perceive that their contact with other groups can prove dangerous or fatal. The Gothic, as Tanya González argues, "is important here [in Latinx Literature] because it is historically a literary genre that not only introduced literary monsters . . . but that also served as the aesthetic space where authors could comment on the socially and culturally aberrant" (González 47). The Barrio Gothic concerns itself with the fears associated with Latinx groups that have been historically painted as aberrant: police brutality, illegality and the looming threat of deportation, the pressures of assimilation, and racial tensions between Latinxs and other marginalized groups. What makes the Barrio Gothic stand apart from the American Gothic is that, while the American Gothic is "fantasy and amusement, games and fancy dress, entertainment that engages with its readers on many different levels from trauma to laughter" (Lloyd-Smith 35), the Barrio Gothic is concerned with the lived stakes of Latinxs as they are under constant social, cultural, and legal threats that can lead to real, corporeal, embodied violence, even proving fatal. In writing on Latinx speculative fiction, Cathryn Merla-Watson and B. V. Olguín proclaim that "we cannot imagine our collective futures without reckoning with the hoary ghosts of colonialism and modernity that continue to exert force through globalization and neo-liberal capitalism" (4).[2] The Barrio Gothic confronts and contends with the specters of colonialism, which have shifted into new forms and shapes, delimiting the physical and economic mobility of Latinxs.

THE GOTHIC BARRIO

Cemetery Boys presents several key elements of the Barrio Gothic. Thomas sets the narrative in East Los Angeles, a section of Los Angeles historically populated by Mexican Americans. Richard Romo recounts the history of this barrio, noting that in the early twentieth century, Mexican Americans began to migrate from Los Angeles proper to the east side, "the vast open spaces, the flat low lands along the Los Angeles River amid old housing tracts belonging to European ethnics of an earlier generation" (viii). These sociopolitical forces cutting off East LA from the city center are further cemented by infrastructure, about which Raúl Villa argues that freeways around East LA created an "urban residential isthmus produced by a historical succession of infrastructural development" creating a "dystopian confines" (157) that trap the residents in the barrio, multiplying the inaccessibility and seclusion of the residents. Spurred on by racist gerrymandering that led to the exclusion of Mexican Americans from the political arena, as well as "poverty and ethnic pride" (García Bedolla 41–43), East LA developed as a barrio where Mexican American—and Latinx more broadly—people found a sense of community within the metropolis, but it also reflected the segregation of Latinxs from the rest of the city. Lisa García Bedolla notes that East LA's coerced isolation as a barrio of Los Angeles proper "allowed for the maintenance of Mexican cultural life and the development of group solidarity, but the concentration of the population was not by choice and limited Mexican Americans' social, economic, and political opportunities" (48). This history of the East LA Barrio from "vast open spaces" of abandoned housing tracts contains within the Gothic frontier that which is at the edge of society, desolate, open, yet seemingly uninhabited. Even as the density of Latinxs grew, this space is still cast as an outside frontier of Los Angeles, an Other space distinct from the city, one that, though now surrounded through increasing urbanization and housing development, still isolates, traps Latinxs—spatially, politically, economically—in this geographic enclave.

The East LA of *Cemetery Boys* reflects this historical reality, imbuing it with the supernatural to reflect the psychic effects of the Barrio Gothic. Yadriel lives within cemetery walls that shroud the brujx community. In relating how the brujx came to California, the narrator recounts that "when the first brujx immigrated to Los Angeles, they had only built a small church and graveyard.

But as the community expanded, so did the cemetery, and eventually, the original church was just too small to hold them all. Finally, a couple of decades ago, the new one had been built, along with Yadriel's home" (Thomas 42). The narrative ties the building of East LA with brujx history, intertwining them. Yet while the brujx cemetery is within the barrio, it is also conspicuously separated from it: "The brujx cemetery was right in the middle of East Los Angeles, surrounded by a tall wall that concealed it from prying eyes. Yadriel could hear dogs barking in the distance and the thudding bass of reggaeton blaring from a passing car" (Thomas 41). Yadriel and the other brujx, then, occupy a space that is seemingly divorced from the rest of the Latinx community: the driver who is blasting reggaetón music and the dogs sounding an alarm are part of the background, presenting mischievous, or perhaps dangerous, interlopers that threaten or could threaten the brujx supernatural community. In resisting the gaze, of being shrouded behind a wall, the cemetery space signals an imagined utopic vision of Latinidad that must be protected, ironically, from both nonbrujx, but also from other Latinxs that roam and reside in the same urban environment. The brujx represent what Keara Goin refers to as a monolithic, "generic Latinidad," the "standard political and representational practice in the United States, Latina/os [sic] are consolidated under the label 'Hispanic' and their heterogeneity masked by a generic and flattened representation" is often presented as "contemporary US pan-Latinidad" (349). Generic Latinidad is imposed on by outside groups, creating the damaging stereotypes of Latinxs, but it also speaks to a predominantly white, patriarchal, heterosexist power structure held by particular groups of Latinxs that seek to control the narrative of what defines Latinidad.

Indeed, the novel depicts an exalted, idyllic pan-Latinidad materialized in the brujx community of "men and women who'd emigrated from all over— Mexico and Cuba, Puerto Rico and Colombia, Honduras and Haiti, even the ancient Incas, Aztecs, and Maya—all bestowed with powers by the ancient gods. A mix of beautifully nuanced, vibrant cultures that came together to make their community whole" (Thomas 9). What is implicit in this description is the notion of a monolithic Latinidad wherein there is the surface recognition of differences, national, cultural, racial, that are linked through a sense of mestizaje—the notion of intermixed Indigenous, European, and African origins that resulted in the Americas through colonization and the slave trade—that binds together, even as references to Haitian brujx are closed off without directly referencing Blackness. Moreover, the language in this description is key for the disruption, the fissure between the brujx and idealized, generic Latinidad and a truly "nuanced" vision of Latinx identity. The collective reference to the community as brujx, through the voice of the narrator, as nonbinary, conflicts with the gendering of the community in these lines. These migrants must be and always are envisioned as "men and women" in a Latinidad that elides discussions of Blackness and sketches gender identity within a binary, heteronormative schema.

The heart of the cemetery lies in the new church built to house the growing brujx. And as the old ruins remain shrouded in overgrowth, dilapidated, "The [new] church itself was made of a variety of differently shaped and colored stones, all patched together with clay. There was a small bell tower on the roof, directly above the wooden door, that didn't seem to house an actual bell anymore" (42). The stones, with their different shapes and colors, speak to the binding of different Latinx experiences that are conjoined under the notion of Latinidad. This mosaic that is bound together offers an appearance of camaraderie, yet the bell tower stands oddly vacant. Bell-less, it becomes a tower that stands above, situated as a marker of observation and surveillance rather than the traditional bell tower that calls the congregation together. Following Michel Foucault, the bell tower in the brujx cemetery is the "perfect disciplinary apparatus" that makes "it possible for a single gaze to see everything constantly" (191). Lacking a bell but having a bell tower reveals that traditional, generic Latinidad is a myth created to maintain particular social performances, much like the brujx maintain binary, cisgendered views of gender, which makes an outcast of Yadriel. As a result, the Latinidad of the brujx, the perceived safe haven for Latinxs of the cemetery and church, is instead a force of policing and surveillance, mimicking the specters outside of the barrio that haunt the brujx/Latinx community. The threat of policing of Latinx bodies through issues of legality permeate the novel. In the search for Miguel, a missing brujo who the brujx sense is dead, the attempts to go to the police become confrontations with dangerous beings that exists outside the walls of the insular brujx community. In addition to the threat of not fitting into the brujx due to his gender identity, Yadriel remains cognizant of state-sanctioned violence: "More and more people in their community—brujx and otherwise—had been deported. Families were split apart and good people were torn away from their homes. People were fearful of the police" (Thomas 172). Although a brief moment in the text, the threat of policing both Latinx and queer bodies comes up when Yadriel and Julian take Rio's car to fulfill Julian's bucket list of activities he wants to accomplish before his soul must cross over on Día de Muertos: Yadriel, fearful of the situation, tells Julian, "Your brother is going to call the police, it'll turn into a car chase" (Thomas 262). After Julian tries to reassure Yadriel and tells him not to fret about taking the car, Yadriel gives him "the death glare" (Thomas 263), read in the text as a sneer for Julian's perceived disregard for the gravity of the situation, yet holding a deeper valence of the fear of what violence could happen to a queer, trans Latino boy should they be pursued by police. The looming threat of this surveillance from both the brujx and institutions such as whiteness, homophobia, and transphobia become what looms over Yadriel and Julian.

QUEER GHOSTS AND FEELING BROWN

Julian's reckless attitude towards stealing his brother's car and towards Yadriel's fears of arrest and detainment serve as instances of how Julian's ghost shifts the lens of Barrio Gothic fears back onto the brujx—and Latinx—community itself. Julian's spirit serves as validation of Yadriel's identity as a brujo, as the summoning of a spirit is the rite of passage that initiates a boy into a brujo, something which Yadriel's father Enrique refuses to let him do, not only by preventing the enactment of the ceremony before the brujx congregation but also by his misgendering of his son; Enrique yells at Yadriel, "You stay here with the rest of the women!" (Thomas 27) when he wants to help find Miguel. Enrique tells Camila, Yadriel's dead mother, "He can't just choose to be a brujo" (Thomas 32). The delegitimization and dismissal of Yadriel's gender identity coincide with him living in a cemetery where ghosts consistently roam around, part of the everyday life of the brujx. Yadriel is surrounded by manifestations that symbolize the perpetuation of a heteronormative Latinidad. María del Pilar Blanco and Esther Peeren argue that "the normative position (of masculinity, heterosexuality, whiteness) is ghostly in that it remains un(re)marked, transparent in its self-evidentiality" (310). Yadriel is surrounded by the spirits of a Latinidad that reject his gender identity; Julian, on the other hand, interpellates Yadriel into being a brujo. In minor instances, such as Yadriel needing to use the restroom, Julian reminds Yadriel, who has been conditioned to use the girls' bathroom at school, that it is the "wrong one, dude" (Thomas 207). Here Julian validates Yadriel's masculinity by simultaneously ushering him into the boys' restroom and referring to him as "dude."

Mirroring his experience in taking Julian's ghost to school, a school that is outside of the confines of the cemetery, Yadriel remembers when he was younger and had a spirit companion at school, Lisa. Yadriel relates that Lisa "was a dead girl who haunted my elementary school" and that they "would play together during recess in the field and hang out during free time in class" (Thomas 93–94). This scene recalls an initial state of alienation for Yadriel, as a brujx who was chided and made fun of by the nonbrujx children. Julian, meanwhile, is a new manifestation, a reminder of a facet of Yadriel's identity that has alienated him from the brujx and puts a target on him amongst heteronormative society. Francisco Galarte points to the trans-Chicano/Latino as a critical figure in Chicanx/Latinx culture maintaining dominant gender regimes: "The figure of the Chicano/Latino FTM exists as a pathologized and almost entirely impossible figure . . . their bodies and existence figure as a battleground for shoring up claims to gender categories" (114). Hesitating to take Julian to school in the first place, Yadriel wonders, "What if he slipped up? What if someone caught him talking to Julian? The last thing he ever wanted was to draw more attention to himself" (Thomas 95). Like Lisa outing Yadriel as a brujo, he fears that Julian's ghost may lead to outing his gender identity. But Julian instead offers connection: feeling Brown.

José Esteban Muñoz describes feeling Brown as "feeling together in difference. Feeling Brown is an 'apartness together' through sharing the status of being a problem. . . . Brownness is a value through negation, the negation projected onto it by a racist public sphere that devalues the particularity of non-Anglo Americans" (444–45). Julian, too, is demeaned and devalued by the school, being seen as a gangbanging drug dealer. Yet Julian reveals he is an orphan, lives with his brother Rio, is queer, and is part of a "gang" of homeless Latinx LGBTQ youth who live in a tunnel beneath train tracks, eschewed from society as if they were human detritus. Whereas the ghostly is often the unseen normativity that is self-evident, Julian becomes a ghostly mirror that shows the ways Latinidad erases and perpetuates violence on queer Latinxs, rendering them criminals and outcasts. Julian is the feeling of being Brown that connects Yadriel to a queer Latinx community he has been sheltered from, which has been shrouded from him, by generic Latinidad, the idealized vision of Latinidad that conforms to the vision of this pan-ethnicity based on those who hold the top tier in a power hierarchy, excluding those that do not fit into these confined, drawn-out lines of what Latinidad "should" be like. These are the ghosts that exist beyond the cemetery gates, which connect to the brujx through their shared spectral nature, but which also challenge its utopic illusion of unity in the face of danger, as in this vision Latinidad is the threat to queer Latinx life.

THE GHOSTS OF LATINIDAD

The barrio both reflects the marginalization of Latinxs in the urban center and is a site of protection. The real fears of the violence from those outside of the brujx—a privileged Latinx—community manifest in the death and disappearance of Miguel. His demise is literally felt through the body of the brujx: "Then searing pain stabbed into Yadriel's chest.... The pain was unbearable. Yadriel's breath came in sharp bursts as he clutched at his chest. His eyes watered, blurring the vision of Lady Death standing above him" (Thomas 18). Here, the site of the body becomes representative of connection. It is felt, viscerally, and is manifested through the body. Yadriel's queer body is in tune with the other brujx; he feels the unbearable pain inflicted onto Miguel. The notion of sensation in his chest becomes a key image in Yadriel's struggle to validate his trans identity—to have a recognition of his trans masculine body—to his family and the other brujx. Without this acknowledgment, Yadriel's attempts to control his body's appearance become painful, difficult moments full of resistance in contestation. For example, "Water had soaked into his [Yadriel's] binder, making it tight and freezing cold, sucking all the warmth from his core" (Thomas 234) and "the tight, stretchy material [of his binder], it clung mercilessly to his wet shoulders. Yadriel gave it a tug, wiggled, and squirmed, but it only seemed to get tighter" (Thomas 248–49).

Binding functions as a mode of embodying masculinity that rejects the cultural coding of gender, allowing trans men to pass and assert their masculine identity while also avoiding incidents of transphobic violence. Thus, trans men, when presented in the public space, can be perceived as a threat to heteronormative, cisgender masculinity (Namaste 592). Tito's attack after becoming maligno—the turning evil of spirits if they remain tied to the earth for too long—signifies that the fears of the Latinx community being attacked by outsiders is mirrored back in the attack on Yadriel. Though it is not intimated that Tito attacks Yadriel because of his queer identity, the saturating rain as he and Julian return, sucking the warmth from Yadriel's "core," speaks to his return to the brujx barrio as a space of danger, one where his core, his identity, renders Yadriel vulnerable to antiqueer violence from his own community. As identity and connection to other brujx are depicted as coming through the body, the binder challenges the body as the sight of brujx identity. Moreover, the assault takes on the valence of a "reinscription" of the trans masculine body, asserting that the victim is not "really" a man, and violates dictates of trying to access masculine power (Namaste 592). Yadriel is able to counter this antitrans violence by a reassertion of his masculinity symbolized in his ritual dagger. Here, the dagger becomes a sartorial marker of brujo masculinity, not merely adornment. Clothing and adornments become critical markers to pass in terms of gender, but also to actively "assert queer and transgender identity" for queer Latinxs (Rodríguez 225). Galarte argues that "the expressiveness of the trans masculinity embodied by [Chicano FTM trans figures] can and should be read as a protest against the pathologization of transsexuality and the violence of hegemonic, heteropatriarchal Chicano masculinity" (114). Through this vanquishing and wielding of brujo power, Yadriel presents a resistant trans masculinity, though this tense moment relates the threats to Yadriel as coming not from the East LA barrio, but his own brujx community.

SANTA MUERTE AND ST. J

The irony in the queerphobia of the brujx community in Thomas's novel lies in that, as they seek to protect their utopic vision of Latinidad, they also worship Santa Muerte, the patron saint of social outcasts. This folk saint, who is not formally recognized, and often demonized, by the Catholic Church, has a strong following and devotion amongst folks in Mexico, Latin America, and in the United States. La Huesita, as she is also named, has become a beacon for Latinxs who feel they stand on the outskirts of mainstream, acceptable Latinx identity. In contrast to other deities, Santa Muerte is nonjudgmental, a deity who instead is accepting of all who devote themselves of her, giving no preferential treatment to any of her adherents (Prower 14). Because of her welcoming of all, this skeleton saint draws many followers who are social outcasts, or those whose work leaves them vulnerable to violence with impunity: thieves, cartels, sex workers, bartenders, and mariachi players (Prower 38). And while the brujx, due to their mystical abilities, seek Santa Muerte's protection as a means to maintain their community, they also gloss over Santa Muerte's adoption and celebration within LGBTQ circles.

It is, after all, Santa Muerte who provides Yadriel with his powers, interpellating him as a brujo when his own father and the other brujx refuse to validate his identity. When Yadriel offers up his blood as part of the ritual of becoming a brujo, he feels "a rush of air brushed against his face and dragged like fingers through his hair. The flames trembled, and the statue of Lady Death suddenly felt alive" (Thomas 14). Santa Muerte, then, regulates and offers up the power to those to whom it belongs. Depicted as the aftermath of death, she is a skeleton whose gender is not defined or confined by social constructions; she defies regulation over her sexuality and is only signified as female through the robes she wears; which is at best a gender—i.e., female—performance (Blackwell 593). Yet, she is still tethered down by the brujx, who simultaneously impose gender policing even when it subverts their deity.

Santa Muerte is the beacon for the brujx community, but Julian, who is painted as a troubled "gang" member by his fellow classmates, also seeks redemption through a different saint: Saint Jude or the patron saint of desperate cases. Tethering Julian's spirit to the earth—he has been killed by an unknown assailant—is his medal depicting this Catholic saint. St. Jude is seen as the patron saint of desperate cases, the saint of last resort, of those who feel hopeless. He is beloved by those seen as outcasts—the destitute, the sick, the frightened, the lonely, the dying. Julian is characterized as the lost cause, first because of the rumors surrounding him as the son of a Colombian cartel leader, but it is further revealed that he is an outcast due to poverty, orphanhood, and sexuality. As Santa Muerte becomes Yadriel's protector, St. Jude serves as the possibility of hope in a world where he is cast off as a "street kid": on Julian's pendant, St. Jude's image is "bright silver, as if it had been polished by someone rubbing their thumb against it over and over" (Thomas 48). A juxtaposition between St. Jude and Santa Muerte reflects the budding relationship between Yadriel and Julian, both outcasted from their respective barrios.

But Julian is also presented as a saint, albeit an unorthodox one. He becomes the patron saint of a group of other LGBTQ kids who are forced to live hidden near some train tracks. Upon going to see Julian's friends—per Julian's demands—to see if they are okay following Julian's death, Yadriel is captivated by a piece of graffiti: "Below in lopsided black letters was HAY NIÑAS CON PENE, NIÑOS CON VULVA Y TRANSFÓBICOS SIN DIENTES. In the lower corner, it read, ST. J." (Thomas 143) This juxtaposition of antitransphobia and religiosity forces an interrogation into the ways religions, such as Catholicism and the brujx clan, use religious doctrine to inflict violence onto gender nonconforming and queer bodies. Divinity is associated with those who must have faith to believe in a world outside of the one that represses and inflicts harm on the queer community. In a reversal, a retaliatory violence is insinuated: transphobes will have their teeth knocked out in this space where Julian and his friends find sanctuary. The St. J here alludes to St. Jude's protection of these destitute outcasts, as Julian has shown his devotion to the saint he believes protects him and his friends. Yet, the ambiguity of the J in St. J demands to be read as St. Julian. And his death becomes a sort of martyrdom, protecting his friend Luca: "Probably tryna mug him or something, which is dumb 'cause he's never got any money.... So, I just ran up on him from behind and shoved him. I thought I knocked him over, but he turned and before I could take off... Everything went black" (Thomas 64). His sacrifice saves his friends from death. He also becomes a patron saint for Yadriel as well. Yadriel has to keep the tethering object, the St. Jude medal around his neck, and in instances where this is brought up in the novel, Julian offers up encouragement and support for Yadriel in accepting his trans identity, unencumbered by the brujx and their expectations or their acceptance. He asks Yadriel "Why do you have to prove anything to anyone?" "You don't need anyone's permission to be you, Yads" (Thomas 183). This is followed by his explanation that Yadriel cannot be the first or the last trans brujx who has existed. Julian then becomes the patron saint to queer Latinxs, proffering protection, encouragement, someone to listen to their struggles and prayers, and also an arbiter of a queer history and queer past that has been rendered invisible by a heteronormative Latinidad, not just in the brujx community, but the wider Latinx community that instead criminalizes, demonizes, and inflicts psychic, spiritual, and physical harm upon queer Latinxs. Julian offers up an alternative narrative that asks Latinxs to examine the ways they have contributed to the violent erasure of queer and trans folks through their need to establish a generic Latinidad.

THE GHOSTS OF QUEER LATINX FUTURES

Cemetery Boys builds a Barrio Gothic world, one where the brujx—Thomas's fictional, magical, mystical, Latinx community of East LA—fear queer Latinxs broaching the walls of the brujx's enclosed, isolated, heteronormative view of Latinidad. Queer Latinxs like Yadriel and Julian struggle to be acknowledged, to survive, and to exist in spite of both a white, American world that marginalizes them for their ethnic identity and their expulsion from their heritage communities. Yadriel is able to gain acceptance through an embracing of his Latinidad, centering how queer Latinxs have existed all along; through his ability to harness the power of a brujo, Yadriel showcases the erased history of queer Latinxs by displaying power not seen in the brujx community since earlier, mythical times. Moreover, Yadriel retraces the existence of queer Latinxs from the earlier, indigenous, mythical times as an integral part of Latinidad, not a threat to it, with divisions in the brujx community leaving them all unprotected from the outside threats of US racial regimes.

But more than simply speaking to the existence of queer Latinxs throughout time, *Cemetery Boys* uses Julian's ghost to further show the ways that queer Latinidad speaks not only from the past, but from a possible queer future. This is especially critical in YA novels whose central characters are children, and in *Cemetery Boys*, queer Latinx children. Angel Matos and Jon Wargo argue that "Because children have not been restricted, hampered, or defined by the influences of knowledge and experience, their futures are therefore more open—full of promise, potentiality, and the ability to imagine a place and time different from the present" (2). While the image of the child is "contingent on White, middle-to-upper-class frameworks" (Matos and Wargo 5) of temporality, one that is heteronormatively linear in that it leads to reproduction, queer Latinx children represent a challenge to this conception of a linear time that necessitates the death of queer Latinxs due to the threat of the notion that reproduction of whiteness is the only possible future. Throughout the narrative, Julian is thought to be dead, but when Yadriel confronts Catriz, it is revealed that "it was Julian, and he was alive, but barely. . . . Sticking out of his chest, right above his heart, was a dagger" (Thomas 295). Julian's simultaneous existence between corporeality and spirituality, his ability to exist simultaneously in two planes, represents the possibility for queer existence beyond the present. By being both ghost and living body, existing contemporaneously, Julian disrupts straight time, instead showing both the existence of queer present/presence and queer future. Yadriel falls in love with Julian as Julian normalizes Yadriel's gender identity, though a troublesome and irksome pest, Julian models an embrace of queerness as Other to heteronormativity. In seeking to be accepted as a trans boy, Yadriel desires interpellation into masculinity; Julian instead offers up no notion of wanting to adopt culturally dictated performances of masculinity. Through his alternate spiritual form, Julian speaks to a queer life and future in light of the dangers that threaten queer life.

Ghosts haunt from the past, but they also represent an afterlife, one that is beyond the current present of antiqueer violence. To imagine queer life beyond the now is needed for queer survival. Julian's ghost transforms the ghost from relic of the past to messenger of a future. In this way, Thomas disidentifies the notion of the ghost as harbinger of past wrongs bubbling up to torment those living in the present. For José Esteban Muñoz, "Dominant signs and symbols, often ones that are toxic to minoritarian subjects, can be imagined through an engaged and animated mode of performance or spectatorship" (169). For Muñoz, the symbols that seek to destroy, harm, or erase queer peoples become moments to refashion them, showcase the way heteronormativity is itself a performance that can be altered to reveal its social constructed nature. As mentioned, there are toxic ghosts, those that turn maligno—evil—in the brujx cemetery and attack Yadriel. These ghosts function to control the queer Latinx child ghost of Julian, inverting the narrative of heteronormativity that renders queer futurity as "horrific and spectral in and of itself" (Matos and Wargo 11).[3] Julian makes the liminal ghost one that serves as proof that queer futurity is possible. Julian here is performing as a ghost, for he is not dead, but merely incapacitated. In this moment, he is able to sit within a liminality of being that allows him to transmit messages to other queer folks, protecting and encouraging them to not subsume themselves to heteronormative Latinidad, not to become queer ghosts that are buried in the margins of the past.

Through his return to the living realm through Yadriel, Julian materializes a queerness that is visible, that is part of the Latinx community, not an antagonist or threat to it. This moment disidentifies queer death as not an inevitable and tragic end. Now once again fully embodied, Julian represents an envisioning of a different time and place of queer identity that can be realized in the now, and one that allows for queer survival and queer futurity, expanding the barrio and its possibilities. This blurring of queer identity as between life beyond the now is further developed when Julian and Yadriel are recuperating in a hospital following Catriz's attack and Yadriel's performance of resurrecting the dead. Upon seeing Julian, "Luca openly gaped like he was staring at a ghost" (Thomas 325). Even as Julian is pinned back into his body, his spirit reconnecting with his physical form, he still wears the traces of his ghost form. He is simultaneously an insertion into and subversion of the normative, being alive but also containing the traces of the ghost. By this disidentification of life and death, Julian as queer subject gestures towards a possible future, providing a different version of a queer existence and world that could exist.

In the novel's final scene, where Yadriel is finally presented as brujo before the larger brujx community, he brings Julian to the ceremony with him. This is a bridge of the brujx barrio and the queer barrio; what was once seen as two distinct spheres of Latinidad are merged. Upon seeing Julian, he is described by Yadriel's mother as "a ghost boy who came back from the dead, thanks to my Yadriel" (Thomas 336). Camila's description here revels Julian as a bridge; he is not just a boy that was resurrected but a ghost boy, one who reveals the alternative possibilities of Latinidad that exist, if only the Latinx community would open its eyes and see beyond its patriarchal, machista, heteronormative present.

NOTES

1. In his novel, Thomas uses brujx to refer to both the larger community and to when referring to more than one brujx. I maintain this nomenclature rather than pluralizing the term in these cases so as to maintain consistency with the novel.

2. Merla-Watson describes Latinx speculative fiction as "texts [that] often blend speculative genres, such as sci-fi, fantasy, horror," which then "create new, hybrid forms reflective of cultural mestizaje." Thomas's text while arguably incorporating fantasy, maintains many of the hallmarks of the Gothic, marking it outside of this definition of speculative fiction.

3. Matos and Wargo build on the work by Mason Derritt and Joshua Whitehean in "When Everything Feels Like the Horror Movies: The Ghostliness of Queer Youth Futurity." *Research on Diversity in Youth Literature* 2, no. 1, Article 3 (2019): 1–21.

WORKS CITED

Blackwell, Brent Adam. "Devotional Politics as States of Exception: Santa Muerte's Challenge to Church and State Sovereignties." *Political Theology* 21, no. 7 (2020): 591–605.

Blanco, María del Pilar, and Esther Peeren. *Popular Ghosts: The Haunted Spaces of Everyday Culture*. Continuum, 2010.

Foucault, Michel. *Discipline and Punish: The Birth of the Prison*, edited by Alan Sheridan. Penguin, 2020.

Galarte, Francisco J. *Brown Trans Figurations: Rethinking Race, Gender, and Sexuality in Chicanx/Latinx Studies*. University of Texas Press, 2021.

García Bedolla, Lisa. *Fluid Borders: Latino Power, Identity, and Politics in Los Angeles*. University of California Press, 2005.

Goin, Keara K. "Marginal Latinidad: Afro-Latinas and Us Film." *Latino Studies* 14, no. 3 (2016): 344–63.

González, Tanya. "The (Gothic) Gift of Death in Cherríe Moraga's 'The Hungry Woman: A Mexican Medea (2001).'" *Chicana/Latina Studies* 7, no. 1 (2007): 44–77.

Lloyd Smith, Allan. *American Gothic Fiction: An Introduction*. Continuum, 2004.

Londoño Johana. *Abstract Barrios: The Crises of Latinx Visibility in Cities*. Duke University Press, 2020.

Matos, Angel Daniel, and Jon Michael Wargo. "Editors' Introduction: Queer Futurities in Youth Literature, Media, and Culture." *Research on Diversity in Youth Literature* 2, no. 1, Article 1 (2019).

Merla-Watson, Cathryn Josefina. "The Altermundos of Latin@futurism." *Alluvium*, 2017. www.alluvium-journal.org/2017/03/15/the-altermundos-of-latinfuturism/.

Merla-Watson, Cathryn Josefina, and B. V. Olguín, eds. *Altermundos: Latin@ Speculative Literature, Film, and Popular Culture*. UCLA Chicano Studies Research Center Press, 2017.

Muñoz, José Esteban. "'Chico, What Does It Feel Like to Be a Problem?' The Transmission of Brownness." *A Companion to Latina/o Studies*, edited by Juan Flores and Renato Rosaldo. Wiley, 2007.

Muñoz, José Esteban. *Cruising Utopia: The Then and There of Queer Futurity*. 10th Anniversary ed., New York University Press, 2019.

Namaste, Viviane K. "Genderbashing: Sexuality, Gender, and the Regulation of Public Space." *The Transgender Studies Reader*, edited by Susan Stryker and Stephen Whittle. Routledge, 2006, 584–600.

Peréz, Gina M. "Barrio." *Keywords for Latina/o Studies*, edited by Deborah Vargas et al. New York University Press, 2017.

Prower, Tomás. *La Santa Muerte: Unearthing the Magic and Mysticism of Death*. Llewellyn, 2015.

Rodríguez, Sonia Alejandra. "'Fierce and Fearless': Dress and Identity in Rigoberto González's The Mariposa Club." *MeXicana Fashions: Politics, Self-Adornment, and Identity Construction*, edited by Aída Hurtado and Norma E. Cantú. University of Texas Press, 2020, 216–34.

Romo, Richard. *East Los Angeles: History of a Barrio*. University of Texas Press, 1983.

Santos, Adrianna M. "Broken Open: Writing, Healing, and Affirmation in Isabel Quintero's *Gabi, A Girl in Pieces* and Erika L. Sánchez's *I Am Not Your Perfect Mexican Daughter*." *Nerds, Goths, Geeks, and Freaks: Outsiders in Chicanx and Latinx Young Adult Literature*, edited by Trevor Boffone and Cristina Herrera. University Press of Mississippi, 2020, 45–60.

Thomas, Aidan. *Cemetery Boys*. Swoon Reads, 2020.

Villa Raúl. *Barrio-Logos: Space and Place in Urban Chicano Literature and Culture*. University of Texas Press, 2000.

Chapter Two

WHEN BISEXUALITY IS SPOKEN

Normalizing Bi Latino Boys in Adam Silvera's
They Both Die at the End

Trevor Boffone

In 2019, culture reporter Gwen Aviles, writing for NBC News, published an article signaling a groundswell of interest in queer Young Adult (YA) Literature. Aviles's article, "The Rise of Young Adult Books with LGBTQ Characters—and what's next," demonstrates how, within the already burgeoning field of YA literature, the market for novels that feature queer characters is also expanding. This growth signals an increased demand among readers of YA fiction for characters and stories that speak to identities and experiences that have been traditionally left out of literature marketed towards young people. This push for more diverse and #ownvoices YA literature specifically focuses on three things—race, ethnicity, and sexuality. Aviles recognizes how transgender, intersex, and asexual readers still lack representation while work by Latinx YA authors such as Benjamin Alire Sáenz, Gabby Rivera, and Adam Silvera are filling gaps for queer Latinx teens. It seems the road to nuanced queer representation in the realm of YA literature has its lows, but there are plenty of highs that must be celebrated.[1]

By any measure, queer Latinx YA fiction is having a moment, with a rapidly flourishing canon of novels that speak to not only a full spectrum of Latinx identity but also a multifaceted portrayal of queer sexualities.[2] This growing corpus of Latinx YA literature focusing on queer teens includes representative examples such as *Aristotle and Dante Discover the Secrets of the Universe* by Benjamin Alire Sáenz, *Tommy Stands Alone* by Gloria Velásquez,

Rainbow Boys by Alex Sanchez, *Down to the Bone* by Mayra Lazara Dole, *The Mariposa Club* by Rigoberto González, *Chulito* by Charles Rice-González, *More Happy Than Not* by Adam Silvera, and *Juliet Takes A Breath* by Gabby Rivera. Indeed, this list, in tandem with Aviles's article, signals a changing-of-the-guard so to speak, although there is still one identity that remains almost entirely excluded from the narrative—bisexual Latino boys.

If I have learned anything from teaching LGBT studies and engaging with Bisexual Twitter (not to mention being bisexual myself), bisexuality is one of the most frequently misunderstood queer identities. As such, let's begin with some definitions and statistics. Bisexuals are people that can be attracted, both romantically and/or sexually, to people of their gender and people of other genders; they can be attracted to these people at different times, in different ways, and to different degrees (Ochs).[3] Furthermore, bisexuals make up more than half the LGB community and over 40 percent of bisexuals also identify as people of color (Gates; Human Rights Campaign). Despite these large numbers, in nearly every facet of US popular culture, bisexuals face challenges regarding representation. For instance, bisexual characters in film and television are few and far between.[4] More specifically, it's no secret that bisexuality is underrepresented in YA fiction and, whereas there is a growing corpus of YA lit focusing on bisexual girls, there is a noticeable void of books written about bisexual boys of any race or ethnicity.[5] Aside from novels such as *Honestly Ben* by Bill Konigsberg, *Boyfriends with Girlfriends* by Alex Sanchez, *Double Feature: Attack of the Soul-Sucking Brain Zombies/ Bride of the Soul-Sucking Brain Zombies* by Brent Hartinger, *Boy Meets Boy* by David Levithan, *Cut Both Ways* by Carrie Mesrobian, *It's Our Prom (So Deal With It)* by Julie Anne Peters, *The Gentleman's Guide to Vice and Virtue* and *The Gentleman's Guide to Getting Lucky* by Mackenzi Lee, *Grasshopper Jungle* by Andrew Smith, and *Deposing Nathan* by Zack Smedley, representative examples are scarce.[6] As Bonnie Kneen highlights, "The absence of bisexuality in YA fiction thus follows (and reinforces) a broader invisibility that is likely to shape most teenagers' lived experience of bisexuality" (363). A 2009 study by Kosciw supports this, revealing that over half of LGBT high school students identify as bisexual (10). And, according to the Pew Research Center, just 19 percent of bisexual males are fully out. Moreover, Epstein comments that when bisexuality does appear in YA fiction, it is oftentimes seen as less desirable than being heterosexual or homosexual ("The Case" 111).[7] By any measure, cultural production by, for, and about queer Latinx youth has been "underestimated, overlooked, and undervalued" (Perez 141). If we know this to be true, that is, that bisexual male representation is almost nonexistent on the page and on screen, the stories of one demographic in particular—bi

Latino boys—are even more noticeably absent. Indeed, by any means, the road to bisexual representation in YA literature is indeed an uphill climb.[8]

Ultimately, these facts led me to question—where are the stories about bisexual Latino teens? When do Latino boys get to be bisexual? If bisexuality is to truly achieve mainstream visibility, then YA literature must become responsive to this systemic lack of representation. And part of this responsiveness is creating an ecosystem that supports a plurality of bisexual identities that stretch across markers of race and ethnicity. This is to say, Latino boys rarely get the chance to be bisexual on YA pages. As this article title states, there is power "when bisexuality is spoken." Although bisexuality does not need to be named to exist on YA pages, there is power in texts that openly name it, as these normalize bisexuality and refuse its erasure. Despite bisexuals making up the largest demographic of the LGBT community in tandem with the United States' growing Latinx population, we can count instances of Latino teenage bisexuality in YA literature on one hand. Latinx YA novels such as *Boyfriends with Girlfriends* by Alex Sanchez, *Dragonlinked: Dragonlinked Chronicles, Volume 1* and *The Bond: Dragonlinked Chronicles, Volume 2* by Adolfo Garza Jr., and *They Both Die at the End* and *Infinity Son* by Adam Silvera remain part of only a handful of books that explicitly write Latino teen bisexuality into the narrative.[9][10] That said, there is a sizeable corpus of YA novels that portray Latina bisexuality such as *Wild Beauty* by Anna-Marie McLemore, *Labyrinth Lost* by Zoraida Córdova, and *The Resolutions* by Mia García. Although these novels do important work in terms of identity and representation, this is beyond the scope of my work in this article.[11] Moreover, queer Latinx YA literary scholarship has largely excluded Latino bisexuality. While studies by scholars Carolina Alonso, Cecilia J. Aragón, Laura Jiménez, Marilisa Jiménez-García, and Angel Daniel Matos have made key interventions into our collective understanding of gay and lesbian Latinx identities as they materialize in YA fiction, these studies do not fully address the intersections of boyhood, bisexuality, and Latinidad.[12]

Although all the aforementioned texts are ripe for scholarly analysis, I now turn my attention to Adam Silvera's 2017 novel, *They Both Die at the End*. I argue that *They Both Die at the End* pushes against bisexual erasure in Latinx YA fiction while also presenting a blueprint for how Latino bisexuality might be rendered discursively spoken. As this article demonstrates, bisexuality is the norm in Silvera's novel. While this might seem inconsequential, as the aforementioned research and statistics indicate, the mere act of writing Latino bisexuality into the narrative remains a radical—and powerful—act of inclusion. Novels that do so push against the mainstream erasure of bisexuality that is all too common. The intricate and subtle ways that *They Both Die at the End* addresses bisexuality render the book singular in both Latinx and YA literatures. The novel challenges some of the expectations that people have of queer Latinx representation in YA, and in bisexual representation more specifically. As such, *They Both Die at the End* merits our critical attention.

WHEN LATINO BOYS GET TO BE BISEXUAL: *THEY BOTH DIE AT THE END*

Born and raised in the Bronx, Puerto Rican writer Adam Silvera (1990–) has burst onto the scene as a veritable force in the field of young adult literature. He has achieved something rare in young adult publishing—writing queer Latinx stories that routinely make the *New York Times* Best Seller list. And these aren't watered down depictions of Latinidad or queerness either.[13] His novels *More Happy Than Not* (2015), *History Is All You Left Me* (2017), *What If It's Us* (2018, coauthored with Becky Albertalli), and the Infinity Son series (*Infinity Son*, 2020; *Infinity Reaper*, 2021) all draw on Silvera's own positionality as a gay Latino while offering nuanced portrayals of characters who have largely been excluded from the YA canon. Silvera has already cemented himself as both the present and future of queer Latinx YA—all before his thirtieth birthday.[14]

They Both Die at the End takes place in what looks and feels just like present-day New York City. But something is different. In this alternate universe, Silvera paints a dystopian world in which people receive a phone call from Death-Cast on the day they are going to die, giving them anywhere from a few seconds to nearly twenty-four hours to live. The phone call doesn't give any details—just that they are going to die. At the start of the book, we meet the two protagonists—Mateo, an eighteen-year-old gay Puerto Rican homebody, and Rufus, a seventeen-year-old bisexual Cuban American who has faced many of life's challenges in recent years, including becoming a foster kid after he witnesses his family die. These two teenage boys are going to die, and there is nothing they can do to stop it. Silvera's novel doesn't rely on a single narrator; rather, the point of view frequently flips back and forth between Mateo and Rufus in addition to vignettes from other supporting characters.[15] While some of these brief interludes from other characters may seem unnecessary at first, all the stories converge at some point, influencing Mateo and Rufus's narrative. Once Mateo and Rufus get the infamous call, they become known as "Deckers," join a social media app called "Last Friend," meet each other, and eventually spend their last day filled with the highs and lows that one would expect from such a story. As the two boys become friends throughout the day, they build community. According to Juan Flores, the Spanish term "comunidad" is comprised of two parts—"común," or what people have in common; and "unidad," or what unites them (193). In the case of Mateo and Rufus, they are drawn together by their similarities (age and death, for example) and they are united by the queer friendship that is intrinsically tied to their Latinx identities. That is, they come together through a shared sense of what José Esteban Muñoz calls "feeling brown," a "manera de ser, a way of being in the world" that ties people together through their shared sense of "feeling like a problem, in commonality" (39). Muñoz adds, "Feeling Brown is feeling together in difference" (39). Rufus and Mateo come together through sharing the same problem—they are two queer Latinos who are going to die. Naturally, this leads everyone in their lives to pity the two boys, wishing they could help but ultimately knowing that there is nothing that can be done. While feeling Brown, the two boys process grief, imagine what could have been, make peace with the past, check off items on their bucket lists, and fall in love. Oh, and they both die at the end.

While this might seem like a depressing story—after all, it is about two teenagers who are about to die—it is more a book that celebrates the reasons we live.[16] We live for the people we love. We live for the experiences we get to have. As Mateo and Rufus come to learn, their Death Day is truly about embracing popular sayings such as carpe diem, YOLO (you only live once), and "no day but today," to borrow from the musical *Rent*. Their final day on earth is about living their life to its fullest extent and, as is often the case, it's about doing that with people you love. Moreover, within this universe, there is no surprise regarding death. During a January 24, 2021, Twitter question and answer session, Silvera responded to several reader questions about how Rufus and Mateo view death. People can opt out of the Death-Cast phone call, meaning that the two boys both accepted the rules of this universe and didn't try to avoid it (@AdamSilvera A). A follow up question asks if Silvera is afraid of dying. His response surely influenced his writing: "I wrestle with mortality a lot, especially dying ahead of my time. That's how I conceived Death-Cast to KNOW when it's your last day" (@AdamSilvera B). Another reader asks Silvera if Rufus and Mateo are happy in the afterlife, to which Silvera responds, "I like to think so" (@AdamSilvera C). This Twitter conversation reveals Silvera's motivations for writing his novel while also conveying Rufus and Mateo's approach to their Last Day. Dying, then, is simply another part of life and, although their day has moments of dread and defeat, ultimately they are able to celebrate the day in queer community.

They Both Die at the End is noteworthy for the ways that Silvera allows bisexuality to be spoken. Whereas Mateo's queerness is never explicitly addressed or given a name—he never says he is gay—Rufus's bisexuality is frequently presented in a very matter-of-fact way. Although bisexuals can exist without being named, as queer YA literature scholar Jennifer Colette proposes, texts that do not name bisexuality are not "effective representation" of bisexuality (86). Moreover, Mateo spends his Last Day coming to terms with being gay, which is a radically different experience compared to Rufus, who has already accepted this integral part of his Latinidad. Given these premises, Silvera's rendering of Rufus recalls Latinx studies scholar Lázaro Lima's proposal that queer identity practices "provide alternative social imaginaries and templates from which to envision forms of national inclusion that establish greater continuity between the past, the present, and the futures of queer Latino communities and aesthetics" (10). Rufus's characterization offers a key intervention into unraveling the nuances of Latinx queerness. Much like the protagonist Mila in Emilio Rodriguez's 2017 play *Swimming While Drowning*, who is battling homelessness while coming to terms with his queerness, Rufus pushes against traditional racial and ethnic scripts by troubling the notion of masculinity and what it entails to live a life on the streets. As Latinx cultural studies scholar Boffone posits in "Young, Gay, and Latino: 'Feeling Brown' in Emilio Rodriguez's *Swimming While Drowning*," "Although these urban youths wrestle with the expectations of masculinity, they both actively reject the major identity script of Latino urban identity: the cholo, which has all-too-often become the stereotypical image of Latino men" (146). As *They Both Die at the End* and *Swimming While Drowning* demonstrate, writing alternative identity practices works to push against the stereotypes of Latino urban youth identity. This is to say that cultural work such as *They Both Die at the End* is a process of "broadening the identities of young Latinos" (Boffone 146).

Rufus's narrative begins in an unexpected way. When we meet him, he is jumping his ex-girlfriend's new boyfriend, Peck. He is surrounded by the "Plutos," who at first appear to be a gang, but in reality are anything but that—they are a group of teens who live at the same foster home and have become a chosen family. Or as Chicana queer theorist Cherríe Moraga proposes in her play *Giving Up the Ghost*, they "make familia from scratch" (58). That is, Rufus imposes a queer chosen family structure on the Plutos. This group rejects the heteronormative family unit that Latinx studies scholar Richard T. Rodríguez proposes has always traditionally existed in Latinx cultures and dominated community structures (2). Rodríguez suggests that we reimagine family structures by unpacking what family means for those who don't fit within its traditional confines (3). In the case of Rufus, as a bisexual family leader, he encourages his friend group to create familia from scratch with him. Although we do not know the sexualities of his friends, they inevitably queer popular notions of what urban life is like for youth of color. For example, Silvera initially paints Rufus as a stereotypical (straight) cholo before unraveling the character's identity in such a way as to create something entirely original. In fact, Rufus's bisexuality would likely be shocking to a reader who entered the text without any previous knowledge. When we meet Rufus, he is entrenched in machismo and toxic masculinity. It is in this stereotype that Silvera disrupts the notion of masculinity and effectively forges Rufus's queerness. Here, Silvera's depiction of the cholo stereotype reveals the complexities of identity and how, more often than not, youth identities don't fit neatly into a box. They are nuanced and full of contradictions.

As a bisexual Latino, Rufus's journey parallels Chicana queer theorist Gloria Anzaldúa's concept of Nepantla. Nepantla is a Nahuatl word signifying being between different spaces. According to Anzaldúa, this in-between space, despite being "unstable, unpredictable, precarious," and "always-in-transition," is a site in which transformations can materialize (1). Nepantlerxs are a threshold people who "move within and among multiple, often conflicting, worlds and refuse to align themselves exclusively with any single individual, group, or belief system" (Keating 6). As a place of in-between-ness, invisibility, and transition, Nepantla particularly speaks to the bisexual coming-of-age experience. Nepantla can signal confusion, pain, a loss of control, and anxiety—all things that are embodied in stories of teenagers working through their bisexuality. In the case of Rufus, following the death of his family, he is left on the streets and, therefore, must develop survival skills and new forms of queer family. Yet, as we see from his relationship with the Plutos, the struggles he endures are matched by the brotherly bonds he creates with his friends. When Rufus meets Mateo, he moves through Nepantla, coming out on the other end as a more self-assured queer teen who has accepted his place in the world and his fate.

In *The B Word: Bisexuality in Contemporary Film and Television*, Maria San Filippo theorizes the issue of visibility in her exploration of bisexuality in media: "Bisexuality is both visible and invisible . . . due to the slippage between its representational pervasiveness and the alternating measures of tacit acceptance, disidentification, or disavowal that render bisexuality discursively un(der)spoken" (4). Effectively, bisexuality is both unspoken and underspoken. Silvera's novel pushes against this invisibility and underspokenness shortly after the reader meets Rufus. His violent turn soon leads to a clash with the police, who unexpectedly show up at the foster home looking for him. Rufus flees out the backdoor, finds himself alone, and downloads Last Friend in a last-ditch effort to find company with another Decker. From this profile, he puts his sexuality on full display alongside other key identity markers. Silvera writes,

> **Name:** Rufus Emeterio
> **Age:** 17.
> **Gender:** Male.
> **Height:** 5'10".
> **Weight:** 169 lbs.
> **Ethnicity:** Cuban-American
> **Sexuality:** Bisexual.
> . . .
> **Final Thoughts:** It's about time. I've made mistakes, but I'm gonna go out right. (72–73)

In this instance, Rufus's profile pushes against the ways that bisexuality is rendered discursively unspoken and underspoken. Doing this, San Filippo posits, resists "the monosexist assumptions of dominant cultural discourses," assumptions which largely (re)inforce a gay-straight binary of sexuality (35). This binary renders bisexuality invisible, which is particularly concerning for teenagers since it limits queer teens' understanding of their plural desires (Kneen 362). We can see how Silvera pushes against this binary through Rufus's openness and outness. Indeed, in this moment Rufus is confident in his sexuality; he puts himself out there in such a way as to reject the notion that bisexual males must be in the closet or on the down low. Yes, he admits to having made mistakes, but he's not making them anymore. His Last Day will be done the right way, as he is an out bisexual Cuban American teen.

Rufus's outness counters Mateo's closetedness. In this case, Silvera flips the traditional script in which gayness is easier to name and is thus a more viable identity than bisexuality. In *They Both Die at the End*, bisexuality is the norm and gayness is messy. Routinely, Mateo attempts to give voice to his queerness, but continues to fall short. When the two boys visit Mateo's father. who is in a coma at the hospital, Mateo attempts to finally come out to his father:

> It's time I tell you a story for once. You were always asking me—begging me, sometimes—to tell you more about my life and how my day was, and I always shut down. But me talking is all we've got now, and I'm crossing my fingers and toes and unmentionables that you can hear me." I grip his hands, wishing he'd squeeze back.
> "Dad, I . . ."

I was raised to be honest, but the truth can be complicated. It doesn't matter if the truth won't make a mess, sometimes the words don't come out until you're alone. Even that's not guaranteed. Sometimes the truth is a secret you're keeping from yourself because living a lie is easier. (Silvera 117–8)

Gayness is unspoken. It is hidden. Even with his father who can't hear him, Mateo can't say it; he can't say those three words—"I am gay." In contrast, Rufus's coming out is very matter-of-fact and something he feels he *must* do once his parents and sister get the call from Death-Cast telling them they will die within twenty-four hours. After Rufus casually mentions that his sister was the first person he came out to, Mateo asks if he ever came out to his parents:

"On our last day together, year. I couldn't put it off any longer." My parents had never hugged me like they did on their End Day. I'm really proud I spoke up to get that moment out of them. "My mom got really sad because she'd never get a chance to meet her future daughter- or son-in-law." (Silvera 176)

Admittedly, coming out to one's parents on their Last Day is not a normal situation, even in the alternate universe that Silvera constructs. Perhaps knowing that you will never see your child again influences the queer rite of passage. Even so, Silvera flips the trope of Latinx parents being unaccepting of queerness with the love that Rufus is met with after coming out. In this instance, the only thing that matters to his parents is supporting their child and ensuring that he knows they love him for who he truly was.

Although *They Both Die at the End* is not a romance, at least in the traditional sense, the narrative does hinge around Rufus and Mateo falling in love. Neither boy is a fully reliable narrator, but each leaves the reader with nuggets of flirtation and questioning the other boy's motivations and romantic interest. In perhaps the novel's most euphoric moment, Rufus and Mateo go to Clint's Graveyard, a club for Deckers to celebrate their final day on earth. At the club, the two boys sing karaoke to "American Pie" by Don McLean before being whisked offstage. While the two boys have danced around kissing throughout the day, in this moment Mateo finally takes Rufus's signals and kisses the boy he has fallen in love with. Silvera writes,

I drag him offstage, and once we're behind the curtain, I look him in the eyes and he smiles like he knows what's about to go down. And he's not wrong.

I kiss the guy who brought me to life on the day we're going to die.

"Finally!" Rufus says when I give him the chance to breathe, and now he kisses me. "What took you so long?"

"I know, I know. I'm sorry. I know there's no time to waste, but I had to be sure you are who I thought you were. The best thing about dying is your friendship. . . . And even if I never got to kiss you, you gave me the life I always wanted." (308–9)

While Mateo initiates the kiss and appears to have been the most influenced by the unexpected friendship, Rufus has been affected just as much. After the kiss, he admits that he had been "so damn lost the past few months" and was filled with doubts (Silvera 309). He needed help to find himself again. And as evidenced in the novel, the intrinsic bonds of queer love and friendship are exactly what Rufus needed to become a better version of himself. Although he had accepted his bisexuality and, in turn, been accepted by his family, something was missing—Mateo.

As Rufus nears death, the spokenness of his bisexuality has one remaining act. While the duo are about to kiss again backstage, Rufus's eye drifts away and he smiles. His friends have arrived at the club. Up until this point in the narrative, it has been hinted that his friends know he is bisexual, but it has never been explicitly mentioned. The forwardness that Rufus exhibits by naming his bisexuality in his Last Friend profile implies a certain level of outness. When the Plutos see Rufus and Mateo embracing, there is uncertainty as to how the open display of queerness will be accepted. The Plutos group hug Rufus. Rufus narrates, "'I love you guys,' I say. No one cracks homo jokes. We're past that" (Silvera 317). In this world, in this friend group, being bisexual is normal. Being bisexual isn't taboo. Latino boys can be bisexual. Latino boys can kiss cute boys that they have been flirting with all day. They can even do it in front of their posse and ex-girlfriend.

They Both Die at the End imagines a new normal. It envisions a new world in which queerness is not frowned on or something that should be hidden. It doesn't have to be worked through or figured out. It simply is. It just exists. That Adam Silvera paints the rules of this world through a bisexual character is all the more noteworthy. It is bisexual Rufus who provides gay Mateo with a roadmap to understanding and accepting his sexuality. Gone is the trope of the bisexual teen realizing they are different and working through their sexuality before ultimately realizing that it's okay to be bisexual. It's normal.

CONCLUSION: IMAGINING A MORE INCLUSIVE PUBLISHING INDUSTRY

In the introduction to *Ambientes: New Queer Latino Writing*, Lázaro Lima argues that "Queer Latino writing, understood as such, functions as narrative acts against oblivion" (8), effectively signaling the resistant and dissenting character that queer Latinx writing embodies. The act of writing by queer writers of color exemplifies the sociopolitical activism in which the pen becomes a weapon to redefine "gender, sexuality, race, ethnicity, class, economics, and political inclusion" (Lima 8). By inserting a bisexual Latino teen into the narrative, *They Both Die at the End* by Adam Silvera offers an alternative route to resisting oppressive systems and structures, calling attention to Lima's notion that queer Latinx aesthetics not only offer resistance, but (re)imagine, (re)construct, (re)member, and (re)envision an original, unconventional branch of queerness that takes into account the full spectrum of Latinidad (8).

But even so, despite Silvera's successes with *They Both Die at the End*, I return to the central questions that led me to begin this research in the first place. Where are the stories about bisexual Latino teens? And, when do Latino boys get to be bisexual? As the demographics of the LGBTQ+ community in tandem with the queer community's increased level of acceptance in the United States reveal, there is no shortage of readers who are interested in stories about bisexual teens. The Latinx population continues to grow at a rapid clip, showing there is also a growing body of young readers who want to see their identities represented on the page. And, of course, young adult literature is one of the few genres of publishing that continues to become more relevant. Adam Silvera is no stranger to this, as *They Both Die at the End* experienced a renaissance of sorts in 2020. As BookTok—the TikTok subculture dedicated to YA literature—exploded during the COVID-19 pandemic, Silvera's novel became one of the more popular novels on the short-form video app. Naturally, TikTok's influence extended into the commercial realm, as well. The novel reentered the prestigious *New York Times* Young Adult Paperback Best Seller list, steadily climbing throughout 2020 and even reaching second on the list in January 2021, a position higher than when the book debuted over three years prior. As teen TikTok readers know, there is a hunger for queer Latinx stories like those penned by Silvera.

So, if the readership exists, then where are these stories? Why aren't they being told? Ultimately, the answers to these questions are beyond the scope of this article even if they are within the realm of my current research project.

If we are to make the change we wish to see in the world—if we are to create an inclusive world—then we must interrogate the gaps in the publishing record. We must shape a world in which bisexual Latino boys get to be the protagonists in their own stories. We must shape a world in which these young readers know that, yes, they can be Latino *and* bisexual. The possibilities are endless. We just have to imagine them.

NOTES

1. In terms of the lows, the number of books published annually remains low. For instance, in 2017 and 2018, only eighteen of the published young adult books were written by queer authors of color (Cooperative Children's Book Center).

2. Although some see Latinidad as an inclusive term, others believe the term erases Indigenous and Black portions of the Latinx community. Throughout this article, I work with an understanding that Latinidad encompasses all Latinx identities. That said, queer theorist José Esteban Muñoz notes, "Identity is indeed a problematic term when applied to Latinas/os—groups who do not cohere along the lines of race, nation, language, or any other conventional demarcation of difference" (38).

3. I use the term bisexual to refer to a person who is attracted to more than one gender. This definition corresponds with theorist Surya Monro's understanding of bisexuality as a "strategic move that overlooks the binary composition of the word" (2).

4. Notable bisexual characters on television include *Grey's Anatomy*'s Dr. Callie Torres (Sara Ramirez); *Brooklyn Nine-Nine*'s Rosa Diaz (Stephanie Beatriz); *Broad City*'s Ilana Wexler (Ilana Glazer) and Abbi Abrams (Abbi Jacobson); *Schitt's Creek*'s David Rose (Dan Levy); *Big Mouth*'s Jay Bilzerian (Jason Mantzoukas); *Riverdale*'s Cheryl Blossom (Madelaine Petsch), Toni Topaz (Vanessa Morgan), and Moose Mason (Cody Kearsley). There are more bisexual characters and film, but, by and large, bisexuality is rarely represented on screen compared to gay and lesbian identities.

5. While my criteria for what amounts to a bisexual novel is perhaps restrictive, this is intentional. I do not mean to reduce novels that don't name bisexuality. Rather, I seek to shed light on ones that do give the importance of representation in YA literature. Moreover, my work here specifically focuses on Latinx YA literature that names bisexuality. Bisexuality is rare within YA literature. Even so, YA lit websites queerbooksforteens. com and yapride.org both feature many titles that fall within the umbrella of bisexuality. Few of these texts, however, depict the intersections of bisexuality and Latinidad.

6. As Bonnie Kneen notes, some of these novels lack multidimensional depictions of bisexual characters and fall into the trap of stereotyping. For more on the lack of bisexual representation in YA lit, see Epstein, Colletta, and Kneen.

7. What is more, although there is potentially a wealth of bisexual+ literature, many books are not marketed as such, which can impede the process of finding representative literature; if the books that do exist are too difficult to find, they are essentially rendered invisible to the community that needs them the most.

8. Although youth today have embraced the umbrella term "queer," in my work as a high school teacher, Gay-Straight Alliance club sponsor, and university professor of LGBT

Studies, I find that many young people identify as bisexual in addition to using queer to label their identities.

9. Some readers and scholars view books such as *Aristotle and Dante Discover the Secrets of the Universe* and *More Happy Than Not* as bisexual texts. My focus here is on novels that explicitly name bisexuality.

10. It is worth noting that few of these books are written by openly bisexual Latino writers.

11. Notably, Latino bisexuality, while largely underspoken in YA literature, is not the only sexual identity that faces issues of representation. Trans Latinx teens remain underrepresented, for example. This, however, is perhaps changing as the expanses of Latinx youth identities continue to penetrate the publishing world. The critical and commercial success of Anna-Marie McLemore's *When the Moon Was Ours* (2016) and Aiden Thomas's *Cemetery Boys* (2020) signals a changing of the guard so to speak.

12. See, for example, Carolina Alonso, "The Coming-of-Age Experience in Chicanx Queer Novels *What Night Brings* and *Aristotle and Dante Discover the Secrets of the Universe*"; Cecilia J. Aragón, "Representations of Sexual and Queer Identities in Chicana/o-Latina/o Children's Literature"; E. Sybil Durand and Marilisa Jiménez García, "Unsettling Representations of Identities: A Critical Review of Diverse Youth Literature"; Laura Jiménez, "Representations in Award-Winning LGBTQ Young Adult Literature from 2000–2013"; Angel Daniel Matos and Jon Michael Jon Michael, "Editors' Introduction: Queer Futurities in Youth Literature, Media, and Culture."

13. Some critics view the Latinidad in Silvera's body of work to be "atmospheric." That is, atmospheric Latinidad lacks nuance and only paints Latinidad onto the characters rather than fully exploring the complexity of Latinx identities. José Esteban Muñoz touches on this concept in his discussion of playwright María Irene Fornés, whose works rarely, if ever, feature Latinx characters yet are definitively Latinx works (14). That is, Latinx literature does not need to be entrenched in identity markers to effectively convey Latinidad.

14. For critical studies of Adam Silvera's work, see Alyssa Chrisman and Mollie V. Blackburn, "Interrogating Happiness: Unraveling Homophobia in the Lives of Queer Youth of Color with More Happy Than Not"; E. Sybil Durand and Marilisa Jiménez-García, "Unsettling Representations of Identities: A Critical Review of Diverse Youth Literature"; William Orchard, "Endless Happy Beginnings: Forms of Speculation in Adam Silvera's *More Happy Than Not*."

15. This narrative tactic leads to something common in YA literature: the unreliable narrator.

16. Notably, the novel engages with the way that death is perceived and approached in many Latinx cultures. This influences the tone of the book and adds another layer of nuances that engages readers with Latinidad.

WORKS CITED

@AdamSilvera A. "People can opt out of the Death-Cast call. There was more emphasis on this in an earlier draft. It's something I will revisit if I get to return to this world." *Twitter*, 24 January 2021, 3:41 p.m., https://twitter.com/AdamSilvera/status/1353457835674279938?s=20.

@AdamSilvera B. "I wrestle with mortality a lot, especially dying ahead of my time. That's how I conceived Death-Cast to KNOW when it's your last day." *Twitter*, 24 January 2021, 3:15 p.m., https://twitter.com/AdamSilvera/status/1353451446063124481?s=20.

@AdamSilvera C. "I like to think so." *Twitter*, 24 January 2021, 3:14 p.m., https://twitter.com/AdamSilvera/status/1353451218283028482?s=20.

Alonso, Carolina. "The Coming-of-Age Experience in Chicanx Queer Novels *What Night Brings* and *Aristotle and Dante Discover the Secrets of the Universe*." In *Nerds, Goths, Geeks, and Freaks: Outsiders in Chicanx and Latinx Young Adult Fiction*, edited by Trevor Boffone and Cristina Herrera. University Press of Mississippi, 2020, 175–89.

Anzaldúa, Gloria E., and AnaLouise Keating. *This Bridge We Call Home: Radical Visions for Transformation*. New York: Routledge, 2002.

Aragón, Cecilia J. "Representations of Sexual and Queer Identities in Chicana/o-Latina/o Children's Literature." In *Voices of Resistance: Interdisciplinary Approaches to Chican@ Children's Literature*, edited by Laura Alamillo, Larissa M. Mercardo-López, and Cristina Herrera. Rowman and Littlefield, 2018, 105–119.

Aviles, Gwen. "The Rise of Young Adult Books with LGBTQ Characters—and What's Next." *NBC News*, 10 March 2019, https://www.nbcnews.com/feature/nbc-out/rise-young-adult-books-lgbtq-characters-what-s-next-n981176. Accessed 30 March 2020.

Boffone, Trevor. "Young, Gay, and Latino: 'Feeling Brown' in Emilio Rodriguez's *Swimming While Drowning*." In *Nerds, Goths, Geeks, and Freaks: Outsiders in Chicanx and Latinx Young Adult Fiction*, edited by Trevor Boffone and Cristina Herrera. University Press of Mississippi, 2020, 145–58.

Brown, Anna. "Bisexual Adults Are Far Less Likely Than Gay Men and Lesbians to Be 'Out' to the People in Their Lives." Pew Research Center, 18 June 2019, accessed 28 March 2020.

Coletta, Jennifer. "The Missing B Word: Compulsory Binarization and Bisexual Representation in Children's Literature." *Jeunesse: Young People, Texts, Cultures* 10, no. 1 (2018): 85–108.

Chrisman, Alyssa, and Mollie V. Blackburn. "Interrogating Happiness: Unraveling Homophobia in the Lives of Queer Youth of Color with *More Happy than Not*." In *Engaging with Multicultural YA Literature in the Secondary Classroom: Critical Approaches for Critical Educators*, edited by Ricki Ginsberg and Wendy J Glenn. Routledge, 2019, 83–92.

Cooperative Children's Book Center. "Data on Books by and about People of Color and from First/Native Nations Published for Children and Teens." Cooperative Children's Book Center, School of Education, University of Wisconsin-Madison, https://ccbc.education.wisc.edu/books/pcstats.asp, Accessed 30 March 2020.

Durand, E. Sybil, and Jiménez García, Marilisa. "Unsettling Representations of Identities: A Critical Review of Diverse Youth Literature." *Research on Diversity in Youth Literature* 1, no. 1 (2018).

Epstein, B. J. "'The Case of the Missing Bisexuals': Bisexuality in Books for Young Readers," *Journal of Bisexuality* 14, no. 1 (2014): 110–25.

Flores, Juan. *From Bomba to Hip-Hop: Puerto Rican Culture and Latino Identity*. New York: Columbia University Press, 2000.

Gates, Gary J. "How Many People Are Lesbian, Gay, Bisexual and Transgender?" *The Williams Institute*, 2011, http://williamsinstitute.law.ucla.edu/research/census-lgbtdemographics-studies/how-many-people-are-lesbian-gay-bisexual-and-transgender/. Accessed 30 March 2020.

Human Rights Campaign Foundation, Ché Juan Gonzalez Ruddell-Tabisola, and Lake Research Partners. "At the Intersection: Race, Sexuality and Gender," Human Rights Campaign, 2009, http://www.hrc.org/resources/at-the-intersection-race-sexuality-and-gender/. Accessed 30 March 2020.

Jiménez, Laura. "Representations in Award-Winning LGBTQ Young Adult Literature from 2000–2013." *Journal of Lesbian Studies* 19, no. 4 (2015), 406–22.

Keating, AnaLouise. "From Borderlands and New Mestizas to Nepantlas and Nepantleras: Anzaldúan Theories for Social Change," *Human Architecture: Journal of the Sociology of Self-Knowledge* 4, no. 3 (2006): 5–16.

Kosciw, Joseph G., Emily A. Greytak, Elizabeth M. Diaz, and Mark J. Bartkiewicz. "The 2009 National School Climate Survey: The Experiences of Lesbian, Gay, Bisexual and Transgender Youth in Our Nation's Schools." New York: Gay, Lesbian and Straight Education Network, 2010.

Kneen, Bonnie. "Neither Very Bi nor Particularly Sexual: The Essence of the Bisexual in Young Adult Literature." *Children's Literature in Education* 46 (2015): 359–77.

Lima, Lázaro. "Genealogies of Queer Latino Writing." Introduction. *Ambientes: New Queer Latino Writing*, edited by Lázaro Lima and Felice Picano. University of Wisconsin Press, 2011, 3–13.

Matos, Angel Daniel, and Jon Michael Wargo. "Editors' Introduction: Queer Futurities in Youth Literature, Media, and Culture." *Research on Diversity in Youth Literature* 2, no. 1 (2019).

Monro, Surya. *Bisexuality: Identities, Politics, and Theories*. Basingstoke, Palgrave Macmillan, 2015.

Moraga, Cherríe. *Giving Up the Ghost*. West End, 1986.

Muñoz, José Esteban. *The Sense of Brown*. Edited by Joshua Chambers-Letson and Tavia Nyong'o. Duke University Press, 2020.

Ochs, Robyn. 2014. "Bisexual." *Robyn Ochs*. http://robynochs.com/bisexual/. Accessed 30 March 2020.

Pérez, Daniel Enrique. "Entre Machos y Maricones: (Re)Covering Chicano Gay Male (Hi)Stories." In *Gay Latino Studies: A Critical Reader*, edited by Michael Hames-Garcia and Ernesto Javier Martinez. Duke University Press, 2011, 141–6.

Rodríguez, Richard T. *Next of Kin: The Family in Chicano/a Cultural Politics*. Duke University Press, 2009.

San Filippo, Maria. *The B Word: Bisexuality in Contemporary Film and Television*. Indiana University Press, 2013.

Silvera, Adam. *They Both Die at the End*. New York City, Harper Teen, 2017.

Chapter Three

LATINX QUEER WORLDMAKING

Boys Loving Boys in Latinx Children's and
Young Adult Literature and Film Adaptations

T. Jackie Cuevas

In their introduction to *Nerds, Goths, Geeks, and Freaks: Outsiders in Chicanx and Latinx Young Adult Literature*, coeditors Trevor Boffone and Cristina Herrera point out that, "In recent years, the field of Latinx children's and YA literature has exploded with new imprints specifically dedicated to the field" (5). They rightly suggest that "the need for scholarship centered on Latinx children's and young adult writing has become more pressing" (5). Responding to this gap, this chapter explores two texts and their film adaptations that take seriously narratives of queer Latinx boys. While they differ in their narrative and filmic strategies, *We the Animals* (2018) and *La Serenata* (2019) partake in Latinx queer worldmaking through narratives that center Latinx boys who love other boys.

Queer theorist José Esteban Muñoz describes queer worldmaking as a key practice performed by queer of color cultural producers who reject the constraints of heteronormativity by imagining new worlds. According to Muñoz, "Queers of color and other minoritarians have been denied a world" (200). In response, through strategic "disidentificatory performances," queer of color performers "use the stuff of the 'real world' to remake collective sense of 'wordless' through spectacles, performances, and willful enactments of the self for others" (200). Muñoz's approach to performances can also help us read the queer worldmaking practices in literary texts and film adaptations that resist heteronormativity for Latinx subjects and imagine otherwise—other ways of being for queer Latinx boys.

Directed by Jeremiah Zagar and based on the 2011 novel by Justin Torres, *We the Animals* adapts a coming-of-age novel into an avant garde film that relies on a child's point of view and drawings to tell its complex story. Directed by Adelina Anthony and written by Ernesto Javier Martínez, *La Serenata* is a short film based on a children's book written by Ernesto Javier Martínez and illustrated by Maya Christina Gonzalez. A winner of HBO's LatinX Short Film Competition, *La Serenata* focuses the viewer's attention on the young protagonist as he expresses his desire to serenade another boy. These adaptions strategically mobilize the filmic medium to convey the challenges as well as beauty of queer Latinx young lives. Both films and the texts on which they are based engage in Latinx queer worldmaking strategies. *We the Animals* and *La Serenata* engage in Latinx queer worldmaking practices by deploying strategies such as posing questions about the relationship between individual identity versus family belonging and positing writing as integral to the process of queer self-making.

Here, I am interested in the strategies of Latinx queer worldmaking aspects that cohere around the question of whether familial disruption or personal distance is required in order to create a queer world or space of being and living queerly. This theme has circulated in the writings of many queer Latinx authors, such as Gloria Anzaldúa, Cherríe Moraga, Richard Rodríguez, Felicia Luna Lemus, and many others. Marivel Danielson, in *Homecoming Queers*, reads the literary phenomenon of what I am referring to as an individual versus collective dilemma as a question of home. Richard T. Rodríguez, in *Next of Kin*, deftly analyzes this recurring theme as a critique of the Chicano family as an idealized heteronormative institution. Ernesto Javier Martínez, in the book *On Making Sense*, terms this commonly represented struggle as a form of queer migration and "queer migrant labor" (78). Martínez clarifies that his usage of such terms does not necessarily refer to the transnational flow of workers: "Queer migrant labor references strategies practiced at various geographic scales by people searching for ways to express themselves sexually and socially in forms not sanctioned by the communities in which they reside" (78).

WE THE ANIMALS

We the Animals narrativizes this dilemma—the experiences of a Latinx individual growing queerly at odds with and potentially leaving the heterocentric family unit—in a troubling but complex way. In the intensely dramatic ending to the novel, the family discovers the queer boy's private journals, in which he graphically describes erotic queer desires, and they commit him to an institution, presumably a psychiatric hospital.

Prior to the dramatic closing chapters, the narrative's perspective is that of the first-person plural, with the narrative told through the vantage point of the three young brothers as a collective unit constructed through the pronoun "we." We see the "we" in the book's perspective right from the beginning with the following opening sentence: "We wanted more" (1). In that first scene, the boys are hungry and wanting: "We knocked the butt ends of our forks against the table, tapped our spoons against our empty bowls; we were hungry. We wanted more volume, more riots . . . we were brothers, boys, three little kings locked in a feud for more" (1). The majority of the novel is told using the "we" perspective to show the collective experiences and plight of the boys as they grow up together.

As the book builds toward its dramatic close, the perspective shifts into a first-person narrative told from the perspective of the queer Latinx boy. After many chapters of seeing through the lens of the collective "we," the shift to the first-person "I" seems arresting, signaling a break in the collective perspective. The narrator expresses awareness of this shift in the chapter called "The Night I Am Made," in which he invites the reader to look at his brothers and then to look at him, to watch his painful individuation process unfolding. In a passage in which his brothers hold him as they threaten to beat him, the narrator says, "Look at us three, look at how they held me there—they didn't want to let me go" (110). The older brothers let him go and reveal that their mother has asked them to protect the young boy for being "bright" (111) and as fragile as "a fucking crystal vase" (111). The narrator later says, "Look at me, how I itched to leave that loading dock; how I itched to leave that snowy hour" (111). The chapter ends with the young boy narrator contemplating his isolating feeling of difference with the following thought: "Maybe it was true. Maybe there was no other boy like me, anywhere" (112). The focus of the narrative shifts into his singular "I" perspective in the final chapters, during which the young queer boy begins to realize the singularity of his own experience. The "I" emerges as he realizes his experience differs dramatically from that of his brothers, with whom he has been so intertwined, and as he realizes that his queerness exceeds the confines of the family's heteronormativity.

In the final, brief, one-page chapter called "Zookeeping," we gain a mere glimpse into the queer boy's institutionalized experience. He laments, "I've lost my pack" (125). He describes his days by saying, "I sleep with other animals in cages and in dens," and "They adorn me, these animals—lay me down, paw me, own me—crown me prince of their rank jungles" (125). The suggestion here is that the boy may be having sexual experiences with other boys in the institution, but that he is caged against his will and has lost the familiar space of his brotherly "pack." The language in the passage describes the people as animalistic and suggests a highly physical, erotic, violent environment echoing the desires the boy has written in his discovered journal.

After the queer boy has expressed wanting to be away from his close-knit family, what emerges in the end is a kind of ambivalent longing. Elsewhere, I have argued that the protagonist in *We the Animals* resists the hegemonic forms of toxic masculinity in his family and that the text works "to delink violence from queer Latinx masculinities" (Cuevas 131). In this chapter, I am concerned with how the text figures the young character as a queer child and how this figure is constructed as navigating the dynamic between individual self and relationality along the axis of queer difference. The narrator's ambivalence in the end of the book seems to stem from the collision among his sense of belonging to the family, his ejection from the family home through institutionalization, and his queer desires.

His ambivalent longing echoes what critic Leticia Alvarado might refer to as an "ambivalent belonging." In the book *Abject Performances*, Alvarado uses the term "ambivalent belonging" (133) to describe how some Latino Mormons have carved a sense of belonging in their faith community despite historically being seen as abject racialized others in relation to white members and the church's "ideologically embedded white heteropatriarchy" (155). For our purposes, the term "ambivalent belonging" provides a productive way to think about the tension between a yearning to belong to the Latinx family fold and a distancing sense of difference around sexual orientation or identity. This contradictory position can produce a dilemma for Latinx queer people if their familial group subscribes to heteropatriarchal or homophobic values that circumvent queer expressions or identities. In *We the Animals*, the family operates as a paradoxically violent yet protective space for the young boy, who then starts to see how his family sees him differently as he ages and develops queer desires.

The film adaptation of *We the Animals* takes a different tack to the ending. Rather than having the family commit the queer boy to a mental institution, the film version ends with the boy leaving home. Importantly, the film also names the protagonist, who remains nameless in the novel. While the older brothers, Manny and Joel, are named in the novel, it is only in the film that the narrator is given a name—Jonah. Toward the end of the movie, Jonah takes money from one of his brother's backpacks and goes alone to visit Dustin, a white neighbor boy who had previously talked about wanting to move to Philadelphia. Dustin tells Jonah he is welcome to stay the night at his house. Jonah asks Dustin, "How much money do you need to go to Philly? Can I come?" Dustin responds with a casual, "Sure."

After this exchange, the camera focuses on Jonah as he eyes Dustin's neck, chin, and mouth while in the background we hear the sound of blood pumping or water rushing. The live action scene melds into a mixture of live action and animation in which Jonah and Dustin are suddenly depicted underwater. While the boys are looking at each other under water, Jonah reaches out to touch Dustin's hair, and the boys kiss. The film cuts away from the underwater dreamlike sequence back to the live action scene of the boys merely sitting next to each other, suggesting that the underwater moment had been Jonah's interior imagining. In the live action scene, Jonah then indeed does reach out to touch Dustin's hair, Dustin turns to look at him, Jonah leans in, and the boys kiss. The next scene cuts to Jonah walking home with a smile.

When Jonah returns home to the bedroom he shares with his older brothers, he sees that their mattress has been removed from their bed, exposing the hiding spot where he had stashed his journal. While searching desperately for his journal, he finds his parents and brothers gathered in the living room with Jonah's journal pages spread out across the floor. The camera focuses on Jonah's journal pages, filled with drawings of sex scenes he has sketched. Several of his drawing depict two masculine bodies with penises engaging in sexual acts with each other.

While Jonah tries to gather up his journal pages, one brother shakes his head at him. The mother takes Jonah's face in her hands while asking, "Jonah, where were you?" Jonah starts crying and flies into a rage, hitting his mother. The father, Paps, pulls him off her, telling Jonah to calm down. Jonah tries to swing at his father while Paps holds him down. Turning to self-harm in this crisis moment, Jonah bites his own arm until it bleeds. His father continues, saying, "Just breathe. Calm down. Tranquilo, tranquilo . . ." In an unusual moment of physical tenderness, Paps kisses Jonah's forehead gently while the brothers stand by watching.

We next see Jonah watching his brothers while they sleep, and he has a brief flashback of the three of them playing together. The contrast between nondiegetic sounds from the flashback and the visual of the currently sleeping brothers further amplifies the emotional disconnect between the past closeness of the brothers and the current moment, in which Jonah watches them at a distance after their betrayal in giving their parents Jonah's journal. Jonah then goes to the living room and tucks in his mother while she sleeps on the touch. He then leaves the house.

Outside in a trash can, he digs out his discarded journal pages. He again has a flashback, this time to his own journal entries, drawings that have been flashed across the screen as feverish red and blue animated sketches at various points in the film. Some of the images include three figures with red targets that appear amidst the background sounds of boys chanting "More!" as the brothers did at the movie's start. Some of the images are unclear, with ambiguous bodily figures shifting from being intertwined in embraces, violence, sexual acts, or combinations thereof. With these images, the film gives visual texture to the boy's somatic, sadomasochistic desires and his imaginings about the interplay among domination, submission, violence, and sex.

Jonah gathers up his journal pages and walks away from the camera. He pauses to turn toward the camera, then looks upward toward the sky. The audio track flows into the sound of a heartbeat or perhaps wings rhythmically thumping while in the sky there appears a silhouette of a body flying over the snow and trees. The shadowy figure soars overhead toward a bright sky mixed with dark clouds on the horizon. This striking visual scene situates the queer boy as moving toward a queer horizon.

Given that viewers do not get to see whether Jonah makes it to Philadelphia or somewhere else, the ending—although tinged with hopefulness for a queer future—also remains suspended in ambiguity and uncertainty. Zorimar Rivera Montes, in considering the relationship between queerness and Latinidad in Torres's novel, builds on Édouard Glissant's notion of opacity by arguing that, "Using the lens of opacity allows us to read Torres's unique engagement with Latinidad, queer sexualities, and masculinity, both politically and aesthetically" (220). According to Rivera Montes, "engaging with opacity allows Torres to enact a politics of queer liberation" (220). Rivera Montes locates this opacity largely within the novel's subversion of the coming-of-age genre, elusively of expectations around Latinidad, and ambiguity of the ending.

I agree with Rivera Montes's astute analysis and would like to extend this line of inquiry to consider how Torres deploys opacity or ambiguity specifically through suggestiveness and sparseness of detail around sex—and the film adaptation counters this ambiguity by animating drawings from the queer boy's diary. The novel indeed oscillates between frankness by stating the action matter-of-factly and receding into lyrical ambiguity by glossing over any further description that would reveal specific details. For example, when the family discovers the boy's journal in the novel, we learn only generally what it contains: "In bold and explicit language I had written fantasies about the men I met at the bus station, about what I wanted done to me. I had written a catalog of imagined perversions, a violent pornography with myself at the center, with myself obliterated" (116). While the gist of the journal is conveyed in the novel, the film clarifies the desires further by illustrating and animating drawings of the fantasies on screen. What the novel states generally and categorically allows the specificities of the sex acts to remain unsaid, but the film visualizes the taboo scenes. In the novel, it is immediately after Jonah has sex with a stranger at the bus station that his family finds his journal and institutionalizes him. In the film, the family finds the journal after Jonah kisses a boy. By sequencing the narrative in this way, both the novel and film enact nightmarish, worst-case-scenario approaches to a queer coming-of-age story, all the while attempting to leave room for ambiguous interpretations of what happens to Jonah once the narrative closes.

There is no institutionalizing the queer boy in the film adaption. In this version of the narrative, the family does not gather Jonah up and whisk him off to a psychiatric ward. Instead, the film ends with Jonah walking away with his journal—a boy and his "catalog of imagined perversions" (116). Thus, the ending also stakes a claim for writing and drawing as a crucial component of Jonah's individual queer self-making. By taking his private journal back, Jonah retakes ownership of his personal narrative by holding tight to the pages where he has imagined his own queer ways of being. While this version of the ending for *We the Animals* does not necessarily resolve the ambivalence or ambiguity of the novel's ending, it does create a more generous space for the possibility of Jonah's making a queer life. Hence, we can read the movie's ending as opening up the narrative toward a greater possibility of Latinx queer worldmaking.

LA SERENATA

Another text that produces possibilities for young boys and their Latinx queer worldmaking is the children's book called *Cuando Amamos Cantamos/When We Love Someone We Sing to Them* (2018), authored by queer theorist Ernesto Javier Martínez, illustrated by Maya Gonzalez, and translated by Jorge Gabriel Martínez Feliciano. Martínez is also the author of *On Making Sense: Queer Race Narratives of Intelligibility* and the coeditor (with Michael Hames-García) of *Gay Latino Studies: A Critical Reader*. Martínez also founded the Femeniños Project, which is "a children's literature and narrative film initiative exploring the relationship between queer Latino/x youth and their familias" (38). Martínez adapted the children's book into a short film called *La Serenata*, which was directed by Adelina Anthony, a widely acclaimed Two Spirit, Xicana, Lesbian filmmaker, actor, and writer.

The picture book tells the story of a young boy who wants to serenade another boy in the style of the traditional Mexican serenata. The boy's father teaches him that the serenata is a way of communicating one's love to another person. The father says, "When we love someone . . . we sing to them, we send our love through song" (2). The father says, "We call this a serenata" (2) and asks the boy to remember when they sang together to serenade the boy's mother for Mother's Day.

When the father describes to the boy the emotions associated with a serenata, the father says of serenading, "It's our way to hug with sounds . . . We call this Xochipilli's joy, when the feeling of blooming flowers and dancing butterflies abound" (4). The book's backmatter contains an extended explanation of Xochipilli:

> Xochipilli is the mesoamerican Nahua god of creativity, art, song, writing, and dance. His name is made up of two Nahuatl words: xochitl ("flower") and pilli ("prince"/"child"). He was often depicted in a cross-legged and/or seated position with sacred, magical flowers covering his body. Flowers carried very important ritual meetings for the Nahua of Mesoamerica. Among other things, flowers represented love, fertility, growth, and enchantment and were sometimes associated with queer/two-spirit people in Nahua culture. The Nahua people still continue to inhabit Central Mexico to this day. (39)

By connecting the serenata tradition to the concept of Xochipilli's joy, the book identifies the serenata form as a Mexican expressive practice that emerges from indigenous Nahua peoples.

The father tells the boy, "I promise you, my son . . . when you start to feel the Xochipilli way, I will sing with you" (11). The boy shares with his father that he already feels love for someone. For several pages, the story switches perspectives to focus on the boy's experience as he shares with his father how he feels about the other boy. A series of Gonzalez's beautiful illustrations depict two young boys spending time together. In one illustration, the boys are reaching for each other's hands, and the protagonist addresses his feelings directly to the other boy by saying, "My heart fluttered like the wind in the grass when you held my hand" (15). In a two-page illustrated spread without text or a caption, the boy who loves another boy is shown with his eyes closes and sound waves, flowers, and mariposas fluttering out of his open mouth. As Daniel Enrique Pérez points out, the figure of the mariposa is used by some Chicano/Latino cultural producers "to affirm queer Chicano and Latino identities" (100).

Prior to this part of the story, the narrative has focused on the father-son interactions and their serenading of the mother. In the first part of the story, the first-person plural pronoun "we" is used repeatedly. When the father speaks of a "we" and "our way," he seems to be suggesting a collective sense, referring to the family as singers but perhaps extending that plurality to a larger cultural sense of Mexican tradition. Unlike young adult books for older readers that tend to deal with the details of young queers coming out, facing homophobia, bullying, and self-doubt, this children's book models a parent's positive response to the boy's expression of love for another boy. The father does express a form of either surprise or concern: "Papi remained quiet after I told him. He sighed, turned his head, and looked out the window" (24). Yet the story does not linger on the father's pause. The narrative moves toward a swift resolution when the boy says to his papi, "Teach me a song for a boy who loves boys" (26). Papi helps the boy write himself and his own feelings into the serenata tradition by offering to help the boy "make a new song, a great song, for your butterfly-garden-love-joy" (26).

Unlike many children's books with queer characters, this book centers a queer child rather than a queer adult. As Jill M. Hermann-Wilmarth observes, queer books for younger readers tend to have queer adult characters rather than queer children as the locus of their queer characterizations. Hermann-Wilmarth says, "What is clear about the history of LGBTQ+ books written for children is that, while the numbers of publications increase alongside cultural expansions in the acceptance of queerness, there are still relatively few queer-inclusive books available for young readers." She cites the now classic *Heather Has Two Mommies* as an example and suggests that this approach has not necessarily changed much since that book's publication in 1990 (495). According to Hermann-Wilmarth, "Themes in LGBTQ+ picture books are often, as in *Heather Has Two Mommies*, of normality, and to show that, indeed, LGBTQ+ people exist, often in the form of an adult" (Hermann-Wilmarth 495). Martínez's book resists this tendency by focusing instead on a young queer protagonist.

Like Torres's novel, Martínez's children's book draws on autobiographical elements to develop a fictional narrative.[1] Martínez's book deploys what Isabel Millán terms autofantasía. Millán defines autofantasía "as a literary technique whereby authors deliberately insert themselves within a text in order to fantasize solutions or responses to hegemonic structures" (202). In the author's biography at the end of the book, Martínez mentions that he grew up singing with his family trio and those experiences influenced his desire to write this book. Despite being involved in the singing group, he did not learn any songs representing his queer perspective: "Unfortunately, none of the songs I was taught included love between boys" (34). Reflecting on the past, Martínez shares how the exclusion of queer perspectives in the musical tradition he participated in drove him away from singing:

> As a young gay boy, this brought me sadness and left me concerned that my feelings were not important to those around me. I grew up loving music, loving my community and family, but I was so sad about not being included that at one point, I stopped singing. Inside, I wanted a song—a healing, loving song all my own—and a community that I could trust would listen (34)

The book becomes an expression of healing for readers of any age wishing to see queerness incorporated into cultural traditions such as the serenata. Martínez says, "Working with Maya and writing this book, I learned that creating children's books can be a form of cultural medicine, both with a queer person of color revisiting their past and for the larger community eager to see themselves represented" (34).

In the short film adapted from the book, the boy becomes aware of the historical exclusion of boys who love boys in the serenata tradition. When the boy tells his parents that he wants to serenade another boy, the mother responds in a supportive manner, but the father says, "Is this a joke?" The father's negative reaction prompts the boy to ask, "Is something wrong?" The second time the historical exclusion is made evident to the boy is when his parents cannot find any songs about boys who love boys. The boy looks on as his parents search through their collection of musical scores, but their search comes up empty. The boy asks his parents, "No one has ever written a song for a boy who loves a boy?"

After arguing about whether to explain homophobia to the child, the father offers to help the son write a song. The father asks the son to explain why he loves the boy. The son shares the following response: "He makes me feel like it's my birthday everyday. He saved a ladybug at recess. He never laughs when the other boys make fun of me. He stops the other boys from spitting on me. I guess he makes my heart hum." By incorporating homophobic bullying into the narrative, the short film addresses an important topic that goes beyond the simplicity of the original version of the story offered by the children's book.[2]

As the son, called Luis in the film, arrives at his friend's house to perform the serenade, Luis says in a voice-over that his father told him his love is sacred: "Papi tells me that my love is like a garden inside of me, that it is sacred, that it blooms butterflies. Papalotl. He says that gardens like mine even through droughts have persisted. He says that gardens like mine have always existed." The final scenes show Luis singing his new Xochipilli song and smiling as he holds a small bundle of flowers.

With this appeal to a transhistorical existence of boys like Luis, boys who love other boys, the short film beckons to what Emma Pérez terms "decolonial queer interpretations that obligate us to see or hear beyond a heteronormative imaginary" (129) and Carolyn Dinshaw refers to as a "queer desire for history." The family's collective search for the presence of queer love songs is a search for a queer archive, an archive of queer desire. Their response to the gap in the archive is to insist that either the songs exist and cannot yet be found—or that they must write new songs that honor the boy-loving-boy experiences. In this way, the text also makes use of a common trope in Chicano literature in which the individual seeks to connect his own experience as a Chicano with a larger historical and collective framework, such as in canonical texts like *Yo Soy Joaquin/I Am Joaquin*, by Rodolfo "Corky" Gonzales. *La Serenata* writes the Latinx boy who loves boys into the history and tradition of the serenata as a cultural practice.[3] The short film transforms a cultural tradition that has historically maintained heteronormative boundaries into a cultural practice where a queer boy can express his love as he participates in Mexican cultural and familial traditions.

La Serenata actively works against erasure of the queer subject in serenata history by creating an actual song celebrating boy love. At the end of the short film, Luis sings a song called "Jardín de Mariposas," composed by Héctor H. Pérez for use in *La Serenata*. The film brings the song into the serenata tradition by showing the young singer's embodiment and performance of dedicating the original song to the boy he loves, publicly serenading him. Through this performance of Latinx boys expressing love for other boys, *La Serenata* makes an exquisitely multilayered contribution to Latinx queer worldmaking.

CONCLUSION

In this chapter, I have put two seemingly disparate types of children's and young adult texts and their film adaptations into dialogue as a means of blurring what constitutes or demarcates imagined boundaries between children's and young adult literature, particularly when nascent queerness comes into play in the characters' lives. As Frederick Luis Aldama and Christopher González observe, despite making up over 18 percent of the population in the US, Latinxs "appear in less than three percent of all media, and this includes children's book, young adult fiction, TV, film, and all else" (13). The texts and film adaptations analyzed in this chapter infuse young adult fiction and film with Latinx perspectives. Given the contemporary attempts to ban LGBTQ books in public schools, film adaptations become an even more critical medium for making queer Latinx narratives available to young adult audiences. Through film adaptations, Latinx queer youth can imagine queer possibilities beyond mainstream white heteronormative narratives.

We the Animals (the novel and film), *Cuando Amamos Cantamos*, and *La Serenata* center the experiences of young Latinx boys who love other boys. These important cultural products expand the available narratives for young people, including Latinx boys who love other boys, who deserve to see themselves represented in books and films. Despite featuring young boy protagonists, these children's and young adult narratives do not shy away from contemplating and honoring the messy bundles of emotions, hormones, attractions, and fleshly desires of queer Latinx boys. As I have shown here, these texts and films are not merely representations of Latinx queer experiences, they are indeed exemplars of Latinx queer worldmaking.

NOTES

1. See Justin Torres's TED Talk called "My Story, and 'We the Animals'" for his personal story about his family discovering his personal journal when he was a teenager.

2. Daniel Enrique Pérez counts the short film *La Serenata* as among "progressive responses and interactions between Chicanx and Latinx fathers and their queer sons" (243–44).

3. M. Roxana Loza, in an article discussing how "Contemporary Latinx children's and YA literature is filled with artist protagonists," lists Martínez's book *Cuando Amamos Cantamos* among the many examples.

WORKS CITED

Aldama, Frederick Luis, and Christopher González. *Reel Latinxs: Representation in US Film and TV*. University of Arizona Press, 2019.

Alvarado, Leticia. *Abject Performances: Aesthetic Strategies in Latino Cultural Production*. Duke University Press, 2018.

Boffone, Trevor, and Cristina Herrera, eds. *Nerds, Goths, Geeks, and Freaks: Outsiders in Chicanx and Latinx Young Adult Literature*. University Press of Mississippi, 2020.

Cuevas, T. Jackie. "Fighting the Good Fight: Grappling with Queerness, Masculinities, and Violence in Contemporary Latinx Literature and Film." *Decolonizing Latinx Masculinities*, edited by Arturo J. Aldama and Frederick Luis Aldama. University of Arizona Press, 2020, 131–50.

Danielson, Marivel T. *Homecoming Queers: Desire and Difference in Chicana Latina Cultural Production*. Rutgers University Press, 2009.

Dinshaw, Carolyn, et al. "Theorizing Queer Temporalities: A Roundtable Discussion." *GLQ: A Journal of Lesbian and Gay Studies* 13, no. 2 (2007): 177–95.

La Serenata. Directed by Adelina Anthony. Written by Ernesto Javier Martíinez. AdeRisa Productions and Rebozo Boy Productions, 2019.

Loza, M. Roxana. "'He Doesn't Talk:' Silence, Trauma, and Fathers in *Aristotle and Dante Discover the Secrets of the Universe* and *I Am Not Your Perfect Mexican Daughter*." *Label Me Latina/o*, Special Issue on YA Latinx Literature 11 (2021). Edited by Trevor Boffone and Cristina Herrera.

Martínez, Ernesto. *On Making Sense: Queer Race Narratives of Intelligibility*. Stanford University Press, 2012.

Martínez, Ernesto Javier. *Cuando Amamos Cantamos/When We Love Someone We Sing to Them*. Translated by Jorge Gabriel Martínez Feliciano. Reflection Press, 2018.

Millán, Isabel. "Contested Children's Literature: Que(e)Ries into Chicana and Central American Autofantasías." *Signs: Journal of Women in Culture and Society* 41, no. 1 (September 2015): 199–224.

Muñoz, José Esteban. *Disidentifications: Queers of Color and the Performance of Politics*. University of Minnesota Press, 1999.

My Story, and "We the Animals": Justin Torres at TEDxStanford. Directed by TEDx Talks, 2012.

Pérez, Daniel Enrique. "Like Father, Like Queer Son? Gay Chicanx and Latinx Males and Their Fathers." *Fathers, Fathering, and Fatherhood: Queer Chicano/Mexicano Desire and Belonging*, edited by Adelaida R. Del Castillo and Gibrán Güido. Springer International, 2021, 233–54.

Pérez, Daniel Enrique. "Toward a Mariposa Consciousness: Reimagining Queer Chicano and Latino Identities." *Aztlan: A Journal of Chicano Studies* 39, no. 2 (September 2014): 95–127.

Pérez, Emma. "Queering the Borderlands: The Challenges of Excavating the Invisible and Unheard." *Frontiers: A Journal of Women's Studies* 24 (2003).

Pérez, Héctor H. "Jardín de Mariposas." *La Serenata*, 2019.

Rivera Montes, Zorimar. "'For Opacity': Queerness and Latinidad in Justin Torres' *We the Animals*." *Latino Studies* vol. 18, no. 2 (June 2020): 218–34.

Rodríguez, Richard T. *Next of Kin: The Family in Chicano/a Cultural Politics*. Duke University Press, 2010.

Torres, Justin. *We the Animals*. Houghton Mifflin Harcourt, 2011.

We the Animals. Directed by Jeremiah Zagar. Cinereach/Public Record, 2018.

Chapter Four

"EVERYONE IS GAY"

Queer Latina Identity in Isabel Millán's *Chabelita's Heart* and Gabby Rivera's *Juliet Takes a Breath*

Sonia Alejandra Rodríguez

In 2022, several states across the country created and/or passed legislation to limit, challenge, or ban LGBTQIA+ content in the K-12 classroom and LGBTQIA+ rights outside of the classroom.[1] PEN America's recent report on banned books show that out of 1,145 books (2022) banned or challenged in the United States, 467 had protagonists of color and 379 books had LGBTQ+ characters and topics. The rise of attacks in the last few years on LGBTQIA+ people, especially people of color, serves to maintain the country's white, Christian, and heteronormative agenda. In 2014, I wrote a brief essay for "Gay YA"[2] discussing Mayra Lazara Dole's *Down to the Bone* (2008/2012), in which I stated, "Despite the increased awareness for the need of diverse children's literature many gaps still exist—diversity in queer and gay YA literature being one of those gaps. *Down to the Bone* remains one of the few YA novels with a Latina lesbian character written by a Latina/o author." Much has changed in children's literature publishing since writing about *Down to the Bone*, but I still assert that there remains a large gap when it comes to representation of Latinx queer youth, but specifically queer[3] Latinas. Additionally, many of the representations of queer Latinas are in speculative fiction, and while the genre affords its own potentiality for queer futurity, it is the lack of representations of queer Latinas in realist fiction that has prompted my analysis for this chapter.[4] In "The Invisible Lesbian in Young Adult Fiction"

(2020), Malinda Lo shares a similar, and broader, concern for the lack of representation for queer girls. In an inconclusive analysis of the Stonewall Book Award for YA novels, Lo finds that from 2010–2020, more often than not, the award was given to books that centered cis male characters. Lo says about her findings,

> Cis queer women have always been marginalized because we exist at an intersection of misogyny and homophobia, at minimum. Add in race, disability, class, etc., and things become even more complicated. We are dismissed for being irrelevant (lesbians, because we aren't in sexual relationship with men). We are denied as impossible (bisexual women) or erased because we're invisible (feminine-presenting queer women).

Now more than ever, it feels imperative to discuss and share LGBTQIA+ children's and young adult books with youth. It is the marginalization, dismissal, denial, and erasure of queer young girls that Lo mentions above that has drawn me to focus on queer Latinas for this chapter.

The books I analyze in this chapter are realist and contemporary fiction that center cisgender Latinas spanning from elementary age to college age.[5] In my analysis of Isabel Millán's picture book *Chabelita's Heart* (2022), I employ her own term *autofantasía* alongside Jennifer Miller's concept of "new queer children's literature" to discuss the ways *Chabelita* queers home and childhood and in turn presents an empowering queer Latina experience for the young readers. In my discussion of the graphic novel version of Gabby Rivera's *Juliet Takes a Breath* (2020) with illustrations by Celia Moscote, I engage with Jasbir Puar's concept of *homonationalism* to discuss Juliet's literal and emotional journey away from her family and back to her family as part of the construction of her queer identity. Throughout this chapter, I argue that Millán and Rivera challenge notions of what it means to be queer and Latina. Furthermore, I argue that these books showcase the role of the Latinx family as shifting from an exclusively oppressive space for queer Latinx youth to a type of Latinx family that encourages and embraces messy changes.

In the editors' introduction to the special issue "Queer Futurities" in *Research on Diversity in Youth Literature*, Angel Daniel Matos and Jon Michael Wargo ask, "How can we view tomorrows as times that are so full of potential and promise when the past and present are riddled with hurt, oppression, and violence?" (7). I see Millán and Rivera as presenting two different and similar ways to "view tomorrows as times that are full of potential and promise." I specifically chose to analyze these books because they contest the tropes of queer death and violence that is perpetually common in coming-out and coming-of-age LGTBQIA+ literature for young people. While the protagonists in Millán's and Rivera's stories do experience instances of violence due to their sexuality, their gender, their class, and/or their race and ethnicity, nonetheless, love and joy abound throughout the stories, including at the end. It is precisely narratives that challenge oppressions due to gender and sexuality while still centering love and joy that make books like Millán's and Rivera's powerful tools for social change.[6]

"YES, GIRLS CAN LIKE GIRLS": *CHABELITA'S HEART*

There are few picture books that present LGBTQIA+ themes and center Latinx characters. Some of the books include *Antonio's Card/La tarjeta de Antonio* (2005) by Rigoberto González, about a young boy and his two moms; *Call Me Tree* (2014) by Maya Christina González, about a nonbinary child; and most recently, *When We Love Someone We Sing to Them: Cuando amamos cantamos* (2018) by Ernesto Javier Martínez with illustrations by Maya Christina González, about a boy who likes a boy and who, with the help of his father, writes a love song about it. Isabel Millán's *Chabelita's Heart/El corazón de Chabelita*, helps fill a void in LGBTQIA+–themed picture books by introducing two young girls who like girls.

Chabelita, who is of Mexican descent, meets Jimena, who is Honduran and Garifuna, for the first time when Jimena joins the classroom as a new student. They like spending time with each other, playing, doing homework, and sharing lunch (11). For picture day, Chabelita decides to wear a black bow tie with printed pink conchas. Jimena is impressed by the bow tie and asks to borrow it so she can also get her picture taken with it. Jacob, the only white character in the book, teases Chabelita for liking Jimena. For a split second, Chabelita panics but is quickly pulled back when Jimena takes her hand and rebukes Jacob. After picture day, they celebrate Jimena's birthday, and Jimena's mom, who had been deported to Honduras, sends Jimena a blue bow tie with yellow stars to match Chabelita's. The story of *Chabelita* is a tender and powerful one about friendship but also desire. It can be easy to read it as a story about female friendship alone especially because the story is presented as a picture book for young children. However, Millán is tactful when showing that this is a story about more than friendship and that "girls can like girls" is more than being amicable but about having feelings for girls. For example, when Jimena enters the classroom for the first time, Chabelita says that Jimena's "eyes sparkle like stars" and that she "[hopes] she sits next to me" (Millán 4). Also, when Jimena expresses wanting to take a trip to Honduras and invites Chabelita to join her, "Chabelita blushes" (13). Additionally, when Chabelita shares her bow tie with Jimena, Millán draws them close to each other, cheeks touching, one of Chabelita's arm draped on Jimena's back, the other holding an end of the bow tie and resting on top of Jimena's hand, while both smile and gaze into each other's eyes (15). Finally, Chabelita chooses to draw Nancy Cárdenas, after learning about her from Papá, for her school role model project because they "both like reading, writing, and girls" (22). In her foundational text on Chicana lesbians, *With Her Machete in Her Hand* (2006), Catrióna Rueda Esquibel argues, "The ways in which female friendships are socially perceived and encouraged provide a space, however restrictive, for lesbian desire in these texts. The intimacy itself provides a context for lesbian desire" (125). The lesbian desire of which Esquivel writes is also evident in *Chabelita*, although I read Chabelita and Jimena's intimacy as having "queer" contexts in order to provide the characters, and readers, access to the wider spectrum of sexuality, especially because Millán does not give the characters a label to describe their sexuality other than "girls can like girls." Again, to echo Malinda Lo, it can be very easy to marginalize, dismiss, deny, and erase queer young girls and read Chabelita and Jimena's intimacy, for example, as friendship. By referring to *autofantasía* in her author's note, Millán further asserts the social and political importance of reading *Chabelita* as a queer text.

In "Contested Children's Literature: Que(e)ries into Chicana and Central American *Autofantasías*," Millán writes about Gloria Anzaldúa's picture books, *Friends from the Other Side* (1993) and *Prietita and the Ghost Woman* (1995), stating that "by writing herself as a child within her stories for children, Anzaldúa recreates her childhood past in order to demonstrate what would have been. In doing so, she is creating *autofantasía* that is autobiographical in her insertion of self and fantasy fiction in her rewelding of the past" (204). Elsewhere I have written about the importance of young Latinas using the act of writing prose and poetry as part of the healing process from systemic oppression.[7] Writing is an opportunity to name a truth, to ask readers to bear witness, and for the potential of more liberating futures by reimagining the past. Millán follows in Anzaldúa's path by creating her own *autofantasía* in *Chabelita*. In the author's note for her debut book, Millán says,

> When I was in first grade, my mom gave me an earring and necklace set for picture day. To my mom's surprise I was not wearing the necklace in my class photo because I had lent it to a little girl I liked. Although I did not come out as queer until I was much older, I often wonder what my childhood would have been like had I found books with queer characters of color in loving, supportive communities. (36)

In *Chabelita*, Millán borrows from her life to give her protagonist a bow tie to lend to Jimena for picture day. In creating this *autofantasía*, Millán creates a ripple effect wherein reimagining the past can heal the future. *Chabelita* exists now and contemporary children of color, and in the future, will have one more book to see "queer characters of color in loving, supportive communities."

In *The Courage to Imagine: The Child Hero in Children's Literature*, Roni Natov writes, "Childhood stories align the imagination with memory so that all parts of the self, past and present, feel connected and coherent. These stories help children imagine things that they may not otherwise be able to. They can tell the story that provides courage, offers inspiration, inspires hope, and provides an escape from moments of pain and sorrow" (187). The alignment between "imagination with memory" echoes Millán's theory of *autofantasía* and her praxis of it in *Chabelita*. While Natov speaks more generally, and not specifically about queer children of color and the importance of childhood stories having the potential for children to imagine otherwise, to have hope, and to process "pain and sorrow," their sentiments still ring true about the power of a story like *Chabelita*. Because of the lack of representation of Latinx children in children's literature, and more specifically because of the gap in representation of queer Latinas in picture books, *Chabelita* "provides courage, offers inspiration, inspires hope" where there might be none. *Chabelita* not only offers solace to an individual queer child but also presents an opportunity to challenge and change larger institutions of oppression like the family and the home.

In "For the Little Queers: Imagining Queerness in 'New' Queer Children's Literature," Jennifer Miller argues that "new queer children's literature" offers a queering of childhood, a queering of home, and potentially a queering of society. For Miller, old queer children's literature is literature where queerness happens around the child. For example, Rigoberto González's *Antonio's Card* could be considered "old queer children's literature" because queerness is happening outside of Antonio, as the story is about Antonio's two moms and not about Antonio's own sexuality. Millán's *Chabelita*, on the other hand, might be considered "new queer children's literature" because "[new queer children's literature] represents queer children as desiring subjects and knowledge makers, while representing the vulnerability and, at times, the inadequacy of the heterosexual family unit. In doing so, childhood itself is queered in the new queer children's literature" (1646). In this way, books like *Chabelita*, offer new ways to read queer childhood and how to exist as a queer child that calls into question fraught institutions like "the heterosexual family unit." That is not to say that *Antonio's Card*, for example, doesn't continue to center queer families by providing queer representation within the overwhelming inundation of books centering white heterosexual families. However, it is also powerful to see queer child characters, especially queer child characters of color, as "desiring subjects and knowledge makers." By giving queer child characters agency over their identity and sexuality, authors like Millán also contest dominant heteronormative ideologies. Miller further argues,

> New queer children's literature creates an imaginative space to think about the ethics and politics of a universalizing view of queer and straight definition in which normativity, the center frequently used to define and maintain the distinction between straightness and queerness, can be seen as in flux. Norms are constantly negotiated and renegotiated. (1646–1647)

Again, by centering the queer child and recognizing the queer child as a subject with desires and with the capability to create knowledge, normativity is decentered and examined. The "distinction between straightness and queerness" and the negotiation and renegotiation is present in *Chabelita*. For example, after Chabelita agrees to let Jimena borrow her bow tie, the narration goes as follows: "'Of course!' [Chabelita] exclaims as she takes off her bow tie and offers to put it on Jimena. Jacob spots them by the big oak tree. As he walks by, he taunts, 'Ohhh, Chabelita likes Jimena, Chabelita likes Jimena'" (15). In Millán's illustration, Jacob, white with blonde and green eyes, is an interloper on Chabelita and Jimena's intimate and queer moment. He is partially hidden behind the oak tree looking at the young girls. I do not read Jacob's action as innocent teasing because doing so would further align innocence with white childhood; instead, I read Jacob as an ambassador for white heteronormativity, especially because his taunting causes Chabelita to question herself. After the taunting, "Chabelita feels her whole face turn bright red like the tulips surrounding the playground. She wants to hide behind a tree or run away" (16). It is important to note here that despite the positive reinforcement Chabelita receives at home about being her truest self, it is the public, outside world that seeks to shame and marginalize her. Miller further asserts that new queer children's literature offers

> Representations of home as an affirmative space in queer children's literature [that] provide a template for modeling queer affirmation in the home. The queer-affirming home is an important part of a queer worldmaking project that seeks to celebrate the queer child and reject

the home as a site of gender surveillance and policing by recreating it as a space that facilitates gender creativity. (1654)

In other words, the home can serve as a site of queer liberation. In *Chabelita*, Millán is intentional in presenting both Chabelita's and Jimena's guardians as supportive adults. Chabelita's papá teaches her about queer historical icons for a class project; Chabelita's parents welcome Jimena into their home to celebrate her birthday; and Jimena's mom gifts her a bow tie to go with Chabelita's. These moments of a queer-affirming home are what no doubt give both girls the strength and courage to stand up against outside oppressive forces that seek to silence, marginalize, and erase them. As Cristina Herrera posits, "In fact, [*Chabelita*] insists on portraying the radical possibilities of liberation when Latinx families love, protect, and celebrate their queer kin."

Following Jacob's taunting, Millán illustrates Chabelita's shame in a two-page spread, zoomed in on the upper half of Chabelita's face with wide eyes and two hot pink circles on her cheeks. Chabelita's instinct to "hide behind a tree or run away," to hide behind a tree like the one Jacob hides behind, further reinforces that the Jacob character is a representation of harmful messages of white heteronormativity. The norms are "negotiated and renegotiated" in *Chabelita* when Jimena steps in: "To Chabelita's surprise, Jimena holds out her hand and smiles back at her. 'So what if Chabelita likes me. I like her, too,' she proclaims. Emboldened, Chabelita adds, 'Yes, girls can like girls!' Jimena and Chabelita walk away holding hands, leaving Jacob behind as they get in line for their photos" (18). Jimena's affirmation as a queer child of color shakes Chabelita out of her moment of insecurity brought on by the violence of white heteronormativity and allows both queer Latinas to exist fully in their queer desire. While it is Jimena who holds Chabelita's hand, Chabelita also raises her voice to reaffirm, "Yes, girls can like girls." Millán's beautiful illustration of two queer Latinas staring into each other's eyes and holding hands while standing next to a giant oak tree surrounded by red tulips is a powerful reminder that heteronormativity is a construction that can be dismantled and love can win.

"EVERYONE IS GAY": *JULIET TAKES A BREATH*

Gabby Rivera's debut novel, *Juliet Takes a Breath*,[8] centers Juliet Palante, a queer Puerto Rican young woman from the Bronx. The graphic novel version of *Juliet*, which will be the focus of this section, is an abridged version of the story with beautiful new illustrations by Celia Moscote. The graphic novel of

Juliet opens in the Bronx with Juliet on her way home for a farewell family dinner before her internship in Portland, Oregon, with the renowned white feminist author Harlowe Brisbane. On this trip, Juliet learns more about her queer identity and the ways it is much more aligned with her family than she initially thought. I employ Jasbir Puar's concept of "homonationalism" to discuss the ways Juliet experiences her queerness as separate from her Latinidad. It is only after Juliet "engages in epistemic disobedience" that she recognizes that the answers she looked for were with her family all along.

Jasbir Puar explains in *Terrorist Assemblages: Homonationalism in Queer Times* (2007) that homonationalism

> is a form of sexual exceptionalism—the emergence of a national homosexuality ... that corresponds with the coming out of the exceptionalism of American empire. Further, this brand of homosexuality operates as a regulatory script not only of normative gayness, queerness, or homosexuality, but also of the racial and national norms that reinforce these sexual subjects. (2)

In other words, homonationalism establishes a dominant form of homosexuality that dictates which sexual subjects have access to national and cultural citizenship and which subjects are outside of this national imaginary and, therefore, disposable. Furthermore, this dominant sexual discourse makes certain queer experiences complicit with the violent erasure and marginalization of "other" racial and ethnic queer identities. Such forms of sexual exceptionalism are evident in *Juliet* by contrasting her Bronx home with Portland and by comparing queer representations in Portland and in Miami. I employ homonationalism because throughout most of the novel, Juliet experiences forms of violence that are related to her nationality and her sexuality, even if tangentially. At the beginning, Juliet understands her gender and sexuality through the white lens of Harlowe Brisbane and her book, *Raging Flower*. It is that representation of queerness, of white queerness, which draws Juliet to Harlowe and ultimately to Portland. While Juliet meets queer people of color in Portland, it is important to note that many of them warn Juliet about Harlowe's toxic whiteness, and it is that toxicity that will have Juliet running from Harlowe and to a queer cousin in Miami. By contrast, Juliet's home of the Bronx and her family are initially represented as riddled with toxic hypermasculinity and homophobia that are associated with her Puerto Rican culture. The dichotomy between Harlowe and Juliet's mom and Portland and the Bronx in the graphic novel point to the ways homonationalism is a pervasive ideology that suggests that in order to be queer and out, one must leave their ethnic community for whiter spaces, as if queerness undoes white supremacy.

The illustrations in the graphic novel make the contrast and separation between queerness and Latinidad that Juliet feels much more apparent. At the beginning of the story, Juliet questions whether feminism, particularly the white feminism that Harlowe Brisbane touts, is even for her. As she walks through the subway exit to her stop in the Bronx and to the crowded street, Juliet ponders the word "feminism" and its inaccessibility. Juliet, depicted as a thick and curvy Latina young woman with black rimmed glasses, dressed in jeans and a white tank and jacket, with her hair in a messy curly bun, takes her earbuds out as she walks through her neighborhood. Speech bubbles capture her thoughts: "Feminism. I'm new to it. The word still sounds weird. Too white. Too structured. Too foreign. Something I can't claim. Wish there was another word for it. Maybe I need to come up with my own." I find it powerful that Juliet's instinct, even if she is at the moment unaware of the overwhelming whiteness of women's feminist movements in the United States, is to feel that something is "weird" about the term "feminism" and that it will be up to her to find a word and an identity that best fits her. Interestingly, the same spread where Juliet questions the word "feminism" is also the one where Juliet reveals she has a secret. Juliet receives a text message from her mother asking her to go to the supermarket just as Juliet is about to reveal to the reader her secret: "How do I tell everyone that I'm . . ." The interruption serves as an opportunity to remark on how her mother "refused to read Harlowe's book because it says 'vagina' too many times" but remains proud of her nonetheless, which Juliet fears will change once she comes out. While Juliet contemplates the multilayered complexities of her intersectional identity as she makes her way home, she's experiencing street harassment in the background. A man whistles at her, which Moscote represents with the word "whistle" nearing Juliet's head, a vivid representation of the ways street harassment is an attack. Juliet is cornered by four men who are drawn as bigger than her; in most of these panels, Juliet is drawn only from head to shoulders. One of the men propositions her and slaps her behind. In a full rage, Juliet responds with: "No, I'm gay, you asshole. Don't freakin' touch me!" The harasser says, "Ha, gay. That's nothing what I got right here can't fix" and he takes Juliet's hand and places it on his genitals. Juliet tries to push her way out, but the men get more aggressive with their language, and it's not until a woman bumps into the harasser with her shopping cart that Juliet is able to get away. The hit with the shopping cart is made to look like an accident as the woman does not look at Juliet and the woman's children ask for cereal. However, I read this moment as active feminist resistance against violence and the patriarchy even if it is a small gesture. It is these subtle moments in the graphic novel where the reader can also see that the feminist empowerment Juliet searches for is around her in the Bronx since the beginning. At the entrance of her family home, Juliet expresses gratitude at having found *Raging Flower*, and while not mentioned in the panel, there's also gratitude for leaving the toxic hypermasculinity of the Bronx behind, even if only for the summer.

When Juliet does eventually come out during dinner, her mother doesn't respond well: "Enough! There aren't any lesbians at this table. Ok?" The panel zooms in on Juliet's round face with speech bubbles coming at her. In the next page, Juliet takes up the full page, smacks one hand on the table, and places the other hand on her chest as she says: "Stop! There is a lesbian at this table. It's me. I'm gay. Gay. Gay. Gay." For a second time in one day, Juliet's queerness is denied even as she demands to be seen and heard. Moscote's illustrations, however, force the reader to witness Juliet's queerness in both instances. In the panel with the harasser, Juliet is visibly angry with furrowed eyebrows and a growl in her mouth forcing the reader to take note. When she literally stands up to her mother in another panel to say she is gay, Juliet's thick body, now more vulnerable without a jacket, takes up the majority of the page while her face is pleading. Again, when Juliet interacts with characters who represent and uphold heteronormative patriarchy, the illustrations force the reader to bear witness to Juliet's queerness, showing the power Juliet does not know she has yet. Juliet's mother responds: "That vagina book has you all messed up in the head. Confused." Blaming the "vagina book" for Juliet's queerness is an example of the subtle ways homonationalism constructs an imagined homogenous queer identity where queerness is associated with whiteness. Furthermore, Juliet's mother distances queerness from Latinidad, more specifically, from her Puerto Rican family, asserting that queerness is a white construct and therefore does not belong in their home. The irony in Juliet's mother's sentiment is revealed later in the story as Juliet learns that there are indeed multiple queer people in her Puerto Rican family.

In "Lesbian 'Growth' and Epistemic Disobedience: Placing Gabby Rivera's *Juliet Takes a Breath* within Puerto Rican Literature and Queer Theory," Consuelo Martínez-Reyes says about the novel, "Nationality and queerness are linked through their social conceptualization, definition, and delimitation, which, for Juliet, in the context of this Puerto Rican diaspora and as a woman of color in the United States, prove to function as exclusionary instead of welcoming spaces" (339). For Juliet, what she learns about what it means to be Latinx and what it means to be queer clash with one another. As Boffone and Herrera reaffirm, "Juliet is an outsider both within her community and among the white, feminist, lesbian enclave of Harlowe's Pacific Northwest" (71). Put differently, based on the difficult day Juliet had before heading to the airport for her internship, street harassment, sexual assault, and homophobia are associated with her Latinx family and community in the Bronx and tokenism, marginalization, and classism are associated with the predominantly white queer space in Portland. Juliet is both Latinx and queer but does not feel welcomed in either space because of the sexism, homophobia, and homonationalism she experiences and witnesses.

Juliet's mother's rejection at the beginning of the story and later Harlowe's white savior tokenism[9] serve as catapults that thrust Juliet to search for a third space that challenges homonationalism where she can explore her queer identity. In writing about *Aristotle and Dante Discover the Secrets of the Universe*, Angel Daniel Matos says that gay coming of age novels "are in some way connected to or dependent on familial structures; even when they are focused on a protagonist's abandonment of their families in their search for alternative models of kinship and belonging, the family nonetheless serves as the element by or against which queer protagonists define their subjectivities" (41). The familial structures in the graphic novel *Juliet* play into that process of helping or hindering Juliet define herself. Juliet's abandonment of her family in the Bronx, while happening under the guise of an internship, is nonetheless a desire and an opportunity to search for a place where she can be unapologetically queer. Unfortunately, Harlowe and Portland do not result in the imagined "alternative models of kinship" for which Juliet had hoped. I argue that Juliet has abandoned her family in the Bronx, not as a judgment, but as a recognition of the difficult position in which homonationalism puts children and youth of color—that of choosing between their ethnic family and being queer. *Juliet Takes a Breath* demonstrates how homonationalism is a double-edged sword where on one side Juliet's Puerto Rican mother equates queerness with whiteness and on the other where Harlowe associates Juliet's Puerto Ricanness with otherness. That Juliet needs to leave her family to explore her queerness is not much of a choice.

Juliet's transformation and full embrace of her intersectional identity take place when Juliet decides to travel to Miami to visit with her bisexual cousin Ava and escape Harlowe. The transformation begins the night before her trip when she spends the night at Kiara's apartment, and they have sex. Moscote undoes Juliet's iconic messy bun and draws her hair down with curls framing her face representing the ease, or breath, Juliet has been needing. The trip to Miami is a significant contrast to the oppression experienced in Bronx and in Portland. At the onset, Moscote draw the panels demonstrating tenderness and love with Juliet being embraced and caressed by her cousin and aunt. It is also Juliet's family in Miami who openly discuss gender, sexuality, and sex with her. They share intimate moments of asking questions, learning about past queer loves, and express complete and whole acceptance of one another. Ava takes Juliet to a "QTPOC Babes Only" party where Juliet witnesses and experiences a beautiful safe space with queer people of color who fully embrace all parts of their intersectional identities. It is also at this party where she shaves part of her hair giving readers the recognizable look on the cover. Juliet leaves Miami aware that queerness is a part of her family history and future. Similar to *Chabelita*, the trip to Miami reinforces for Juliet that home can be a site where queerness can thrive. To echo back to Miller, representations of families loving their queer children is a powerful reminder that these families exist and that these families are possible (1654). Such a possibility is especially important for children and young people of color.

The trip to Miami, however, is not the first time that Juliet has tapped into the knowledge of her family and culture for empowerment. Martínez-Reyes discusses Juliet's epistemic disobedience in relationship to Juliet's visits to the Portland Library, where she learns about feminist heroes including Lolita Lebrón, and how learning one's own history is liberating. I argue that the same process of epistemic disobedience is happening with her family in Miami, and those moments allow Juliet to participate in a decolonial healing practice. Martínez-Reyes says about the library in *Juliet*:

> This move from colonial knowledge is key for colonized subjects like Juliet. It implies that the "facts" about Puerto Rican and American history that she has access to were always already mediated by the socio-political relationship between colonizer and colonized. She discovers these "facts" to have been "censored" or altered, and by breaking with them she engages in epistemic disobedience. (332)

During these library scenes Juliet learns more about the history of colonization and liberation movements in Latin America, and it is the act of absorbing that new knowledge that transforms her and how she sees herself. It is that transformation that allows her to break with a filtered, colonized version of a history that tells her who she can and cannot be. By engaging with epistemic disobedience, as Martínez-Reyes puts it, Juliet has opened herself to alternative knowledges and different ways of being. Juliet's time with her family in Miami is part of her epistemic disobedience where she rejects what she's learned about what it means to be Latinx and queer from her mother and from Harlowe and instead embraces alternative and liberating knowledges.

By the end of the graphic novel, Juliet's mother gives her a gift with a note that says "Dear Juliet, Reading will make you brilliant. But writing will make you infinite." With this note, her mother is also practicing a decolonial healing that allows her to unlearn heteronormativity and give her room to embrace Juliet. Juliet also learns that her brother is queer and exclaims, "Everyone is gay!" While Juliet is being hyperbolic, it is that sentiment that challenges homonationalism and creates a possibility for queer Latinx homes, childhoods, and futures.

CONCLUSION

bell hooks concludes her foundational essay "Love as the Practice of Freedom" by stating, "The moment we choose to love we begin to move against domination, against oppression. The moment we choose to love we begin to move towards freedom, to act in ways that liberate ourselves and others. That action is the testimony of love as the practice of freedom" (250). Isabel Millán's picture book *Chabelita's Heart* and Gabby Rivera and Celia Moscote's graphic novel *Juliet Takes a Breath* are examples of how choosing love can lead to transformative ways of being. In both texts, choosing love, as demonstrated in simple and complicated acts like Chabelita holding hands with the girl she likes and like Juliet taking chances on romantic, platonic, and familial love, has led the protagonists to a "practice of freedom" and away from oppressive knowledges that limit who they can be and who they can love. Chabelita and Juliet are years apart in age, and come from different cultural backgrounds, but their journeys have similarities. Most significantly, both protagonists navigate their queer identity with the support of their family and friends. Additionally, it's important that both stories conclude with a happy ending that affirms their queer Latina identities. Carolina Alonso states about queer coming of age novels that "it is important not only that these queer stories are told, but also that they are narrated in a positive way and avoid falling into the past tropes where the queer characters rarely managed to empower themselves from their subjectivity" (186). Again, *Chabelita* and *Juliet* are significant contributions to representations of queer Latina identity because they queer home and childhood, challenge homonationalist ideologies, and present possibilities for a queer future where queer and Latinx children and young people are alive, loved, and empowered. Literature alone cannot protect queer children. But positive and affirming literary representations can provide queer children of color support and vocabulary to understand their subjectivities. We need more worlds, even if for the moment only literary ones, where children like Chabelita can grow up to embrace their full queer selves and young people like Juliet can grow up to be writers to tell more LGBTQIA+ stories.

NOTES

1. See "Freedom for All Americans: Legislative Tracker: All Anti-LGBTQ Bills."
2. The site has since changed its name to "YA Pride."
3. Throughout this essay I use the terms LGBTQ, LGBTQIA+, gay, lesbian, and queer. When citing a reference, I use whichever term the author used originally. Oftentimes, I default to "queer" throughout the essay as an attempt to write about a broader experience.
4. In this chapter, I don't compare, contrast, or pit speculative fiction against realist fiction. Nor am I suggesting that one genre does or doesn't do more than the other. My focus on realist, contemporary fiction simply follows my larger research trajectory.
5. The focus on cisgender Latinas was not intentional. As much as I argue that there is a lack of representation of queer Latina girls, there is an egregious omission of trans Latina girls. There is a secondary character in *Juliet Takes a Breath* who has a minor role in the story, Frikitona Luz Angel, who is trans: "I'm queer. Cuban. And trans AF."
6. Some other realist, contemporary novels that center queer Latinas include *No Filters and Other Lies* (2022) by Crystal Maldonado; *Ophelia After All* (2022) by Raquel Marie; *The Lesbiana's Guide to Catholic School* (2022) by Sonora Reyes; and *Just Your Local Bisexual Disaster* (2022) by Andrea Mosqueda.
7. See Rodríguez, "Conocimiento Narratives."
8. *Juliet Takes a Breath* was first published in 2016 by Riverdale Avenue Books and then again in 2019 by Dial Books. The novel is considered as "New Adult" fiction because Juliet is a nineteen-year-old college student.
9. For more on the role of white woman allyship in *Juliet Takes A Breath* and literacy instructions see Shea Wesley Martin.

WORKS CITED

Alonso, Carolina. "The Coming-of-Age Experience in Chicanx Queer Novels *What Night Brings* and *Aristotle and Dante Discover the Secrets of the Universe*." In *Nerds, Goths, Geeks, and Freaks: Outsiders in Chicanx and Latinx Young Adult Literature*, edited by Trevor Boffone and Cristina Herrera. University of Mississippi Press, 2020, 175–89.
"Banned in the USA: Rising School Book Bans Threaten Free Expression and Students' First Amendment Rights." *PEN America*, https://pen.org/banned-in-the-usa/#genres.
Boffone, Trevor, and Cristina Herrera. *Latinx Teens: U.S. Popular Culture on the Page, Stage, and Screen*. University of Arizona Press, 2022.
Esquibel, Catrióna Rueda. "Memories of Girlhood: Chicana Lesbian Fictions." *With Her Machete in Her Hand: Reading Chicana Lesbians*. University of Texas Press, 2006, 91–127.

Herrera, Cristina. "'Girls Can Like Girls, Too': Celebrating Queer Latina Girlhood." *Latinx Spaces*, 13 April 2022. https://www.latinxspaces.com/latinx-literature/girls-can-like-girls-too-celebrating-queer-latina-girlhood.

hooks, bell. "Love as the Practice of Freedom." *Outlaw Culture: Resisting Representations*. Routledge, 2006, 243–50.

"Legislative Tracker: All Anti-LGBTQ Bills." *Freedom for All*. https://freedomforallamericans.org/legislative-tracker/anti-lgbtq-bills/.

Lo, Malinda. "The Invisible Lesbian in Young Adult Fiction." *Malinda Lo*, 10 February 2020. https://www.malindalo.com/blog/2020/2/4/the-invisible-lesbian-in-young-adult-fiction.

martin, shea wesley. "What Do We Do with the White [Cis] Women?: *Juliet Takes a Breath* as the Blueprint for Reimagining Allyship in Literacy Instruction." *Research on Diversity in Youth Literature* 4, no. 1, Article 3 (October 2021): 1–26.

Martínez-Reyes, Consuelo. "Lesbian 'Growth' and Epistemic Disobedience: Placing Gabby Rivera's *Juliet Takes a Breath* within Puerto Rican Literature and Queer Theory." *Centro Journal* 30, no. 2 (Summer 2018): 324–46.

Matos, Angel Daniel. "A Narrative of a Future Past: Historical Authenticity, Ethics, and Queer Latinx Futurity in *Aristotle and Dante Discover the Secrets of the Universe*." *Children's Literature* 47, no. 1 (2019): 30–56.

Matos, Angel Daniel, and Jon Michael Wargo, eds. "Editors' Introduction: Queer Futurities in Youth Literature, Media and Culture," *Research on Diversity in Youth Literature* 2, no. 1, (June 2019): 1–16.

Millán, Isabel. *Chabelita's Heart/El corazón de Chabelita*. Reflection Press, 2022.

Millán, Isabel. "Contested Children's Literature: Que(e)ries into Chicana and Central American *Autofantasías*." *Signs: Journal of Women in Culture and Society* 41, no. 1 (2015): 199–224.

Miller, Jennifer. "For the Little Queers: Imagining Queerness in 'New' Queer Children's Literature." *Journal of Homosexuality* 66, no. 12 (2019): 1645–1670.

Natov, Roni. *The Courage to Imagine: The Child Hero in Children's Literature*. Bloomsbury Academic, 2018.

Puar, Jasbir. *Terrorist Assemblages: Homonationalism in Queer Times*. Duke University Press, 2007.

Rivera, Gabby, and Celia Moscote. *Juliet Takes a Breath*. BOOM! Box, 2020.

Rodríguez, Sonia Alejandra. "Latinx Gay YA." *Gay YA*, 12 June 2016. https://www.gayya.org/2016/06/latinx-gay-ya/.

Rodríguez, Sonia Alejandra. "YA Latina Lesbians: On Mayra Lazara Dole's *Down to the Bone*." *Gay YA*, 14 January 2014. http://www.gayya.org/2014/01/ya-latina-lesbians-on-mayra-lazara-doles-down-to-the-bone/.

Rodríguez, Sonia Alejandra. "Conocimiento Narratives: Creative Acts and Healing in Latinx Children's and Young Adult Literature." *Children's Literature* 47, no. 1 (2019): 9–29.

Section Two

Queerness and Bodies in Transformation

Chapter Five

TRANSFORMATION AND THE QUEER LATINX BODY IN THE COLLECTED WORKS OF ANNA-MARIE McLEMORE

Cristina Rhodes

In their remarks upon winning the American Library Association's Morris Award for their debut novel, *The Weight of Feathers* (2015), Anna-Marie McLemore notes, "As a teen, I made the decisions that shaped who I was and who I would become. As a teen, I came out as queer. As a teen, I decided to stop spending so much of the life I had in me trying to pass for white" ("Anna-Marie McLemore—Morris Award Remarks" 1). McLemore's paralleling of their Latine identity and their queerness not only intimately ties the two together, but this assertion also connects those identities with transformation.[1] While McLemore has certainly always been Latine and certainly always been queer, their conscious choice to inhabit those identities is revelatory and reparative. As a result, nearly all of their books and short stories bear these concepts as a leitmotif.[2] McLemore's work privileges queer bodies that experience corporeal or phenomenological change resulting in ameliorative action outside of the characters themselves.

For example, McLemore's debut novel *The Weight of Feathers* (2015), though lacking in the overt queer content of their later novels, still contains the queered context within which I read the body and change in McLemore's corpus of work. The novel, a magical realist retelling of *Romeo and Juliet*, pits the Paloma family against the Corbeaus. Lace Paloma, who works as a real-life mermaid in her family's traveling show, is rescued from a factory explosion by Cluck Corbeau, but his touch, as foretold by her family, is "poison" (McLemore, *The Weight of Feathers* 2). Exposure to Cluck transforms Paloma's body. The birthmarks (or scales) she is born with are shed when he touches her. However, instead of changing Paloma's body in an irreparable or negative way, Cluck's touch reveals the truth, that he is not poisonous, nor are the other Corbeaus. Rather, his touch is reparative, healing. Though Lace's body is radically altered, the feud between the families is alleviated because of that change. Unlike its source material, which ends in tragedy, *The Weight of Feathers* proffers an alternate future, one in which embodied transformation precipitates collective betterment. In my prior analysis of queer Latinx speculative fiction, I observed that "reading for queer Latinx futures means accepting the necessity for imagination and the promise of a better tomorrow" (8). McLemore's books, through their fantastic and magical realist worldbuilding, bring that future into the present.

In this chapter, I will demonstrate the myriad ways McLemore utilizes metamorphosis to facilitate positive and ameliorative queer realities. While many of McLemore's books and short stories follow this pattern, I focus most closely on *When the Moon Was Ours* (2016), *Wild Beauty* (2017), *Blanca y Roja* (2018), and *Dark and Deepest Red* (2020). McLemore's books, though popular in social media circles, have yet to receive much critical attention.[3] Through my focus on a few key examples of transformation and queer Latinx bodies in McLemore's work, I underscore how embodied change operationalizes amelioration.

MAGICAL REALISM AND FAIRY TALE TRANSFORMATIONS

Magical realism, according to Lois Parkinson Zamora and Wendy B. Faris, "serves the purpose of political and cultural disruption: magic is often given as a cultural corrective, requiring readers to scrutinize accepted realistic conventions of causality, materiality, motivation" (3). As a Latin American literary tradition, magical realism responds to oppression on social and geopolitical scales and seeks to redress that injustice. Writing about Latinx youth literature, Jesus Montaño and Regan Postma-Montaño likewise argue, "[transforms] themselves and their contexts to reflect their lived experiences and the shared dreams of their communities" (2). The confluence of magical realist Latinx youth literature proves an apt canvas for remedying oppression and seeking change. Further, of importance to my discussion of McLemore's work, is their additional emphasis on fairy tale retellings. While traditional European fairy tales are often linked with didactic or moralistic endeavors, McLemore's Latinization of their adaptations queers these stories. Rather than teach a lesson, McLemore's fairy tales provide a space for growth and renewal. Through the melding of magical realism and fairy tale adaptation, McLemore creates a landscape for their characters that is ripe for revolution.

What's more, transformation is woven into the fabric of being Latinx and being young. In her introduction to *Figurations: Child, Bodies, Worlds*, Claudia Castañeda explains, "What is distinctive about the child is that it has the capacity for transformation" (2). Childhood is a time of perpetual transition: bodily maturation, emotional and cognitive growth, burgeoning civic responsibilities, and confrontations with socio- and geopolitics. This transition often denies children and adolescents agency, but its motion and malleability conversely make adolescence the best possible space within which to engage with rebirth and restoration. Thus, in the following sections, I will address several iterations of McLemore's rendering of embodied transformation and the ensuing betterment of justice. José Esteban Muñoz opens his *Cruising Utopia: The Then and There of Queer Futurity* with the assertion that "queerness is not yet here. Queerness is an ideality" (1). If queerness is that ideal to strive toward, I argue McLemore's characterizations of change and reformation bring us closer to a future in which queerness is reality. To do so, I will first examine the ways that McLemore has written bodies that experience holistic shifts—that is, bodies that are entirely changed rather than just individual parts. I will then discuss how McLemore's works depict the uncontrollable body as a site of agency and reclamation. Finally, I will examine how McLemore's oft-used conceit of growth and flowering impacts embodied transformation.

FULL BODY TRANSFORMATIONS

Queer Chicana theorist Gloria Anzaldúa often utilized the figure of la nagula or shapeshifter in her theoretical and autoethnographic writing to surrogate internal change which leads to creative action and social justice.[4] Anzaldúa's invocation of a fully embodied transformation coincides with McLemore's regard for whole-body metamorphosis in their fictional work.[5] Anzaldúa's la naguala is "a mode of consciousness that's emotionally complex, diverse, dense, deep, violent, and rich, one with a love of physicality and the ability to switch bodies" (105). For the case studies I examine, Aracely in *When the Moon Was Ours* and Roja from *Blanca y Roja*, embodied shifts are reactions to familial trauma and result in mended relationships and senses of self.

When the Moon Was Ours (2018), perhaps McLemore's most popular novel, features two transgender characters, one of whom, Aracely, undergoes a magical transformation.⁶ Aracely serves as the guardian to the novel's protagonist Miel, but is also secretly her sister. Importantly, Aracely was assigned male at birth. Miel, as I will discuss later, is regarded as an abomination because of the roses she seemingly unnaturally grows from her wrists, but Aracely acts as a buffer between Miel and those who would harm her. In fact, Aracely's desire to protect Miel spurs her transmogrification. In an attempt to cleanse her of this dangerous magic, Miel is nearly drowned as a child and Aracely, then living as her brother, tries to save Miel. Both are taken by the water and assumed dead. Miel spends time suspended in a state of hibernation in the water, but the water takes the child brother and returns her transformed into the adult Aracely.

Their shared trauma may initially trigger Aracely's embodied changes, but their similarities end there. Whereas Miel is unchanged, McLemore explains, "The water made the outside of [Aracely] show the truth in all ways" (*Moon* 102); and Aracely "[came] out of the water soaked and a stranger in her own body. Surfacing as someone older than when she'd gone in, while the water had kept Miel the same age. Back then, Miel had the sorrow of a child. But Aracely's heart carried the sadness of the woman she had become" (*Moon* 253–54). Finally, Aracely clarifies, "It wasn't about [the water] making me older. . . . It just gave me back as what I was meant to be" (McLemore, *Moon* 214). The complexities of Aracely's transformation are magnified when we consider that Aracely isn't just transgender, but trans-aged. Children's literature scholar Nabilah Khachab notes, "Ethnic bodies are . . . on display in Western culture in violent ways that mark them as deviant, Other, and freak" (5). Aracely's otherworldly transfiguration magnifies Khachab's warning because Aracely's changes signal several transgressions against hegemonic power—not only does she supersede adolescence, but she moves from a male-assigned to a female-assigned body. In this way, Aracely's transformation is at once intimate and radical. In its connection to her body and gender identity this evolution dwells squarely within Aracely herself, but it also has a wider impact on her relationship to her sister, Miel. When Miel learns that Aracely is her sister, she is taken aback, but their relationship is made stronger by the change. Aracely is much more able to relate to and care for Miel as an adult woman than she was as a male child. While Aracely's only function isn't just to serve Miel, the parallels between her embodied change and the positive shifts they precipitate in her relationships and home life cannot be understated. In this way, the connections facilitated by embodied change epitomize the reparative function of transformation.

Aracely's isn't the only body to fully transform in service of her family. *Blanca y Roja* (2020) follows cursed sisters Blanca and Roja del Cisne, one of whom will be cursed to spend the rest of her life as a swan. Roja has predicted since before the book's beginning that she will be the one taken to become a swan, but Blanca, her elder sister, resists this narrative. The sisters share a closeness that extends beyond typical sisterhood. Indeed, when Roja appears to be chosen to permanently become a swan, a sacrifice which would allow Blanca to live a full life as a human, Blanca fights back. Page, Blanca's love interest, notes, "No matter what body held it, Blanca's heart would always be true to her sister" (McLemore, *Blanca* 333). And perhaps more importantly, "She wanted a new body—feathered, winged—that would let her fly after the sister she was losing" (McLemore, *Blanca* 333). Blanca corroborates Page's reading of her sororal relationship. She thinks, "I swear Roja and I could feel the things that lived in each other's bodies" (McLemore, *Blanca* 335). Yet the swan curse threatens to sever the bond, as one body will ultimately become a swan and the other will remain human.

At the climax of the novel, as both Blanca and Roja—in their swan forms—grapple with who the curse will claim, the two become a united front, almost a single body: "I felt a spreading heat, shared across my body and my sister's. It bloomed and darkened, like the swans were hollowing us out. The sense of it both filled and emptied me, like they were reaching into us and taking the hearts out of our swan-bodies" (McLemore, *Blanca* 336). Their unity ultimately breaks the swans' curse, and both Blanca and Roja are transformed back into humans mid-flight. Their bodies plummet to the ground, thankfully cushioned by a flooded cranberry bog. Roja is mortally wounded, but Blanca, Page, and Barclay (Roja's love interest) heal her. Their touch knits her body back together (McLemore, *Blanca* 350). Though both fully transform to swans and then back into humans, it is Roja's body that experiences the most radical transformation, as Blanca, Page, and Barclay each pour part of themselves into Roja to heal her. In this way, she is both herself and more than herself. Unlike the metamorphosis into a swan that would have kept her from her family, this transformation cements her bond with her sister and reverses a generation-long curse while simultaneously bringing her out of the del Cisne's insular, accursed world via her newly embodied connection to outsiders Page and Barclay. Ultimately, Aracely's and Roja's bodies each, in some way, confront familial trauma, and their embodied shifts allow for healing between siblings. Put simply, their transformations are what makes reconciliation possible. Even as both Aracely's and Roja's bodies are irreversibly changed, this change is positive on micro and macro levels.

UNCONTROLLABLE BODIES

While the holistic metamorphoses in *When the Moon Was Ours* and *Blanca y Roja* follow a fairly straightforward pattern from transformation to amelioration, not all queered bodies in McLemore's books follow such a linear path. Many of their books feature characters whose bodies act queerly and uncontrollably. For example, McLemore and Tehlor Kay Mejia's coauthored book *Miss Meteor* (2020) sees McLemore's Lita frantically trying to capitalize on the time she has left on earth, as her body is "made of star-stuff" and, alarmingly, is "turning back into the stardust I once was" (Mejia and McLemore 5 and 6). Spurred by the urgency of her disappearing body, Lita seeks to compete in a beauty pageant and must contend with her unruly body being on display. Nevertheless, she seeks to tame said body and reclaim her agency—a pattern which I observe in several of McLemore's other works, key among them *Dark and Deepest Red* and *Mirror Season*.

In *Dark and Deepest Red*, McLemore fuses Hans Christian Andersen's "The Red Shoes" and the historical story of the French dancing plague of 1518. Rosella, whose family are renowned shoemakers, saves the destroyed remains of a beautiful pair of red shoes her grandmother cut up when they were returned to their shop by an angry customer. Rosella keeps the shoes "as a reminder. I would find a way to make sure we never had to destroy something of ourselves just to stop other people from taking it" (McLemore, *Dark and Deepest Red* 22). Rosella repairs the shoes and resolves to wear them to bring her luck, but the shoes take over her body: "I slid into the feeling of being dragged from where I stood, like the red shoes were moving without me moving them" (McLemore, *Dark* 59). The shoes' control over Rosella becomes increasingly violent and uncontrollable. The shoes become stuck to her feet and move her against her will—in one striking scene, the shoes pull her from her bed as she sleeps. They drag her through the woods, and Rosella only awakens when the shoes plunge her into the reservoir. McLemore writes, "I had barely shaken out of sleep when the lack of air blurred my brain, and the shoes took me under again" (*Dark* 192). Rosella's red shoes parallel the dancing plague, which is explored in alternating chapters. The plague is seen as the result of the dark magic of the Romani people in France, a feeling borne of xenophobia. Rosella's own uncontrollable body is likewise rooted in feelings of discontent and prejudice, as the shoes are those that had been returned to her family's shop by a racist customer.

Even as the shoes bring her harm, they become an extension of her body. Rosella explains, "They had sealed to me, like they had become part of my skin" (McLemore, *Dark* 78). When Rosella tries to cut them off, the shoes reform "like a wound healing in seconds" McLemore, *Dark* 209). To be free of the shoes, Rosella must undo their magic. Just as her grandmother, who first cut the shoes to pieces to "save [the customer] the bother of carrying them home," Rosella understands that she must take back control of her body (McLemore, *Dark* 21). She asserts, "I'll save you [the shoes] the trouble of making me dance" (McLemore, *Dark* 281). As Rosella takes back control, she ameliorates her family's legacy. Rosella does not allow the shoes to act on her behalf any longer. Rather than being a passive figure, Rosella usurps power. By disallowing the shoes to move her body beyond her control, Rosella forces the shoes to dance in rhythms all her own. While it may have previously seemed as if her body was uncontrollable, Rosella channels her inherent power over her body to facilitate a revolution for her family's labor.

The Mirror Season likewise positions bodies as influenced by negative external factors yet still pushing for broader restoration and justice. After taking an unknown young man to the hospital following his assault at a summer party, Ciela Cristales attempts to quickly escape before the nurses can notice that she, too, was assaulted at the party. In the dark parking lot as she flees, Ciela notices a strange flower: "Its petals look like glass. No. Not glass. Mirrors" (McLemore, *The Mirror Season* 6). The flower shatters and "[a] shard catches my eye. It's small and coarse as sand, and I try to blink it out. But I feel it go deeper in" (McLemore, *Mirror* 6). This shard of magical mirror, now embedded in her body, distorts Ciela's vision and robs her of her magical power to predict which pan dulce a customer at her aunt's bakery will want. Like Rosella's shoes, the mirror shard in Ciela's eye forces her body to act in ways beyond her control or desire.

Importantly, Ciela isn't the only one afflicted by the mirror shards. Lock, the boy she transports to the hospital following the horrific party, also has a sliver in his eye. Ciela feels compelled to save him—both because of their shared trauma and because she feels a sense of responsibility over the mirror shard. The blight of flowers turning to mirror and shattering, spreading fragments across town and afflicting individuals concerns Ciela. Even more, the confluence of the mirrored foliage and her assault is unignorable. While Ciela and Lock ultimately confront those who sexually assaulted them, they recognize that they are changed. Ciela thinks, "We may never be able to set [the shards and traumas] down for good. They may be in our hands forever, something we're always holding. But we don't have to grip them. We don't have to hold them so tightly that they're forever cutting our fingers" (McLemore, *Mirror* 303). Unlike Rosella's shoes, which are removable, Ciela notes that the trauma she and Lock have incurred is not easily fixed or taken from their bodies. While their bodies are changed and their lives forever altered, Ciela's assertion that they do not need to hold so tightly to the trauma that the wounds can never hope to heal allows her to take back control over her body. By extension, Lock takes back control as well. Even as both transformations began as uncontrollable and traumatic, Rosella and Ciela actively resist dominant narratives that would victimize them and assert their power and agency over their bodies and their circumstances. By making their power manifest through these seemingly uncontrollable bodies, these previously unruly bodies are reclaimed, and the characters demonstrate the feasibility of overcoming harrowing circumstances.

BODIES IN BLOOM

One of the most consistent images throughout McLemore's work is flowers and other plants. Two of McLemore's novels—*When the Moon Was Ours* and *Wild Beauty*—feature characters who magically grow flowers either from or through their bodies. It stands to reason, then, that this motif connects to their rendering of transformed bodies. The metaphor of things growing, transforming from seed to bloom, perhaps demonstrates most succinctly my reading of transformed bodies as being restorative. From something as innocuous as a seed buried in the ground can grow a beautiful flower or a tree that provides shelter and sustenance. The transformation seedlings undergo throughout their life cycles is radical. Likewise, McLemore's emphasis on the connection between flowers and bodies evinces transformative power.

Unlike Aracely in *When the Moon Was Ours*, the water does not facilitate her transformation; rather, her ability to transform is rooted in the roses she grows from her wrists. However, the roses have a precarious past and Miel is distrustful of them. Nevertheless, the primary antagonists of the novel, the Bonner sisters, manipulate Miel, as they see the roses she grows from her wrist as the antidote for their own waning magic. The Bonner sisters' power seems to lie in their untouchability and their superiority, but with their hold slipping, they attempt to steal Miel's magic. They force Miel to cut the roses at the stem and give them the buds, but Miel eventually refuses to give her roses up. She tells Ivy, one of the Bonner sisters, "What do you want with [the roses]? . . . They're not gonna get you what you want. And they're sure as hell not gonna make it so Chloe was never gone" (McLemore, *Moon* 229). In a rage, Ivy retaliates by ripping the rose from Miel's body, causing her to hemorrhage.

Sam finds Miel, bleeding and on the brink of death. The two, whose love has become strained because of the Bonner sisters' interference, reconcile and in the spot on Miel's wrist where once there was a rose, a thorn protrudes and pricks Sam—his own blood magically transfuses through the thorn and heals Miel. Healed, Miel confronts the sisters, divining that the Bonner sisters' "secrets were killing them. They knew it. Speaking them gave the power of those unsaid things back" (McLemore, *Moon* 256). Put simply, the truth will set them free. Miel admits the truth that her family loved her, though she had previously thought that she was hated for her roses. In doing so, Miel spurs the Bonner sisters to confide their own truths: One sister comes out, another attests to her intelligence despite putting on an aloof front, and Chloe speaks the name of her daughter, the child she gave up. Finally, only one sister, Ivy, remains, held by the secret that she believes, "I have nothing that's mine" (McLemore, *Moon* 257). It is this admission of insufficiency and similitude that spurs the transformation in this book that captivates me most. Following this moment, Miel and Ivy trade hair colors. McLemore writes, "Miel's eyes paused on her own collarbone. A wave of copper spilled over her shoulders. Her hair had turned the color of scarlet oak leaves, as deep red as Ivy's," and then, "Miel squinted toward the trees, picking out a dark fall of hair. Ivy looked over her shoulder, the copper that once marked her now as dark as Aracely's eyes. The brown, almost black, made Ivy's face look pale as a cream pumpkin" (*Moon* 259). While this scene does not directly draw on the metaphor of flowers or growth, I read it as a moment of cross-pollination.

Miel's generative magic, manifested through her roses and then through her hair, triggers a physical representation of the equality she now has with the Bonner sisters. By giving something of herself, no matter how unconsciously, the transference of her hair color to Ivy and vice versa signals a shift in the power dynamic between the two. Miel takes a measure of power from Ivy, not necessarily because her new hair color aligns her with whiteness, but because the agency to transform gives Miel power. Likewise, Estrella's power of transformation through floral magic seeks justice in *Wild Beauty*. Estrella's magic, unlike Miel's, means that she can urge flowers to grow from the ground, not her own body. But her generative magic takes on a new meaning when she inadvertently seems to grow a young man from the sunken garden near her home.

Wild Beauty follows the Nomeolvides—a play on the Spanish phrase which translates to forget-me-not—family, who are cursed to live in La Pradera forever, an insular unit of women who bear five daughters each generation. "Only daughters, always five, like the petals on a forget-me-not. And ever since La Pradera had gotten its hold on them, sure and hard as a killing frost, every generation of five daughters had been trapped in these gardens, like their hearts were buried in the earth" (McLemore, *Wild Beauty* 7). But the most recent generation of Nomeolvides women, a set of five cousins often led by Estrella, are on track to break the curse as they "couldn't have five daughters if they were all in love with the same woman" (McLemore, *Wild Beauty* 7). Bay Briar is that woman. Bay is the heir to the La Pradera estate, but her place is tenuous, and Estrella and her cousins are worried for her and themselves because another facet of their curse is that those whom the Nomeolvides women love are doomed. The cousins create a sort of offering to La Pradera, one that will hopefully protect Bay. Estrella plants her offering in the ground and thinks nothing of it, despite that the Nomeolvides' magic allows the women to plunge their hands into the ground and call upward shoots and blooms. But the next morning a boy emerges from the ground where Estrella left her sacrifice.

The boy, whom the cousins come to call Fel, is a mystery. But as the novel unfolds, Fel's past is revealed. Fel was once employed by the Briar family decades ago but was killed in a mining accident the Briars covered up to save face. Fel's body, along with the other miners, is left in the collapsed mine, atop which La Pradera, the garden the Nomeolvides women must tend, grows. McLemore explains, "The Nomeolvides women had no idea that the ravine they made into a valley of flowers had been a quarry. And a graveyard" (*Wild Beauty* 267). Fel's life is imperiled, however, when Reid, another Briar who seeks to usurp Bay's role as heir, wrestles him back into the earth of La Pradera. The earth takes Fel back and "he was nothing but ground" (McLemore, *Wild Beauty* 259). Devastated at Fel's loss, Estrella, who has come to love him over Bay, goes to La Pradera to mourn and repent. McLemore explains, "Fel was gone, and there was nowhere to mourn him. But he had once died in this ground, and now so could [Estrella]" (*Wild Beauty* 286). Estrella tries to sink herself into the earth, to be absorbed alongside Fel. But her magic takes over as she plunges her hands into the dirt; "Estrella was drawing him back" (McLemore, *Wild Beauty* 288). McLemore continues, "She thought she was imagining him, a boy from the earth. Petals and leaves and dirt still half covered him when she made out his shape" (*Wild Beauty* 291). With Fel returned to her, Estrella turns her attention to how her family's powers had been misused to cover up the Briar family's shame.

The Nomeolvides women had once been exploited by the Briars, their magic perverted to ensure the Briars were not held accountable for hundreds of deaths. Estrella and her cousins resolve that "they had to kill all the beauty they'd made" (McLemore, *Wild Beauty* 307). Estrella, Fel, and her entire family all descend upon La Pradera and begin tearing the flowers they had grown with their magic out by their roots. As the women destroy what they created, figures start to emerge from the dirt. Where once their magic pulled beautiful but obfuscatory blossoms from the earth, upon those flowers' destruction the men who were killed in the mine collapse are the ones being pulled forth by the Nomeolvides magic. Via their transformative, floral magic, the Nomeolvides women upend decades of trauma. They channel their magic through their bodies, plunging their arms into the ground to transform that land and themselves.

Just as flowers grow, wilt, and must grow again, the process of evolution and change in McLemore's books is recursive. Embodied transformation facilitates change on wider levels. Miel's shifts bring the Bonner sisters out of their funk, give them something to rely on other than their faltering illusion of superiority. Estrella and the Nomeolvides women may not have the same overt bodily transformation, but the burden of their magic, which they channel through their hands, is rerouted when they begin to destroy the flowers and resurrect the men. The reciprocal nature of these metamorphoses reinforces that embodied change prompts healing more broadly.

QUEERED BODIES AND THE PROMISE OF POSSIBILITY

In the end, the embodied transformations Miel and the Nomeolvides women experience connect with that of Aracely and Roja, Rosella and Ciela. Miel's physical change via the transference of hair colors with Ivy facilitates a similar reconciliation to Aracely and Roja's own evolutions. Similarly, the Nomeolvides women harness their transformative powers to take control over the curse that had plagued their family, just like Rosella and Ciela reclaim agency through transformation. Even as they differ in terms of plot, structure, and queer representation, McLemore's books are woven together with an attention to growth and betterment. While it might be trite to say that McLemore's usage of fairy tale elements culminates in "happily ever afters," the implication that the characters are on paths toward progress or healing is explicit in each novel (and McLemore's queering of this trope is another way they rewrite normative ideals).

That healing is at the fore of their most recent novel, *Lakelore*, published in 2022. Bastián and Lore, both young, neurodivergent, trans, and queer characters, must contend with their individual traumatic pasts in order to stop the mythical world that exists underneath the local lake from creeping to the surface. Bastián, in particular, fears this fate as they have been making alebrijes (papier-mâche sculptures of mythical animals) and attaching all of their trauma and negative feelings and dysphoria to the statues before sinking their creations in the lake. When the novel comes to its denouement, Bastián reclaims their past feelings of despair and dislocation. Bastián thinks, "I'm not fighting it anymore. I went back. [The world beneath the lake is] no longer the place that holds everything I want to keep at a distance. I went back for all those parts of me" (McLemore, *Lakelore* 221). Because Bastián reclaims these disparate parts of themselves, they make themselves whole. They assert that because they are able to fuse these distinct memories and feelings, they are "proof of what exists in between" (McLemore, *Lakelore* 279). Anzaldúa calls this in-betweenness "nepantla," which "is the midway point between the conscious and the unconscious, the place where transformations are enacted" (56). Because they recognize their medial positioning, they enable the shifts that lead to their self-acceptance and their ability to love Lore, as they deserve to be loved.

Much more can certainly be said about *Lakelore* and the rest of McLemore's oeuvre. Nevertheless, queered bodies are regularly at the fore of their work; necessarily so because transformation promises new opportunities. It is important to assert that the changes I discussed in this chapter do not mean that these queer characters *must* shift to be more acceptable within the hegemony. Rather, I read these embodied shifts and the larger changes they facilitate as resetting the dominant order. In the introduction to *Cruising Utopia*, José Esteban Muñoz explains, "Queerness is essentially about the rejection of a here and now and an insistence on potentiality or concrete possibility for another world" (1). Melding Muñoz's theorization with my reading of McLemore's books illustrates that queer bodies in transformation have the ability to bring about that possibility for a better future. Even if that future is still just a potentiality, as Muñoz puts it, McLemore's books bring it closer to reality. As they continue to publish, McLemore's regard for queer bodies and transformation will only grow.[7]

NOTES

1. I use the gender-neutral term Latine to describe McLemore because this is how they identify themself (via their Twitter bio). While Latinx is often favored over the binary gendered Latino/a, there has been pushback against the term. Among many reasons, its unpronounceability in Spanish makes it inaccessible to native speakers; therefore, the pronounceable Latine has been gaining popularity. I will use Latine in this essay when referring to McLemore but will use Latinx in other contexts because it is more widely used at my time of writing.

2. Between 2015 and 2022, McLemore has published eight novels (including a coauthored book with Tehlor Kay Mejia) and nine short stories/essays, available in various anthologies and online. They also have several forthcoming novels.

3. Christine M. Stamper and Mary Catherine Miller's "Arts-Based Approaches to Social Justice in Literature: Exploring the Intersections of Magical Realism and Identities in *When the Moon Was Ours*" is one of the few critical works currently published on McLemore's work. Beyond that, scholarship on queer Latinx youth literature more broadly is a small field, but key articles by Laura Jiménez, Angel Daniel Matos, and Trevor Boffone explore queerness in Latinx literature for young readers.

4. See Kelli D. Zaytoun for more information about Anzaldúa's theorizations of la naguala.

5. While this section details McLemore's novelistic representations of whole-body transformation, McLemore's short story "Glamour" also features Grace/Graciela, an aspiring actress who uses "color glamour" a "borrowed magic, an heirloom her great-grandmother had handed down" to transmogrify her features to be more white and Anglo to be cast in more roles (McLemore, "Glamour," 134). When she is Grace, the aspiring actress, she conceals Graciela's brown skin, but the charade exhausts her. The magic is finite. And Graciela ends the story understanding, "You've gotta wear colors that aren't yours. . . . But if you wear too much of somebody else's colors, there's none of you left" (McLemore, "Glamour," 152).

6. *When the Moon Was Ours* is McLemore's most awarded book, winning both a James Tiptree Jr. Award and a Stonewall Award Honor; it is also their most reviewed book on *Goodreads*, with nearly nine thousand reviews at the time of my writing.

7. McLemore has two forthcoming books, *Self-Made Boys*, forthcoming fall 2022, and *Venom & Vow*, forthcoming 2023 (news posted via McLemore's personal Twitter profile).

WORKS CITED

Anzaldúa, Gloria. *Light in the Dark/Luz en lo oscuro: Rewriting Identity, Spirituality, Reality.* Duke University Press, 2015.

Boffone, Trevor. "When Bisexuality Is Spoken: Normalizing Bi Latino Boys in Adam Silvera's *They Both Die at the End*." *Research on Diversity in Youth Literature* 4, no. 2 (2022): 1–21.

Castañeda, Claudia. *Figurations: Child, Bodies, Worlds.* Duke University Press, 2002.

Jiménez, Laura M. "PoC, LGBTQ, and gender: The Intersectionality of America Chavez." *Journal of Lesbian Studies* 22, no. 4 (2018): 435–445.

Khachab, Nabilah. "Freak Show: Religiously Marginalized Female Bodies as Spectacle in Second-Generation Literature." *Children's Literature Association Quarterly* 45, no. 1 (2020): 4–24.

Matos, Angel Daniel. "A Narrative of a Future Past: Historical Authenticity, Ethics, and Queer Latinx Futurity in *Aristotle and Dante Discover the Secrets of the Universe*." *Children's Literature* 47, no. 1 (2019): 30–56.

McLemore, Anna-Marie. "Anna-Marie McLemore—Morris Award Remarks." *American Library Association*. www.ala.org/yalsa/sites/ala.org.yalsa/files/content/booklistsawards/bookawards/speeches/Anna-Marie%20McLemore.pdf. Accessed April 15, 2022.

McLemore, Anna-Marie. *Blanca y Roja*. Feiwel and Friends, 2018.

McLemore, Anna-Marie. *Dark and Deepest Red*. Feiwel and Friends, 2020.

McLemore, Anna-Marie. "Glamour." *The Radical Element: 12 Stories of Daredevils, Debutantes & Other Dauntless Girls*, edited by Jessica Spotswood. Candlewick Press, 2018, 128–55.
McLemore, Anna-Marie. *Lakelore*. Feiwel and Friends, 2022.
McLemore, Anna-Marie. *The Mirror Season*. Feiwel and Friends, 2021.
McLemore, Anna-Marie. *The Weight of Feathers*. Thomas Dunne Books, 2015.
McLemore, Anna-Marie. *When the Moon Was Ours*. Thomas Dunne Books, 2016.
McLemore, Anna-Marie. "Where Our Magic Lives: An Introduction to Magical Realism." *Diversity in YA*. https://diversityinya.tumblr.com/post/129571372240/where-our-magic-lives-a-queer-latina-on-magical. Accessed May 5, 2022.
McLemore, Anna-Marie. *Wild Beauty*. Feiwel and Friends, 2017.
Mejia, Tehlor Kay, and Anna-Marie McLemore. *Miss Meteor*. Harper Teen, 2020.
Montaño, Jesus, and Regan Postma-Montaño. *Tactics of Hope in Latinx Children's and Young Adult Literature*. New Mexico University Press, 2022.
Muñoz, José Esteban. *Cruising Utopia: The Then and There of Queer Futurity*. NYU Press, 2009.
Rhodes, Cristina. "Imagining the Future: The (Im)Possibilities of Queerness in Two Latinx Speculative Young Adult Novels." *Label Me Latino/a* 11 (2021): 1–10.
Schmidt, Pauline Skowron, and Tricia Ebarvia. "Carpe Librum: Seize the (YA) Book: Possible Impossibilities: The Power of Magical Realism for Adolescent Readers." *English Journal* 106, no. 1 (September 2016): 62–65.
Stamper, Christine M., and Mary Catherine Miller. "Arts-Based Approaches to Social Justice in Literature: Exploring the Intersections of Magical Realism and Identities in *When the Moon Was Ours*." *Engaging with Multicultural YA Literature in the Secondary Classroom: Critical Approaches for Critical Educators*, edited by Ricki Ginsberg and Wendy J. Glenn. Routledge, 2019, 171–79.
Zamora, Lois Parkinson, and Wendy B. Faris. *Magical Realism: Theory, History, Community*. Duke University Press, 1995.
Zaytoun, Kelli D. "'Now Let Us Shift' the Subject: Tracing the Path and Posthumanist Implications of La Naguala/the Shapeshifter in the Works of Gloria Anzaldúa." *MELUS* 40, no. 4 (2015): 69–88.

Chapter Six

"WE ARE SOMETHING NEW"

Disability and Latinx Adolescence in
Mia García's *The Resolutions*

Cristina Herrera

By the time I reached second grade, I had been experiencing tremendous joint pain for several years, and my pediatrician suspected that I had juvenile arthritis (JA), which the Western medical, benchmark testing standards of bloodwork could never officially confirm. The word "disability" was not part of my vocabulary, but as the granddaughter of a fiercely proud Mexican man who lived with polio, disability was a distinct part of my maternal family's history. My grandfather often recalled times that he was disparagingly referred to as "chueco" (crooked) and "medio hombre" (half a man) for his physical disability, and much later in his life he often resisted aiding devices like wheelchairs or orthopedic shoes to reject what would then be visible and undeniable "proof" of his disability. Needless to say, my understanding of disability as a child and teenager was largely shaped by my grandfather's history of trauma that interlocked with poverty, migration, race, masculinity, and normative ideologies around physical differences and bodies. So given these facts of my history, I was struck when I read Mia García's acknowledgments to her 2018 YA novel, *The Resolutions*.

While for some readers an author's acknowledgments might be something to gloss over or skip altogether,[1] it is worth noting that García discloses her own experiences with disability in this message to her readers. Near the end of her acknowledgments, she states, "In addition to a nomadic lifestyle, these past two years brought with them an unwelcome health diagnosis, the result of which led me to concentrate more on my physical and mental health. So to those living with, surviving, fighting, or struggling with a disease, disorder, or illness: I see you, I'm there with you, and I love you. You are not alone."[2] Rather than suggest that García's choice to reference her experiences with disability should be lauded as proof of her "authenticity," an undeniably messy and complicated discussion, I read her disclosure instead as a powerful attempt to destigmatize physical and mental illness to her teen readers. While not a major point that this chapter will explore, I point to García's multiple admissions as her refusal to conceal her disability, which I see as an affirming way to validate what her teen readers (and adult readers, for that matter) may also be experiencing. These open admissions directly challenge the hegemonic imperative to cover up or conceal pain, illness, and disability that maintains restrictive ideologies of the human body. In this regard, I consider *The Resolutions* to be a sensitive and refreshing representation of Latinx teen disability that privileges non-normative bodies, a decidedly subversive, queer move. As this chapter will explore, García's novel queers YA literature through its narrative emphasis and privileging of a group seldom visible in disability studies or YA literary studies: Latinx teens with disabilities.[3] As this scholarship has rarely been undertaken, this chapter lays the groundwork for future study.

Throughout the novel, one of the central characters, Lee, struggles with whether to get tested for genetic markers of Huntington's Disease, an illness that killed her mother, and Jess, her best friend, experiences growing anxiety and depression, culminating in a major panic attack that causes a serious car accident while she is behind the wheel. When Jess is released from the hospital following the accident, it is her queer friend, Ryan, who encourages her to seek therapy. While it would seem at first that he is attempting to "find a cure," a signature debate that scholars in disability studies contest, I read this moment as being far more subversive, as he tells her: "You aren't broken, Jess . . . And neither am I. We are something new" (360). In this gentle but firm statement to his friend, who feels ashamed for her complicated experience with depression, Ryan rejects (hetero)normative, ableist ideologies that render them "broken" and in need of fixing. Instead, Ryan subversively encourages Jess to recognize her lived experience with depression as offering a new, and thus empowering, perspective that affirms disability's presence that can transform life into one that is worth celebrating and living fully.

This chapter contributes to the paucity of scholarship on disability in Latinx YA literature through its engagement with Mia García's novel, *The Resolutions*, which features multiple Latinx teen characters who navigate various forms of disability and its meaning in their lives as young people of color. As this chapter will explore the intersections between disability studies and YA studies, we must question the ways that youth erases one's status as an ideal citizen, particularly when youth intersects with gender, Latinx ethnicity, and disability. As I argue, *The Resolutions* challenges normative, hegemonic standards of adolescent identity through its representation of disability as intrinsic to the Latinx teen characters' identities. Much as Cristina Rhodes has examined how "young Latinxs regard change as integral to their individual and communal well being" (466), this chapter asserts that the Latinx teens from *The Resolutions* signal their journeys with disability as the beginning of a new life, not the end of it. Rather than reinforce ableist tropes that construct disability as an othering, inferior state that one can and should "get over," *The Resolutions* refuses to uphold this ideology, instead positing that the Latinx teens who experience disability are in the process of becoming "something new."[4]

While I center my analysis more closely on Jess and Lee and how the novel foregrounds disability as intrinsic to understanding the full scope of Latinx youth identities, I would be remiss if I did not state that all characters, to some extent, experience disability, particularly anxiety and depression. Although undoubtedly the characters experience many moments of love, joy, and happiness, *The Resolutions* is not always a "happy" text by any means, despite its rather optimistic title. Here, I would suggest, we see the novel's subversive qualities in how it grapples with one of the central tenets that we find in adolescent literature, particularly those that feature disability, the notion of a resolved ending, which I will discuss later in the chapter.[5] Further, the novel's significant efforts to broach the topic of mental and physical disability unsettles one of the signature myths of adolescence, that this group's youth makes them "robust," "healthy," and "strong," to say nothing of how these terms uphold normative ideologies of difference and embodiment. As Suzanne Bost explains, "Foregrounding pain, illness, and disability undermines the myth of self-reliance and demands more expansive ways of understanding individual agency" (5). These ableist tendencies would further suggest that youth and disability are incompatible, despite what we may know to be true. In this light, disability is maintained within hegemonic norms as that which "afflicts" the old, erasing narratives of adolescents who experience and live with disability.

ON DISABILITY STUDIES AND YA LITERATURE

I situate my analysis of García's novel within theories of disability studies, feminist disability studies, and YA literary scholarship. In bridging these perspectives, I point to the novel's insistence that readers recognize how disability, combined with gender, race, sexuality, *and* youth, must be taken into account to fully theorize Latinx adolescent lived experiences. In recognizing the importance of these fields of inquiry, my analysis starts with the central assertion that few scholars have engaged with disability in YA literature penned by Latinx authors.[6] In fact, what Jacob Stratman states in his introduction to the seminal collection, *Lessons in Disability: Essays on Teaching with Young Adult Literature,* is apt: "There is still a dearth of scholarship that explores the intersection of young adult literature and disability" (1).[7] Although disability as a viable lens has grown in studies of YA literature, scholars have seldom paid attention to how it manifests in representations of Latinx teen characters in YA literature. As scholar Julie Avril Minich asserts in her astute work on disability in Chicanx literature, "Nondisabled bodies are believed to indicate robust, sound communities while disabled bodies signify social decay or political crisis. One result of this correlation is an implicit justification for the political exclusion of people with disabilities and others whose bodies do not fit a narrow national ideal (often due to racialized or gendered corporeal attributes)" ("Enabling" 698–99). Markers of otherness related to physical difference, queerness, race, and gender thus demonstrate one's status as an acceptable citizen or member of a family and larger community.

García deftly integrates disability throughout the text to insist on its presence in the teen characters' lives, another facet of identity that equally shapes how they love, think, feel, and negotiate their daily realities. But rather than represent disability as a passing "phase" to work out, eliminate, or reject altogether, the novel captures the characters' navigation of disability as an integral part of their lives as Latinx teen subjects. The novel particularly lends itself to a disability studies approach, as it calls into question the need to "cure" or "fix" illness or that supposed "disease" called adolescence (Trites, *Literary* 1). For example, readers never learn whether Lee is ever diagnosed with Huntington's Disease. There is no resolution to this lingering question, a subtle challenge to Western medical emphasis on diagnosis that does not fully capture a human being's experiences with disability and illness. Jess, in addition, while seeking treatment to address her anxiety, later comes to accept mental and emotional difference not as something that renders her a lesser, "flawed" Latina teenager. Rather, the novel provides a critique of such issues like the exorbitant cost of higher education and demanding expectations of performance as the real culprits that need to be resolved.

Rosemarie Garland-Thompson's pioneering work on feminist disability studies is crucial to our understanding of how disability has been framed within mainstream, dominant discourses. Reminding us that "Disability—like gender—is a concept that pervades all aspects of culture"

(Garland-Thompson, "Integrating" 16), the systems that we inhabit are undergirded by white supremacy, heteropatriarchy, and ableism that demarcate certain bodies "as *beautiful, healthy, normal, fit, competent, intelligent*— all of which provide cultural capital to those who can claim such status, who can reside within these subject positions" (Garland-Thompson, "Integrating" 17–18). Within this system that privileges bodies via their proximity to the normative ideals of white, able-bodied, cisgender manhood, value is ascribed to these bodies, providing entrance to cultural citizenship that excludes queer bodies of color, particularly those with disabilities. Of course, one of the hallmark consequences of this deeply unequal system is how it defines disability and human and bodily diversity as stigmatizing, according to Minich, which then renders disability a product of "individual choices ... [that] coalesces with ideologies of race, gender, and sexuality categorizing certain people as irresponsible, deviant, and ultimately undeserving of health care or public concern" ("Aztlán Unprotected" 168). In this light, systems of white (able bodied) supremacy are essentially let off the hook, reinforcing a bootstrap mythos that encourages rugged individualism rather than structural change. Within these prevailing ideologies, disability is something to be cured, fixed, or even hidden, assuming that is even possible or desired, and the individuals themselves are seen as lesser beings rather than as fully human, autonomous beings.

As a marker of difference that is at worst, excluded from social spaces, and at best, expected to be concealed so as to not "disturb" the social order, disability is rarely, if ever, acknowledged as another facet of a person's identity, like gender or race, as Garland-Thompson reminds us: "Seldom do we see disability presented as an integral part of one's embodiment, character, life, and way of relating to the world. Even less often do we see disability presented as part of the spectrum of human variation, the particularization of individual bodies, or the materialization of an individual body's history" (Garland-Thompson, "Feminist" 1568). Whether it is in the television, film, music, or other dominant industry, disability, when it is represented, is narrativized as an "obstacle to overcome" (Stratman, "Overcoming" 103). Undeniably, this trope of disability as an undesirable affliction to shed permeates popular culture and literature.

In this chapter's examination of Latinx teen disability, I also draw attention to the crucial interventions that YA literature scholars have made to expand our critical conversations on disability and its representation in literature marketed for adolescent readers. Most notably, Stratman's *Lessons in Disability: Essays on Teaching with Young Adult Literature* and Patricia A. Dunn's *Disabling Characters: Representations of Disability in Young Adult*

Literature, are two of the major texts in the discipline, although to be sure, there is much work left to be done. In bridging the work between feminist disability studies and YA disability studies, my aim is to further complicate the conversation by exposing the gap in scholarship that has seldom taken into account how disability intersects with gender, queerness, and Latinx teen identity. In her article, "It Is All in Your Head: Mental Illness in Young Adult Literature," Anastasia Wickham argues that the proliferation of YA texts that centralize the experience of adolescents who experience mental illness is a way to destigmatize these concerns that are often deemed "taboo" (11). García's sensitive treatment of mental and physical illness/disability in her novel, coupled with her own disclosure of disability, supports Wickham's assessment. Disability scholarship disrupts dominant paradigms that ascribe a stigma to disability and to the bodies who experience it. Young adult disability literature can further contribute to this intervention.[8]

But it is equally important to consider how YA disability novels like García's fit within the tradition of so-called YA "problem novels," wherein an ultimate aim is to "'cure' teens of the angst of being an adolescent" (Miskec and McGee 168). Significantly, the underlying message of these problem novels is that adolescence itself is an inherently stigmatizing, troubling period of life, and it is not surprising that these attitudes resemble dominant ideologies that construct disability as a problem or burden that needs resolution. Within this lens, merely being a teenager renders one disabled, meaning all of us have been disabled at one time.[9] Within the problem-novel trope, being an adolescent and thus disabled is undeniably presented as a defect, perhaps a passing phase that will be "solved" through one's eventual transition to adulthood. Barbara Tannert-Smith echoes Miskec and McGee's assessment of YA literature, which at times emphasizes "the 'recovery' of adolescent protagonists as part of a larger coming of age trope" (396). If YA literature has tended to "render adolescence itself as a disability in need of cure" (Markotić 338), my analysis of García's novel suggests that her text challenges this assertion that adulthood is the lofty, idealized goal to which the teens should aspire. Perhaps more troubling is how this ideology implies that one is theoretically "cured" of that other marker of disability, adolescence, once one reaches adulthood, an illogical trope that erases the reality that most humans, at one time or another, experience disability, even long before or after one reaches the supposedly coveted period of adulthood.

While not addressing disability explicitly, children's literature scholar Roberta Trites has argued that YA literature transmits the message that "'there is something wrong with your subject position as a teenager. Grow up and become someone else'" (Trites, *Literary* 1). Trites's argument carries even more significance when we pair it alongside YA "problem novel" scholarship and what Julie Passanante Elman coins "teen sick-lit," wherein "the logics of heteronormativity and ablebodiedness materialize as disciplinary frameworks. . . . In this framework, heterosexuality and health often seamlessly imply one another, while queerness and disability exist as epitomes of abnormality" ("Nothing Feels as Real" 177). Much as problem novels suggest that adolescence itself is in need of curing, teen sick-lit, according to Elman, pushes forth the troubling narrative that vitality and "good health" are only achievable through heterosexuality; queerness can only represent a failure of the body. Teen sick-lit "reaffirms compulsory heterosexuality and ablebodiedness," conveying the troubling narrative that disability is an inherent flaw, much like queerness ("Nothing Feels as Real" 187). Elman builds upon the foundational Crip Theory developed by Robert McRuer, who defined compulsory ablebodiedness as a system that "produces disability, [which] is thoroughly interwoven with the system of compulsory heterosexuality that produces queerness: that, in fact, compulsory heterosexuality is contingent on compulsory ablebodiedness, and vice versa" (McRuer 2). The prevailing system thus defines the able bodied, heterosexual, cisgender being as the norm to which all should ascribe; while not referenced, McRuer's Crip Theory implies adulthood as part of this ideal. Consider, for example, how "gay conversion therapy" uses the language of ableism to advocate for the supposed "curing" of gayness to achieve a normative, heterosexual future (McRuer 13). While the genre of teen sick-lit, according to Elman, often includes plot lines wherein disability is something to be "overcome" to achieve the "happy" heterosexual ending ("Nothing Feels as Real" 187), *The Resolutions*, as a Latinx YA disability text, rejects this alignment of disability as defect that promises only a "doomed" future life of queerness.[10] For the characters Jess and Lee, disability is not positioned as a defective, temporary state of being to "get over," much less something that they actually can simply resolve or avoid through positive vibes, straight coupledom, or through thinking happy thoughts, as the hegemonic, ableist messages of popular culture would have us believe.[11] Undeniably, *The Resolutions* should be read as a Latinx YA disability novel that sharply contrasts the problematic undertones of problem novels and sick-lit, an important fictional contribution to this body of work that considers disability as a significant component in Latinx teen identity offering "something new" to one's lived experiences. Unlike the traditions of problem novels or teen sick-lit that shape disability alongside adolescence as temporary states that require resolution if one has any hope of making it to heterosexual maturation, the Latinx teens in *The Resolutions* actively imagine and construct their present and future selves through an empowered acknowledgment of disability.

"SCARS AND ALL": DISABILITY AND LATINX TEEN IDENTITIES IN *THE RESOLUTIONS*

On its surface, *The Resolutions* appears to follow a fairly straightforward premise: four multiethnic and multiracial Latinx best friends (Nora, Ryan, Jess, and Lee) celebrate New Year's Eve together and commit to making yearly resolutions, but this time, they decide to create resolutions for each other in an attempt to encourage new experiences outside their comfort zones. These resolutions range from a lighthearted "kiss someone wrong for you" to more complicated ones like "choose your own adventure." In their quest to check off the boxes, as we witness, the characters are forced to confront how disability will shape these new life directions and experiences. We see this especially in Lee and Jess, the two characters whose lived realities emphasize the presence of disability and their complex ways of accepting this facet of their identities after much reflection and validation from their friendships with each other.

In the case of Lee, the novel poses fundamental questions regarding disability and the possibility of this lived embodiment. Lee's negotiation of disability is significant in that she does not yet experience living with the actual disease, Huntington's, the major culprit in her mother's death. Rather, *The Resolutions* engages with Lee's decision to get tested for this disease and what a potential diagnosis entails for her life as a Latina subject. Lee's internal debate over whether to get tested for the disease, coupled with her father's ongoing encouragement to determine a diagnosis or not, factor in her daily expressions of her adolescent lived experience, as she grapples with what a potential diagnosis means for her future. For example, early in the novel she visits her mother's grave and speaks aloud her fears of getting tested: "Did it feel like your whole future disappeared when you found out? Dreams just snuffed out of existence?" (94). Lee's struggle to imagine a future for herself reveals a pointed question: "Which youth have the tomorrows that are open, utopic, or even possible?" (Matos and Wargo 6). That is, as a potentially "sick" person, Lee at first internalizes normative and ableist ideologies that essentially align disability with the impossibility of a future, a troubling outlook that aligns disability with only a future of dreams deferred. Lee's internal debate highlights one of the novel's central questions: what does a life with disability mean for a Latinx teen? What might this future entail, and why must disability preclude the possibility of this imagined future?

As a teen who also experiences the joys of first love, Lee's cyclical debate—getting tested or not—poses uncertainties over the possibility of "typical" teen rites of passage, namely sex and the very human desire to live a sexually fulfilling present and future. Soon after becoming sexually intimate with her new boyfriend David (who is also Jess's brother), Lee quickly questions whether she will continue to experience sexual pleasure should she be diagnosed with Huntington's. "It felt good. She felt strong. Like she'd forgotten there was more to her body than the possibility of a future betrayal" (254). Here, sex is a reminder of what the human body can experience, in this case, pleasure, love, and gratification. But while Lee admits feeling empowered after sex with David, the novel also hints at one of the common myths of disability as synonymous with desexuality, "because disabled people are supposedly undesirable in society" (Kim 483). Sex brings feelings of empowerment and strength, the antithesis of what she imagines sex (or life) could be with Huntington's. Significantly, Lee initially views Huntington's as a "betrayal," the opposite of what her body *should* be like or *should* do. If Lee feels "good" and "strong" because of the pleasures her body experiences through sex, then disability is positioned as the antithesis to this heightened embodiment, thus implying that it can only ever mean "badness" and "weakness."

Further, Lee must also grapple with her father's encouragement to get tested, and while his preoccupation is undoubtedly rooted in loving concern for his daughter, his heightened attention to "catch it early" is unsettling for Lee, who has yet to decide whether she actually wants to know the results. For Lee, testing suggests a finality, an end to a life worth living: "I don't want to know how little time I have. I don't want an expiration date just yet" (259). In this deeply unsettling, tragic language, we witness how Lee at first internalizes harmful ideology that renders disabled bodies "expired" and thus marks disability as akin to a social death. The reality, however, is that Huntington's symbolizes more than social death: it raises the possibility of actual death, a life cut short. In a novel that narrates a Latina teen's very real possibility of a youthful death, *The Resolutions* ventures into potentially taboo waters, given that all readers learn is that Lee will eventually get tested. In engaging readers to imagine multiple possible scenarios, the novel resists a narrative of "overcoming" disability I referenced earlier.

Although Lee possesses the outward appearance of youth, Huntington's, or rather, the possibility of it, has already marked her as "past her prime," symbolically stamped with an expiration date like those typically found on food products, or so she believes at first. Significantly, however, it is through her friendships, particularly with Jess, that she discovers that disability need not signal doom and decay: "She was not alone, as her mother had not been alone. Huntington's would not take them from her" (373). Lee does not necessarily deny the real possibility that she may live with the disease, pointing to her eventual acceptance of it as one aspect of her life that makes her who she is. Instead, she finds empowerment through the bonds of friendship and family, reminding her that a potential diagnosis does not negate the presence of love and companionship.

Indeed, while the novel ends with Lee's decision to get tested for Huntington's, readers never learn her diagnosis, rejecting the tidy outcome that is advanced in sick-lit: "To the right there was life without Huntington's; it was still long and green and lush. She could see her friends, her family, and milestones, like college and a career. It was a bit too perfect, and Lee needed to work on that too. To the left was her life with Huntington's" (372). Essentially, Lee reframes the view that Huntington's eclipses the possibility of fulfillment and life, naively believing that living without disability equates to perfection and ease. The language of vegetation and even fertility, such as "long and green and lush," symbolizes the life that Lee imagines without Huntington's, but there are limits to this idealistic image. Storybook images of picket fences and green lawns may hide or obscure what actually lurks beneath the surface, and in Lee's acknowledgment that the image she has conjured "was a bit too perfect," we see the novel's emphasis on disability as offering "something new" that able-bodiedness perhaps cannot. In this stunning example, it is the possibility of a life with disability that allows Lee the space in which to challenge or even altogether reject an idealized, imagined future of lushness that signals comportment to normativity.

While initially Lee suppresses excitement over attending college, yet another teen rite of passage, it is her budding relationship with David that in many ways serves as a catalyst to imagine the possibility of intellectual fulfillment that need not be sacrificed because of a potential Huntington's diagnosis. In one conversation over college applications, Lee downplays David's suggestion to apply to out-of-state colleges, thinking to herself, "And since the future felt so uncertain, why spend four more years in school?" (294). Lee's attempt to squelch excitement, while undoubtedly a mode of self-protection, reflects a belief that as a potentially "sick" person, she has no *right* to a college education if her life may end prematurely. Significantly, this refusal to consider college as a viable option that she is entitled to manifests as a suppression of her interest in horror films, her self-imposed denial that reads as a punishment. Yet David's patient encouragement to investigate a college in New York leads to the discovery of its course offering on horror film, and "it felt like something lit up inside her" (295). While her relationship with David introduces her to newfound pleasures in sex, this youthful Latinx connection simultaneously allows her the possibility to imagine a future she initially believes she does not deserve, much less one in which she will live to see. By experiencing rites of passage that include both sexual intimacy and college admission through this new, loving relationship, Lee's experience of "something new" is facilitated through human connection and intimacy with another Latinx teenager.

Much as Lee arrives at a space of affirmation and acceptance of disability, which is guided by her friendships, Jess must also at first battle internalized views that her body has failed to perform by normative standards of ability. The pressures of seeking college scholarships to fund her education, coupled with a seemingly unending list of activities to perform to mark her as the "ideal" recipient of these funds, lead to profoundly impactful panic attacks that fill her with shame, as she tells herself: "You are drowning in a sea of your own making" (213). I point to this line to emphasize the novel's staunch critique of the pervasive myth of disability as a result of individual "flaws" or "bad choices," that anxiety is merely the result of one's inability to "shake it off," as Taylor Swift would have it. Believing that she has caused this anxiety herself also suggests a failure on her part, an inherent weakness of the mind. Jess at first chides herself, no doubt mirroring normative ideologies that stigmatize mental illness as shameful or embarrassing.

However, the novel is careful to point to Jess's sense of isolation from her friends and family, that is, her insistence on keeping her pain to herself as that which needs correcting, not Jess herself. While the novel in no way suggests that anxiety should be dismissed, my point is that García's text cautions against normative ideologies that one can or should "fix" the person experiencing anxiety. Moreover, given problematic ideologies that classify anxiety and depression as illnesses that are not real, it is important to note the novel's use of medicalized language to legitimize Jess's pain. For Jess, anxiety is something she has always lived with, but "It had never been this bad before. It felt like a virus, infecting anything in its path" (271). While we must be critical of medicalized language that pathologizes and thus stigmatizes those with disability and illness, García's description of Jess's anxiety as feeling "like a virus" is subversive in aligning anxiety not as a matter of personal choice or bad decision making. Instead, much as a virus infects any human in its wake, anxiety is equally experienced by the body. Jess's embodied, lived experience with anxiety, the novel insists, is as legitimate as Lee's potential Huntington's diagnosis; both characters experience disability alongside their lived expressions of teenaged Latinidad.

What is more, the novel allows readers to narratively experience Jess's anxiety, using heightened language to translate a panic attack in uncanny ways. Readers can practically feel the chest palpitations and the deprivation of oxygen that are the signature symptoms of an attack: "She dragged gulps and gulps of breath from her body until she felt ragged, a sob retching free. She shook, a faint part of herself whispering: It's just the cold—you aren't broken. Even though she was certain it was a lie . . . Her heart would not quiet, her breath still labored on like her feet were still pounding away" (270). In this passage rich with imagery, García refuses to use the language of containment or concealment. But rather than use melodramatic language to render Jess a figure of pity, the strong imagery that evokes gasping and the body's struggle to retain oxygen highlights García's subversive efforts to narrate Latina teen embodiment of disability as a refusal to conceal what the body experiences. Readers are not expected to feel pity for Jess; in contrast, the richly packed language is striking, and it is particularly salient for readers who have experienced panic attacks firsthand.

When Jess is hospitalized after an automobile accident, a stunning symbol that implies collision and a necessary confrontation with anxiety rather than a denial of it, her sobs erupt in spite of her attempt to inhibit them: "A sob broke from her throat as she tried to stamp it down, but her body was a traitor that gladly sang out everything she was trying to hide" (347). García's ironic language to describe Jess's inner battle to retain the tears within her body is crucial. On one hand, Jess's body is described as a "traitor," no doubt a reference to mainstream, ableist rhetoric that points to the individual body as culpable for illness or disability. However, this same "traitorous" body "sings" out Jess's tears, a much-needed catharsis that evokes cleansing, even joy. Much as earlier the writer manipulates medical language to compare Jess's anxiety to a virus, here, too García borrows similar wording for subversive purposes. In this passage, Jess's legitimate human emotions refuse to be trapped within her body and the larger body politic that demands containment and concealment.

Earlier in this chapter, I discussed Ryan's crucial role in facilitating Jess's growing acceptance of anxiety as an intrinsic part of her Latina adolescent identity. I point to the significance of one of the novel's queer characters who vocally expresses his fundamental belief that his friend's experiences with disability do not negate her value as a human being. Ryan's simple but affirming language thus queers teen Latinidad through its inclusion of disability as an intrinsic component of their lives:

> Ryan put his arm around her. "Let us be there for you. If it was happening to me or Lee or Nora you would want them to open up, right? You'd want them to get help. So why are you any less?"
> Why was she any less?
> Ryan nudged her. "You aren't a burden. Never think that." (361)

No doubt contesting myths of disabled people as "burdens" on the healthcare system, Ryan rejects this view, subversively defining help as a support system rooted in the bonds of friendship. While for some, Ryan's reference to "getting help" may suggest his need to fix Jess, his earlier insistence that friends should "be there" is a refusal to cast off and isolate their friend. Rather than shame his friend, he insists on walking this path with her. In encouraging her to "open up," Ryan's gentle words additionally contest normative ideologies that demand the concealment of disability, asking her to communicate and vocalize her experiences with her friends. Indeed, the novel concludes with many possibilities for Jess, the anxiety not necessarily "dealt" with finality.

CONCLUDING REMARKS

Late in the novel, Ryan, a burgeoning artist, creates a work on canvas that pays homage to his friends' unique, human complexities. Upon assessing his work, he reflects on what he has created, thinking to himself, "Scars and all. . . . Sky blue for Jess, Lee, and Nora and the bright futures he saw for them regardless of any storm clouds they might see for themselves" (369). Although both Lee and Jess at first associate disability with the impossibility of a future, Ryan imagines a future for them, including their disabilities, and insists on their right to exist. If, as Garland-Thompson argues, "Marks of history such as scarring and impairments are now expected to be surgically erased to produce an unmarked body" ("Integrating" 24), Ryan's artistic envisioning of his friends' scars challenges normative pressures to erase their experiences with disability and pain. Here, Ryan situates his friends' experience with anxiety and mental illness as encapsulating their very being, not as a detriment but as a necessary element that makes them who they are. Ryan rejects the demands of erasure or covering up, articulating acceptance of his friends' whole selves. Further, it is worth remembering, as I pointed out earlier in the chapter, that it is this queer character, Ryan, who utters profoundly impactful words to Jess, facilitating her eventual affirmation of anxiety and depression as part of her lived reality rather than as hindrances that prevent her from fully experiencing life's many complications, both joyous and painful. Although Trites highlights YA literature's common tendency of "employing a wise adult to guide a confused adolescent" (*Disturbing the Universe* 80), it is her friends that facilitate this process of transformation into "something new." Ryan's touching, artistic rendering of his friends' "scars and all" reflects his positioning of disability and scarring as unique road maps of his friends' beautiful, human bodies.

In their well-known theory of narrative prosthesis, David Mitchell and Sharon Snyder explain the ways that disability has been used in narrative "to resolve or correct . . . a deviance marked as improper to a social context" (227). Unlike this well-known trope that depends on a disabled character to propel the story while upholding certain bodies as the "norm," García's novel, I suggest, speaks against this in refusing to treat adolescence as a time to "get better" before one moves on to adulthood. As Mitchell and Snyder explain, "The normal, routine, average, and familiar (by definition) fail to mobilize the storytelling effort because they fall short of the litmus test of exceptionality. The anonymity of normalcy is no story at all" (228). We may presume that *The Resolutions* uses the characters' varying experiences with disability as a narrative prosthesis that moves the novel toward a neat, clean ending, but what distinguishes this text is precisely how it engages in a representation of Latinx teen disability to counter ableist ideologies that demand perfection and bodily normativity for teens if they have any hope to make it to normative adulthood. For the characters, this transition from a perceived sense of doom and gloom that disability supposedly represents to an empowered acceptance and recognition of it as a central aspect of their Latinx identity that offers "something new," is gradual, and as I have argued, facilitated through their friendships with each other. Jess and Lee arrive at a deeply impactful moment in their adolescent lives when they begin to accept disability as a fundamental component of their Latinx lived expressions. In this way, *The Resolutions* queers Latinx YA literature through its exploration of disability. In the end, the characters resolve to shape their lives through disability, a validating and ultimately empowering perspective that recognizes this state of being as an intrinsic and fulfilling aspect of their adolescent Latinidades, a queer element we must not overlook.

NOTES

1. For a discussion on peritexts, including acknowledgments, and their relationship to YA disability texts, please see Megan Brown's chapter, "'Tell Me Who I Am': An Investigation of Cultural Authenticity in YA Disability Peritexts."

2. This is not the first time that García has used a public platform to comment on her lived experiences with disability and illness. For example, in a 2019 interview with *Stay on the Page*'s blog on "shattering stigmas," García says, "I can look back into my memories all the way to the 1st grade and say with certainty I've been having anxiety attacks since then; I just couldn't name it and to be honest, I don't think I would've been believed if I could." ("Q&A").

3. One notable exception is the chapter "Teaching and Reading *Wonder* and *Marcelo in the Real World* with Critical Eyes" by Abbye Meyer and Emily Wender, although curiously, the authors evade a discussion of how disability intersects with Latinx identity.

4. For an insightful discussion of healing and its relationship to creativity, see Sonia Alejandra Rodríguez's "Conocimiento Narratives: Creative Acts and Healing in Latinx

Children's and Young Adult Literature" (2019). This chapter does not engage in a discussion of transformation as a form of healing. See also Jesus Montaño and Regan Postma-Montaño's 2022 book *Tactics of Hope in Latinx Children's and Young Adult Literature*.

5. For the purposes of this chapter, my analysis does not delve into the tropes of (un)happiness, although the novel certainly lends itself to that thematic lens. Please see the important work by Angel Daniel Matos, for example, for an examination of themes of unhappiness in queer YA literature. For further reading on happiness, see Sara Ahmed's *The Promise of Happiness*. Further, this chapter does not engage in an analysis of affect. See, for example, Stephanie Fetta's study, *Shaming into Brown*.

6. However, there is a growing body of important scholarship that examines illness and disability in Chicanx/Latinx literature. See, for example, Amanda Ellis's insightful discussion of what she calls Chicana diabetic poetics in the works of poet ire'ne lara silva, listed in the works cited.

7. Jennifer James and Cynthia Wu's 2006 special issue on disability in *MELUS*, published a whole decade before Stratman's collection, affirms this overwhelming lack of scholarly attention on disability in literature by writers of color, although significantly, not a single essay in this issue addresses children's or YA literature.

8. See Peter C. Kunze's insightful critique of how children's biographies contribute to problematic ideologies of disabled people as "heroic" individuals deserving of pity and admiration, listed under works cited.

9. While not necessarily using a disability framework, please see work by Amanda Ellis and Adrianna Santos for an analysis of writing as a transformative act of healing and agency in *Gabi, a Girl in Pieces* and *I Am Not Your Perfect Mexican Daughter*.

10. This chapter does not exhaustively engage in a discussion of queer futurity in the YA literature genre. For an excellent analysis of this, please see Matos and Wargo, and for a more detailed account of queer YA Latinx futurity, see Matos.

11. While it does not discuss YA literature, Elman's additional research related to how disability and adolescence have been constructed in television aimed for teens as something to "get over" is useful to understand the alignment between growing up and compulsory able bodiedness.

WORKS CITED

Bost, Suzanne. *Encarnación: Illness and Body Politics in Chicana Feminist Literature*. Fordham University Press, 2010.

Brown, Megan. "'Tell Me Who I Am': An Investigation of Cultural Authenticity in YA Disability Peritexts." *Beyond the Blockbusters: Themes and Trends in Contemporary Young Adult Literature*, edited by Rebekah Fitzsimmons and Casey Alane Wilson. University Press of Mississippi, 2020, 140–55.

Davis, Lennard J. "Introduction: Normality, Power, and Culture." *The Disability Studies Reader 4th Edition*, edited by Lennard J. Davis. Routledge, 2013, 1–14.

Dunn, Patricia A. *Disabling Characters: Representations of Disability in Young Adult Literature*. Peter Lang, 2015.

Ellis, Amanda. "Chicana Teens, Zines, and Poetry Scenes: *Gabi, A Girl in Pieces* by Isabel Quintero." *Nerds, Goths, Geeks, and Freaks: Outsiders in Chicanx and Latinx Young Adult Literature*, edited by Trevor Boffone and Cristina Herrera, University Press of Mississippi, 2020, 15–30.

Ellis, Amanda. "Susto, Sugar, and Song: ire'ne lara silva's Chicana Diabetic Poetics." *Kalfou* 7, no. 2 (2020): 308–29.

Elman, Julie Passanante. "*After School Special* Education: Rehabilitative Television, Teen Citizenship, and Compulsory Able-Bodiedness." *Television and New Media* 11, no. 4 (2010): 260–92.

Elman, Julie Passanante. "'Nothing Feels as Real': Teen Sick-Lit, Sadness, and the Condition of Adolescence." *Journal of Literary and Cultural Disability Studies* 6, no. 2 (2012): 175–91.

García, Mia. *The Resolutions*. Katherine Tegen Books, 2018.

Garland-Thompson, Rosemarie. "Feminist Disability Studies." *Signs* 30, no. 2 (2005): 1557–1587.

Garland-Thompson, Rosemarie. "Integrating Disability, Transforming Feminist Theory." *Feminist Disability Studies*, edited by Kim Q. Hall. Indiana University Press, 2011, 13–47.

James, Jennifer C., and Cynthia Wu. "Editors' Introduction: Race, Ethnicity, Disability, and Literature: Intersections and Interventions." *MELUS* 31, no. 3 (2006): 3–13.

Kim, Eunjung. "Asexuality in Disability Narratives." *Sexualities* 14, no. 4 (2011): 479–93.

Kunze, Peter C. "What We Talk About When We Talk About Hellen Keller: Disabilities in Children's Biographies." *Children's Literature Association Quarterly* 38, no. 3 (2013): 304–18.

Markotić, Nicole. "You're Queer? That's So Lame! Queering Disability in Brian Francis's *Fruit: A Novel about a Boy and His Nipples* and Mariko Tamaki's *(You) Set Me on Fire*." *Journal of Literary and Cultural Disability Studies* 12, no. 3 (2018): pp 337–52.

Matos, Angel Daniel, and Jon Michael Wargo. "Editors' Introduction: Queer Futurities in Youth Literature, Media, and Culture." *Research on Diversity in Youth Literature* 2, no. 1 (2019): 1–17.

McRuer, Robert. *Crip Theory: Cultural Signs of Queerness and Disability*. New York University Press, 2006.

Meyer, Abbye, and Emily Wender. "Teaching and Reading *Wonder* and *Marcelo in the Real World* with Critical Eyes." *Lessons in Disability: Essays on Teaching with Young Adult Literature*, edited by Jacob Stratman. McFarland, 2016, 72–99.

Minich, Julie Avril. "Aztlán Unprotected: Reading Gil Cuadros in the Aftermath of HIV/AIDS." *GLQ: A Journal of Lesbian and Gay Studies* 23, no. 2 (2017): 167–93.

Minich, Julie Avril. "Enabling Aztlán: Arturo Islas Jr., Disability, and Chicano Cultural Nationalism." *Modern Fiction Studies* 57, no. 4 (2011): 694–714.

Miskec, Jennifer, and Chris McGee. "My Scars Tell a Story: Self-Mutilation in Young Adult Literature." *Children's Literature Association Quarterly* 32, no. 2 (2007): 163–78.

Mitchell, David, and Sharon Snyder. "Narrative Prosthesis." *The Disability Studies Reader* 4th edition, edited by Lennard J. Davis. Routledge, 2013, 222–35.

Montaño, Jesus, and Regan Postma-Montaño. *Tactics of Hope in Latinx Children's and Young Adult Literature*. University of New Mexico Press, 2022.

"Q&A with Mia Garcia, Author of 'The Resolutions' and 'Even if the Sky Falls.'" *Stay on the Page* (blog). 11 October 2019. https://stayonthepage.wordpress.com/2019/10/11/qa-with-mia-garcia-author-of-the-resolutions-and-even-if-the-sky-falls/. Accessed 25 Jan 2021.

Rhodes, Cristina. "Processes of Transformation: Theorizing Activism and Change Through Gloria Anzaldúa's Picture Books." *Children's Literature in Education* 52, no. 4 (2021): 464–477.

Rodríguez, Sonia Alejandra. "Conocimiento Narratives: Creative Acts and Healing in Latinx Children's and Young Adult Literature." *Children's Literature* 47, no. 1 (2019): 9–29.

Santos, Adrianna M. "Broken Open: Writing, Healing, and Affirmation in Isabel Quintero's *Gabi, A Girl in Pieces* and Erika L. Sánchez's *I Am Not Your Perfect Mexican Daughter*." *Nerds,Goths, Geeks, and Freaks: Outsiders in Chicanx and Latinx Young Adult Literature*, edited by Trevor Boffone and Cristina Herrera. University Press of Mississippi, 2020, 45–59.

Stratman, Jacob. "Introduction." *Lessons in Disability: Essays on Teaching with Young Adult Literature*. McFarland, 2016, 1–7.

Stratman, Jacob. "'Overcoming': Analyzing Motivations in *Shark Girl* and *The Running Dream*." *English Journal* 104, no. 4 (2015): 103–5.

Tannert-Smith, Barbara. "'Like Falling Up into a Storybook': Trauma and Intertextual Repetition in Laurie Halse Anderson's *Speak*." *Children's Literature Association Quarterly* 35, no, 4 (2010): 395–414.

Trites, Roberta. *Disturbing the Universe: Power and Repression in Adolescent Literature*. University of Iowa Press, 2004.

Trites, Roberta. *Literary Conceptualizations of Growth: Metaphors and Cognition in Adolescent Literature*. John Benjamins, 2014.

Wickham, Anastasia. "It Is All in Your Head: Mental Illness in Young Adult Literature." *Journal of Popular Culture* 51, no. 1 (2018): 10–25.

Chapter Seven

BREATHING ROOM

Sustaining Queer Brown Socialities in the Latinx Bildungsroman

Joseph Isaac Miranda

At the center of Gabby Rivera's *Juliet Takes a Breath*[1] (2016) is a sense of entrapment that keeps the protagonist, Juliet Palante, from flourishing. Borne from Rivera's own anxieties of being a young queer Puerto Rican who defies normative expectations of ethnic and gender difference, Rivera sought to write a novel that untangled her sense of self from these delimiting frames. In a 2019 interview, Rivera suggests that her semiautobiographical novel enacts a reconciliation of the multiplicities of being a "messy, emotional, book nerd weirdo, chubby brown human," who fears she cannot be queer and Brown at home (Cornish). Feeling the pressures of familial rejection, Juliet comes out to her family and leaves the Bronx to "breathe out some peace" (Rivera 5). However, this sense of unease only increases after Juliet arrives in Portland to intern for white feminist author Harlowe Brisbane. There, Juliet does not find freedom. Rather, she is further alienated because she is Latinx and working class. Without lingering in abjection, the novel charts an alternative trajectory to the coming-of-age narrative by travelling across different geographies of queerness and Latinidad to find a home where her identities can coexist without shame or isolation.

And yet, the problem of the novel is how to accomplish these goals without reproducing the conventional baggage of individuation at the center of the bildungsroman. Juliet's experience of constraining anxiety emerges from the ways the contemporary coming-out and coming-of-age narrative demand the arrival of the integrated liberal subject by its conclusion; a demand that is predicated on a proximity to white heteronormativity. While the young adult genre typically acts as a staging ground for citizenship, I argue that *JTAB* illustrates the minoritarian struggle with such limiting conceptions of belonging through a repeated motif of constricted respiration and control of one's breath. Represented in the novel by Juliet's real struggle with asthma, the novel's attention to her difficulty breathing reveals the ways the bildungsroman traditionally disarticulates difference, collectivity, and attachment that leaves Juliet isolated from her networks of care and left with a fragmented sense of interiority.

I return to this scene of suspended breath twice in this essay; first, as a metaphor and structure of feeling that the novel deploys to illustrate the constraints of the bildungsroman and the deferred possibility of self-possession for queers of color in the scene of coming out—a scene that should engender narrative liberation; second, I show how the novel uses breath as a thematic orienting device to run away from these demands for individual subjectivity and to reorient the Latinx coming-out novel around the kinship networks and affective ties that sustain Latinx community in the face of ongoing violence.

GROWING PAINS

Juliet, almost twenty, belatedly occupies the conventional time frame of young adult novels. By taking up the time and form of the YA bildungsroman, *JTAB* mimics the logics of apprenticeship represented by her internship with the reality that Juliet should have arrived at a sense of stabilized personhood. Moreover, the bildungsroman is a linear narrative that transforms the child—imagined as wild, attached, and dependent—into the civilized reasonable human who is rational, upstanding, and self-dependent.[2] This narrative trajectory is mired in oppressive forces that deny children of color a sense of the innocence foundational for childhood while also imagining people of color as perpetual children, in need of government assistance and control (Brady 8–9). For queer people, maturation is mired in the feeling that one is not "growing up right" in relation to the norms of desire and gender. Therefore, one's childhood ends in the moment when one realizes they are queer and one's adulthood never arrives at the norms of heteronormative attachments (Stockton 6).

My attention to the meeting point between Latinx young adult coming-out narratives and the bildungsroman reveals the politics of sympathy at the heart of these forms that attempt to make room for Latinx people in the national imaginary through a politics of respectability and assimilation.[3] Hoping that the boundaries of the discursive liberal subject will expand through such performances of individualism, these narratives leave no room for institutional critique—only individual success or failure. Marilisa Jiménez García notes that Latinx YA novels have transformed the relationship of the genre with youth white counterculture of the mid-twentieth century to "[disrupt] narratives of US colonialism" ("[En]countering YA" 233). She notices a rise in Latinx protagonists whose maturation processes hinge on becoming activists in their communities to resist the ongoing effects of coloniality (233). Such attention to coloniality in Latinx YA reveals how the Latinx "young person [transitions] into, though never [reaches], adulthood" (231). Extending this analysis of Latinx suspended development to the withheld sovereignty of Puerto Rico, Jiménez García in *Side by Side* (2022) examines Puerto Rican youth literature in the shadow of US occupation as a growing space of anticolonial critique. In this literature, Puerto Rico is imagined as the "adopted heir" of the United States, a metaphorical stand-in for delayed Puerto Rican sovereignty (27). Such anxieties around belonging, self-possession, and colonial rule at stake in metaphors of Puerto Rico as orphan imagine Puerto Ricans as belated children who cannot govern or possess themselves, in need of—and dependent on—continued intervention (111). If one is imagined as a perpetual child, one cannot authorize one's own narrative of liberal freedom. What then are the possibilities of the Latinx bildungsroman without the promise of freedom and adulthood?

For queers of color, this narrative deferral of liberal subjectivity is also enmeshed in the coming-out narrative, which valorizes the achievement of the "out" LGBT person as liberated from a closet of shame. But this crossing of narrative forms takes queer narratives as implicitly white and not racialized. Rather, this novel is another example of Trevor Boffone and Cristina Herrera's argument about the prevalence of Latinx outsiders in YA fiction who are "caught somewhere between their communities and the Anglo world" ("Weirding Out" 7). These novels offer characters "who write themselves into the community and revise the traditional identity scripts to be more inclusive of outsider identities" (7). Putting Jiménez García in conversation with Boffone and Herrera, I posit that Latinx YA is a space of productive expansion of the form, as wells as a challenge to Latinidad.

Yet, the bildungsroman remains in tension with such progressive goals of representation, critique, and expansion of the liberal subject from marginal positions. However, I propose that *JTAB* moves beyond mere exposure or critique of its form within epistemological regimes of capture, reduction, and alienation of Latinx. I want to examine how Rivera undermines the expected emancipation in coming-of-age narratives by completing the coming-out plot at the beginning of the novel. Born out of Juliet's constricting anxiety, this rush to come out shifts narrative form and concerns by refusing the correlation between self-possession and pronouncements of identification, normatively expected at the climax of the bildungsroman, to make narrative space available for a reparation of self with others—rather than a severing of attachment to perform self-sufficiency. By undermining the destination of the genre as an affirmation of freedom in individuation, the narrative routes Juliet towards her kinship networks needed to sustain her in the everyday.

WAITING TO EXHALE

Juliet feels herself splitting in two. Drawn towards the vision of feminist freedom proffered by Harlowe Brisbane, Juliet decides to come out to her family. Such knowledge of sexuality is the expected destination of coming-out narratives that produce the queer subject in the "emancipation" from the closet into the "light" of discursive liberal identity. I contend with how Rivera's narrative velocity transposes coming out to the beginning of the novel to disrupt this logic—revealing how the alignment of liberation with visibility as the marker of self-production alienates queer people of color. Although such acts of self-realization are expected to produce good feelings, in *JTAB* we are not greeted by such moments of recognition or liberation. Carlos Decena proposes "coming out" has been "severed from collective social change" and unlinked from prior decades of liberation politics to be just another example of neoliberal "individual self-realization through speech.... Today, one comes out not to be radical or change the world but to be a 'normal' gay subject" (339). Juliet senses this uneasy link between identification and visibility when she says she needs to "get it all off my chest so that my lungs wouldn't feel so damn tight.... This dinner could be a straight line, if I wanted: no bumps, no bruises, turbulence-free" (Rivera 23). Juliet's decision debilitates, triggering her asthma and aligning coming out as a deviation from the "straight lines" of a maturation novel and constricting instead of liberating.

And yet, Juliet is trapped in a bind; the closet is constricting, and coming out offers no relief, as it engenders exposure and alienation. Stephanie Clare suggests that coming out is one other area of identity that has becomes depoliticized under neoliberalism. Coming out is "always already too late" (22) and privileges "losing kinship relation" while "[disavowing] the continued presence of inequality, homophobia, and heteronormativity, framing these as problems within the gay or lesbian subject rather than in the world" (25). Juliet articulates her queerness as a form of transgression that would sever herself from her family and her Latinidad. "I had planned my escape—chose to come out and run off into the night. What kind of wolf did that make me? I needed air. I wasn't ashamed. . . . but my family was my world and my mom was the gravitational pull that kept me stuck to this Earth. What would happen if she let me go?" (Rivera 12). For Juliet, coming out does not enact a politics of certainty and self-possession in orienting oneself towards queer desire, rather it articulates a fear of alienation from the social and the very possibility of further disorientation in the figure of the lone wolf and the body lost in space. Juliet's identity is bound to constraint or marginalization in the bildungsroman, not self-possession or acceptance.

When she comes out in the first chapter, she is met by a sense of uncomfortable oversharing. "My words felt like they were being sucked out of me. They lingered in the air. . . . I thought for sure there'd be an earthquake of some kind after my revelation. Nope" (Rivera 25). As if compulsively arriving at a scene of liberal recognition, her moment of identification is constructed in the passive voice and without agency. Instead of engaging with Juliet's disclosure, her family deflates and dismisses a coming out scene that she expects would be a climactic moment of break. Her disclosure is brushed under the table for a narrative of liberal progress and upward mobility, as her mother says "Enough of this crazy talk. . . . tonight Juliet is leaving the Bronx and going away for an amazing internship. Let's toast to her college career, her brave spirit, and to making all of us so proud" (25). Her mother attempts to reorient the dinner around a "turbulence free" coming-of-age narrative. Such attachment to education, as a route to escape systemic poverty and discrimination, is presented as the narrative track the mother wants the novel to take. At once a dismissal of Juliet's desires, her mother still wants to let Juliet go to Portland. Her mother presents a bargain with Juliet by affirming her freedom to leave the Bronx and want something different, but still locates Juliet within a heteronormative framework of liberal uplift and individualism.

But Juliet refuses such a bargain. She stops her mother: "I am gay. Gay gay gay" (26). The repetition, undermining her own declarative clarity, does not engender the arrival of narrative stability that coming-out narratives demand:

> No one moved or laughed, no bottles clinked. From the window, sounds of the #2 and #5 trains screeching away from their shared track filtered into the dining room. . . . I set free the elephant, the falcon, or whatever kind of animal spilled its truth onto dining room tables. Was this what ferocious cunts did? I didn't feel ferocious. The

smoldering discomfort that rose in my chest was humidity: thick, oppressive humidity (26).

The scene's awkward humor subverts the expected narrative freedom of coming-out narratives. Juliet's asthma returns, juxtaposing a sense of expected empowerment and recognition with a growing sense of "oppressive humidity" that produces a sense of disorientation from her desires and her community. Such feelings of alienation constrict Juliet; she recedes from expected agency. Her self-doubts proliferate in the wake of such disclosure. Instead of an affirmation of identity, the narrative time of the plot comes to a screeching halt. Arrested from liberal progress, we move sideways and away from the upright liberated subject of the bildungsroman.

In this moment of suspension, Juliet grows sideways through metaphor. Instead of becoming free, she "sets free the elephant, the falcon, or whatever kind of animal" (26). Kathryn Bond Stockton recognizes how the figure of the child is managed through a process of "*gradual growth* and *managed delay*" towards forms of normative adulthood (40). This progressive drive of maturation is alienating for figures who do not assume the innocence of heteronormative whiteness. Instead, the queer child shares "an estrangement from what they approach: the adulthood against which they must be defined" (31). When grafted onto the expectations of narrative form, Juliet's compulsory desire to find growth in coming out is met with sideways accumulation of animal metaphor, epistemological uncertainty, and bodily discomfort. In the failed movement towards neoliberal liberation, Juliet falls into a belated suspension between adulthood and childhood. Her coming out is imagined not as the pronouncement of rational knowledge. Rather, coming out is imagined as an overshare that unravels as the novel careens towards narrative normativity.

Moreover, her mother's response underscores the ways normativity is valued as growth while queerness is read as a wrongful delay. The mom says, "It's this book, isn't it? This book about vaginas has you messed up in the head and confused" (Rivera 26). *Raging Flower*, the feminist self-care guide by Juliet's idol and boss, Harlowe, posits a universal reductive vision of freedom and desire. Although this inclination towards free expression and self-love inspires Juliet's journey of self-discovery, *Raging Flower*'s imaginary does not account for class and racial difference, and the tensions around identity and belonging are entangled with her mother's desire to have her daughter become socially mobile within the delimitating narrative forms of American belonging.[4] Attaching her daughter's queerness to *Raging Flower* reveals how queerness in the bildungsroman is rendered as disorienting instead of stabilizing.

Transforming the central relationship between knowledge and education in the bildungsroman, Juliet develops the wrong types of attachments in her coming out. The mother's positing of queerness as a sideways relation to learning the "right things" aligns knowledge of sexuality as not liberatory or part of the maturation process but rather irrational or debilitating. In her attachment to things that leave her "messed up in the head," Juliet is imagined as fixated on female sexuality instead of oriented towards the rational liberal subject (26). Through this momentary delay into metaphor, the novel expresses an accumulation of feelings and desires that gesture towards an alternative way of being that is not aligned with narrative progression.

As Juliet finds alienation instead of freedom by coming into the light of discursive identity, the novel spends most of its pages seeking a route of return that offers Juliet room to enmesh herself in a queer Brownness. She observes, "Nothing likes to be split in half so when the 5 train hits that bend, sparks flew out and landed like mini-meteors on the sidewalk" (12). The use of cataclysmic imagery envisions the introduction of queerness alongside the Latinx family as the end of the world. As the 5 train shifts its destination away from the shared path of the 2, this attachment to metaphor articulates an anxiety around coexistence and the introduction of (queer) difference to the vision of her family's narrative of her development. David Eng claims that the aughts culminated in a neoliberal politics that sought to "[cleave] race from (homo)sexuality, and (homo)sexuality from race," to disassemble collective politics and to resist the ways "sexuality and race are constituted in relation to one another, each often serving to articulate, subsume, and frame the other's legibility in the social domain" (3). Eng's framework illuminates how Juliet begins the novel with a sense of anxiety around the impossibility of being both queer and Latinx, as the work of the neoliberal nation succeeded in containing difference in static categories of identity to unsettle any enmeshed socialities from flourishing. As the trains split on the tracks, our attention to the conflict of Juliet's identities combines with the linear image of narrative trajectory, where queerness deviates from the line of her Puerto Rican family. Travelling alone, she fears a greater sense of alienation of the social.

Such a move towards individuation is normatively desirable, but Juliet imagines it as a betrayal of her family and as alienating her Latinidad. Juliet's divergence from the family as a singular heteronormative form breaks the progressive development narrative of the Latinx family, whose children are expected to move beyond the economic sacrifices of their parents towards a vision of a "good life." Such a sense of familial and ethnic betrayal is previewed in the novel's opening letter to Harlowe, whose sense of freedom is tied to being "at all times her true self" without "secrets or self-imposed burdens of shame" (Rivera 3). Such a conception of freedom is placed in opposition to the Bronx, where queerness is imagined to be a secret that will "kill" Juliet because she has to tell the "people who breathed [her] into existence that [she's] the opposite of what they want [her] to be" (3–4). Stifling for Juliet, she imagines herself as a person without shame, "sin vergüenza," "banished from the family" for coming out (4). Coming out is not imagined as a release from shame but rather a looming sense of alienation—where having no shame disarticulates one from social relation.

Richard T. Rodríguez unsettles the collapsed relation between the Chicana family, revolutionary Chicano nationalisms, and heteropatriarchy in *Next of Kin* (2009). By attending to Chicana feminist scholars, he shows how they have rearticulated a Chicana politics around alternative kinship structures to the heteronormative family in order to highlight the "wider range of possibilities and strategies for imagining alliances and constituting a more elaborate genealogical enterprise" to resist state power instead of an accepted accumulation of it (6). By examining how Chicana feminists have queerly "[extended] the family beyond private, domestic space," he "[shifts] the terms of kinship that enable queer models of cultural citizenship," regrounding queer Brown socialities within Chicanx revolutionary politics instead of as a betrayal of them (18). While Juliet is Puerto Rican and not Chicana, the central problem of the family as signifier of ethnic attachment remains, especially as the novel's understanding of Latinidad is tied intimately with the family as its main source of Latinx representation.

The novel begins with this sense of transgression. In Juliet's desire to come out, she fears she will rupture the family form and flees after the perceived "trauma" of queerness is entered into the scene of Latinidad. "In each of their faces, I saw different versions of who I was. This was all happening way too fast. How had I lost my moment?" (Rivera 26). Juliet is split between the identities that make up "who [she] was." In the past tense, she arrives at coming out too late and too fast. By arriving too early to the scene of coming out in the narrative's teleology but arriving too late to the novel's genre, Juliet's search for belonging is suspended in a state of belated disorientation—off rhythm from the white heteropatriarchal expectations of the form of the nation and the novel. However, the repetition of narrative velocity and value reminds us of Juliet's asthmatic breathing that rises in moments of self-articulation with the fear of alienation; coming out triggers a "smoldering discomfort that rose in [her] chest" and "oppressive humidity" constricted her "breathing room" (26, 35).

Juliet's desire to run away to regain self-composure aligns her freedom of movement with freedom as a means of self-determination. And yet,

Juliet's asthma troubles this expression by struggling to move away from such forms of narrative capture. As if Juliet has been running for too long, the novel's movement to different locations in search of a space for more breathing room—Bronx, Portland, Miami, Portland, Bronx—reveals the ways her search is belated and anticipatory of the bildungsroman running at her heels. The locations she visits spatialize her search for identity, as she tries to find a physical home place for Latinidad, feminism, and queerness separately and together, for the first time, in Miami. This constant movement refuses to end the novel dwelling in a space of rupture from form, isolation, or fragmentation from ethnic difference. The novel sutures a means of return for Juliet to delink Latinidad from heterosexuality and reject queerness as a transgression of the Puerto Rican family. In moving towards repair, the novel rejects the drive towards individuation and articulates a form of attachment to queer Brown collective life that sustains, even if they are attachments deemed unvaluable by the state and the bildungsroman form itself.

BREATHLESS

"Maybe America just swallowed all of us, including our histories, and spat out whatever it wanted us to remember. . . . And the rest of us, without that first-hand knowledge of civil unrest and political acts of disobedience, just inhaled what they gave us" (132). Researching Lolita Lebrón and other feminist revolutionaries, Juliet comes to understand the limits of Harlowe's politics and the conditionality of American belonging. America's atmosphere dominates the senses, delimits the possible, and recirculates contained forms of Latinx life through Juliet's compulsory recycling of America's narratives of itself. However, the novel does not choose to linger in such abject possibility. From this moment, the novel unwinds a counternarrative to the typical bildungsroman that reorients the narrative away from a politics of recognition as a means of liberation. I want to connect two key scenes that move Latinx coming-of-age narratives towards enmeshment in queer Brown community and solidarity instead of exposure and visibility. First, I examine the suspension of Juliet's breath that leads to a reparative exhale and rearticulation of coming-of-age narratives at a queer pool party. Second, I read the novel's conclusion, which rejects the bildungsroman's demands for rectitude and the "upright" fixed subject, as a moment that offers Juliet the ability to just breathe.[5]

After a series of racist incidents in Portland, Juliet runs to her cousin Ava in Miami. With her cousin, she voices her frustrations with the delimiting frames of feminism and belonging Portland offered her. Ava affirms her feelings of discomfort while telling her that "we are so much more than Harlowe can even comprehend" (230). What Ava reveals to her is their family's submerged history of activism with the Young Lords and queer desire. Both disclosures offer models of development for Juliet that do not regurgitate the delimiting narrative forms that leave our narrator feeling isolated from the world. Rather, they actively challenge them. Moreover, Juliet experiences such potentialities when Ava brings her to a queer pool party. During the party, Juliet reaches for a sense of her own beauty in the comfort of queer kinship, sharing physical and emotional intimacy with others. In the midst of such joy and pleasure she assumes a collective voice: "We're all okay. We are all beautiful. And you need nights like the one I had, a night to be free and surrounded by queer family" (Rivera 248). Here, Juliet abandons the dream of possessive individuality as the apotheosis of freedom and rearticulates liberation in a form of identity without individualism or what Mary Pat Brady calls an awareness of the "density of connection" within a "queer horizontality" (29). By breaking with the bildungsroman's emphasis on individuality, and the text's expectation of first-person narration, the novel proposes a new composite relation that is enmeshed in a collective network for survival where "we're all okay" in one night "surrounded by queer family" (Rivera 248). Through the queer extension of the individual and the heteronormative family to queer friends, her cousin Ava says it is "a night for us to breathe easier.... It's electric" (235). The control of their breathing does not signify possession of the self and control over one's space, but the calm of recognition that comes with shared experiences of difference. Such collective energy and connection manifests the breathing room found in what José Esteban Muñoz would call a *Brown common*—or "a collectivity with and through the incommensurable" recognition of a "shared wounding" (6–7). In this formulation of entanglement through shared alienation from the social, this electric feeling is ephemeral yet energizing, speaking a new structure of sociality that sustains queer of color life in the face of violence and abjection.

If the party offers a model for queer kinship that affirms collective life over the isolating conventions of the bildungsroman, the novel's final chapter ends in a rejection of the self-sustaining individual all together. After Juliet leaves Miami, she decides to return to Portland and confront Harlowe on a hike through the woods. After Juliet demands Harlowe take accountability for her racist actions she reaches the top of the trail and decides to jump in a river and follow the water downstream. Overcome with a fear of drowning, Juliet is submerged underwater as the river floods her lungs. In this moment she feels "somewhere else," away from Harlowe's world and language, which "sounds weird and wrong. Too white, too structured, too foreign" (256, 2).

Disoriented by the water, Juliet is reminded of her cousin Ava's lessons about the "infinite number of ways to love and be loved, to be queer and brown" (256). Instead of constriction and panic—without "enough air to breathe . . . for a closeted Puerto Rican baby dyke from the Bronx"—Juliet's imagines a horizontal enmeshment of "queer and brown" with her queer of color friends and family in Miami, in the Bronx, and in Portland (4–5). Her feeling of potentiality in the openness towards others is the queer gesture that does not enclose the ending of the novel but opens it up to collective life.

As the current pushes her ashore, she says, "Fear had fucked up my flow. It had flipped me over. I let go of everything I was afraid of and concentrated on my body. I spun myself over" (256). As the water tosses her about, the novel visualizes the conflicting ways in which narrative progression is at odds with Rivera's desire to dodge singular paths of narrative orientation for a theory of enmeshment within multiple identities. Sara Ahmed contends with the orientation of sexual orientation to push identity away from fixed and essential categories of definition and towards an understanding of the self that is situated in space—through the policing of what types of objects one can tend towards. This policing of inclinations naturalizes feelings of being in place and delimits the horizon of the possible. Ahmed's queer investigation of phenomenology posits this structural organization of space, attachments, and relations as turning us towards a straight line of desire. These compulsory lines map similar narrative investments as the bildungsroman and its undergirding narrative objectives to affirm white heteropatriarchy and individuated subjectivity. For Juliet, such demands have produced mental and physical acts of disorientation that messed up her "flow" and "flipped [her] over" (Rivera 256). *JTAB* attempts to follow the compulsory linear movement of the genre and the nation only to queerly turn away from an apotheotic moment of closure. The novel's route, like her body, is "twisted into [new] shapes," threatening "the social ordering of life itself" by failing to "repay the debt of life by becoming straight" in its embrace of disorientation (Ahmed 91).

What takes Ahmed and Juliet's "breath away" is how such acts of narrative and bodily disorientation can produce queer deviant forms of inhabitation (Ahmed 10). Spinning herself over, Juliet reorients herself around queer kinship; recalling an earlier scene that found Juliet unabashedly desiring queer intimacy as a salve to her anxiety, she declared, "I was free falling into the best oblivion. Kira said she saw all my beautiful brown everything. You see my brown? What? Full Stop." (Rivera 277). Arresting narrative momentum, Juliet free falls into suspension. Leaning into the torquing of narrative forms of constraint, the text halts the demands for the straight lines of the bildungsroman that sever race from sexuality. Rather, she sustains a nurturing relation between Brownness and queerness in her pleasurable extension towards the other without shame. Moreover, the shift to direct address extends the affirmation of queer desire towards the reader, entangling us in this reformation of narrative ends towards forms of connection. With this new shape we see how queerness is "not about being fixed into a place, but rather it is about becoming part of a space where one has expanded one's body, saturating the space with bodily matter: home as *overflowing* and *flowing over*." (Ahmed 11). Rather than fixing herself into stable categories of individuation that ultimately affirm the normativity of white-cis heterosexuality, these moment of queer intimacy shifts the narrative horizon of the possible away from straight white attachments and rejects alienation.

Before Juliet reaches the shore, the novel ends meditating on a sense of queer potentiality, not as a means of utopic dreaming, but as a resource for collective survival. "My body flipped over and I was done," Juliet claims as she recounts the long list from Lupe, Lil' Melvin, Zaira, Maxine, Titi Penny, Ava, her mother, and the lessons from Portland and Miami that teach her the "power of being connected to queer people of color" (Rivera 281). Abandoning the dream of the individual subject upstream, Rivera articulates a vision of identity that calls forth the consciousness-raising work of third-world feminist writers like Gloria Anzaldúa, Audre Lorde, and Cherríe Moraga in *This Bridge Called My Back* (1981).[6] In "La Jornada," Moraga narrates the radicalization of her politics as a temporal journey of ethnic discovery and a feeling of proximity to others over time and space. "I wrote in my journal: 'My growing consciousness as a woman of color is surely seeming to transform my experience. How could it be that the more I feel with other women of color, the more I feel myself Chicana, the more susceptible I am to racist attack!'" (xxxvii–xxxviii). Moraga contrasts the before and after of identifying as Chicana with the identification of excess feelings of mistreatment and alienation from whiteness—as the neutral affect that makes one feel like they belong. She feels a sense of proximity created in a growing orientation towards other women of color, first as an observer on a train, then as an activist, organizer, and writer. In becoming Brown, consolidated in action and in writing, her linear unfolding of feelings is posed as a question: feeling closer to women of color makes her feel herself Chicana, which leaves her feeling vulnerable to racism. This openness to relation opens a series of shared resonances of feeling difference and a growing obligation to collective action against the state. Moraga's insistence that we "feel with" women of color instead of "feeling like" them marks a deliberate shift in thinking about identity politics that allows a theoretical framework for being and sharing with others in their difference without coopting or collapsing into singularity one's experience of difference. Moraga's identification as Chicana arrives as a journey alongside her commitment to activism. Her journey towards radical consciousness instead of individuation allows us to read Rivera's novel otherwise. Instead of ending with the failure of Rivera's text to achieve the narrative ends of the bildungsroman, we find space beyond such desires by tending towards a radical Brown queer consciousness as the work of Latinx narrative itself.

Following Moraga's path towards recognizing the enmeshment of the self with others, the novel ends with a final moment that challenges the relation between breath, self-possession, and others. Juliet moves "with the current until it spit me out at its edge. I lay there alone. And in that moment, I finally knew what it was to just breathe" (Rivera 256). Using the conditional phrase and dependent clauses, the text extends this moment of suspension, providing us the stillness and calm Juliet has been barreling towards. The sentence performs the inhale and exhale of breath that is constantly evading Juliet as the interjection of the adverb "just" to split the infinitive "to breathe," slowing the sentence down to a drag. To justly do something, as the OED tells us, is not only about what is appropriate, required, or normative, but also signals a positionality, a time and place where one "just" fits (OED). Juliet's desire "to just breathe" articulates a desire to find her footing in relation to those around her after running away from the delimiting demands of form and feelings of ethnic and familial betrayal (Rivera 256). Here, there are no splitting trains or feelings of constricting anxiety. Without troubled breathing, the attention to rest and respiration—as a circular process of taking in and giving out—mirrors Moraga and Rivera's investments in sustaining a nurturing relation between self and others and the multiplicity of a queer Brown commonality.

CONCLUSION

With this ease of respiration, the novel ends in a pronouncement of belonging without the anxiety Juliet carried throughout the novel. Such flourishing occurs because Rivera chose to eschew narrative expectations to alienate racial, gender, and sexual difference in the assimilation of the individual into the normative rules of the nation. Rather, the conclusion insists Juliet belong within a "queer, Latina, working-class feminism" (Boffone and Herrera *Latinx Teens* 71). A departure from the bildungsroman, such a shift rejects the liberal rules of order to center the alternative forms of obligation in the novel (such as Titi Penny's involvement in the Young Lords or the queer of color organizing in Miami or Portland) that sustain minoritarian life. Moreover, the conclusion allows Juliet the possibility of return, a return to the Bronx and to her Puerto Rican family that was obstructed from possibility earlier in the novel.

In a 2019 interview Rivera speaks about this overwhelming narrative that she had to leave the Bronx and her family in order to thrive. This message, she said, tells us that to be a queer person of color from a working-class neighborhood means one's "neighborhood isn't good enough for you to flourish or find yourself in so you gotta get out. . . . *Juliet Takes a Breath* opens with a welcoming to all round brown girls encouraging them to take up all the space they need and to love themselves and each other" (Vinson). Like Jennie Capó Crucet's *Make Your Home Among Strangers* (2015), Justin Torres's *We the Animals* (2011), and Daniel José Older's *Shadowshaper* (2015), contemporary Latinx coming-of-age narratives struggle with a complex relation to the nation and a homeplace that is inhospitable due to the ongoing systemic violences of gentrification, racism, or homophobia. Reparative in orientation, the novel crafts a way to salve the narrator's sense of alienation—from her body, her attachments, and her kinship networks—and affirm a place for Juliet in queer Brown kinship networks.

Moreover, rejecting the impulses of the young adult genre to uphold self-possession as a form of freedom in adulthood, the novel mediates on the need of others to survive. Instead of severing attachments to the family, *JTAB* returns. At the end of the summer, Juliet calls her mother in the hope of mending their relationship. On the phone they sit, "listening to each other breathe" (272). Her mother says "My love for you is the sun, the sky, and the moon. It's the air I breathe. It lives in everything I do. It's better than good. It's everlasting'" (272). In this final conversation with her mother, the novel turns the individual need for breath into a nurturing and vital interconnection between the self and other. This attention to enmeshment challenges the normativity of Latinidad and expands the possibilities of queerness as coconstitutive of, rather than severed from, the Puerto Rican family. Here, breath transforms from something that is hindered by Juliet's anxiety over her fears of abjection into something that circulates and sustains life. Together, suspended in coconstitutive breath, they breathe.

NOTES

1. Hereafter, *JTAB*.
2. Andrea Fernández-Garcia offers a history of the bildungsroman and its entanglement with Latina subjectivity. Unlike the traditional bildungsroman, the *Latina Bildungsroman* troubles the assumptions of whiteness and masculinity at the center of citizenship to allow

for the temporary "construction and reconstruction" of Latina "lifeworlds" (18). In the post–civil rights era, the bildungsroman became a space to explore the ways marginalized peoples were suspended from the nation in a temporal structural of ongoing deferral from stable identity (21). Moreover, she traces the progression of the genre to account for the creation of a sense of identity that is dependent on "social integration," not just individuation (19).

3. Aesthetic culture, according to Roderick Ferguson, typically is utilized by minor subjects to demonstrate moral fitness for citizenship through the actualization of the protagonist as a "good governable subject." Ferguson suggests that queer of color critique offers an alternative to this narrative progression by using the distance from normative forms of nation and aesthetics to reveal the ways belonging is constructed and produced by these same discourses (24). This methodology uses the aesthetic as a site of rupture to point to how the desires embedded in the bildungsroman, for example, are constructed to fail the minoritarian subject.

4. Amanda Matousek identifies how *Raging Flower* delimits Juliet's imagination—delaying her ability to imagine a more expansive understanding of her queerness and Latinidad. Matousek claims Rivera's novel unsettles Latinidad's limits as a heteronormative relation to posit a form of "Latinidad (and womanhood, for that matter) [for Juliet that] is claimed, uncontained, and not ordained by others" (13). One way this expansion of Latinidad happens in the novel is through Juliet's reckoning with the limitations of Harlowe's feminism as a whitewashed and bourgeois concept. Another is through Juliet's discovery of queer of color spaces with her cousin Ava and Kira, which I discuss later.

5. For a critique of the "upright man" as central to liberal subjectivity, see *Inclinations: A Critique of Rectitude* (2016) by Adriana Cavarero. Her intervention examines the centrality of rectitude as a patriarchal masculine concept and posits attachment and horizontality as grounds upon which to imagine a vulnerable and open subject.

6. shea wesley martin elaborates this connection between Rivera and third-wave feminist writer Gloria Anzaldúa in their reading of the Clipper Queerz Party. wesley martin posits Juliet finds herself a "home" by "[embracing the] confluence" of what Anzaldúa calls "'the emotional residue' of oppression as well as joy and community that arise from that oppression" (martin 18). The party represents a space that celebrates queer and trans people of color without recourse to whiteness, which is at the center of Juliet's experiences with Harlowe in white feminist spaces of the novel's Portland.

REFERENCES

Ahmed, Sara. *Queer Phenomenology: Orientations, Objects, Others*. Duke University Press, 2006.

Boffone, Trevor, and Cristina Herrera. "Introduction: Weirding Out Latinx America." *Nerds, Goths, Geeks, and Freaks: Outsiders in Chicanx and Latinx Young Adult Literature*, edited by Trevor Boffone and Cristina Herrera. University Press of Mississippi, 2020, 3–12.

Boffone, Trevor, and Cristina Herrera. *Latinx Teens: U.S. Popular Culture on the Page, Stage, and Screen*. University of Arizona Press, 2022.

Brady, Mary Pat. *Scales of Captivity: Racial Capitalism and the Latinx Child*. Duke University Press, 2022.

Eng, David L. *The Feeling of Kinship: Queer Liberalism and the Racialization of Intimacy.* Duke University Press, 2010.

Cavarero, Adriana. *Inclinations: A Critique of Rectitude.* Stanford University Press, 2016.

Clare, Stephanie D. "'Finally, She's Accepted Herself!': Coming Out in Neoliberal Times." *Social Text* 35, no. 2 (June 2017): 17–38.

Cornish, Audie. "Life, Love, Coming Out and Culture Shock in 'Juliet Takes A Breath.'" *NPR*, 18 September 2019. https://www.npr.org/2019/09/18/762046606/book-juliet-takes-a-breath.

Decena, Carlos Ulises. "Tacit Subjects." *GLQ: A Journal of Lesbian & Gay Studies* 14, no. 2/3 (April 2008): 339–59.

Ferguson, Roderick A. *Aberrations in Black: Toward a Queer of Color Critique.* University of Minnesota Press, 2004.

Fernández-García, Andrea. "Latina Girlhood: Questions of Identity and Representation." *Geographies of Girlhood in US Latina Writing: Decolonizing Spaces and Identities*, edited by Andrea Fernández-García. Springer International, 2020, 9–52.

Jiménez García, Marilisa. "En(Countering) YA: Young Lords, Shadowshapers, and the Longings and Possibilities of Latinx Young Adult Literature." *Latino Studies* 16, no. 2 (July 2018): 230–49.

Jiménez García, Marilisa. *Side by Side: US Empire, Puerto Rico, and the Roots of American Youth Literature and Culture.* University Press of Mississippi, 2021.

"Just, Adj." *OED Online*, Oxford University Press. *Oxford English Dictionary*, http://www.oed.com/view/Entry/102189. Accessed 5 August 2022.

martin, shea wesley. "What Do We Do with the White [Cis] Women?: *Juliet Takes a Breath* as the Blueprint for Reimagining Allyship in Literacy Instruction." *Research on Diversity in Youth Literature* 4, no. 1 (October 2021).

Matousek, Amanda L. "Selling Spectacle and Airing Identity: Latinidad in American Dirt and Juliet Takes a Breath." *Label Me Latina/o* 12 (Spring 2022): 20.

Moraga, Cherríe, and Gloria Anzaldúa, eds. *This Bridge Called My Back: Writings by Radical Women of Color*, fourth edition. SUNY Press, 2015.

Muñoz, José Esteban, et al. *The Sense of Brown.* Duke University Press, 2020.

Rivera, Gabby. *Juliet Takes a Breath.* Dial Books, 2019.

Rodríguez, Richard T. *Next of Kin: The Family in Chicano/a Cultural Politics.* Duke University Press, 2009.

Stockton, Kathryn Bond. *The Queer Child or Growing Sideways in the Twentieth Century.* Duke University Press, 2009.

Vinson, Arriel. "Gabby Rivera Wants Queer Brown Girls to Feel Seen." *Electric Literature* 21 (October 2019).

Section Three

(Alternative) Spaces of Queer Latinidades

Chapter Eight

QUEERING TIKTOK

Gen Z's Latinx BookTok and Adam Silvera's
They Both Die at the End

Trevor Boffone

In the fall of 2020, gay Puerto Rican young adult (YA) writer Adam Silvera noticed that something interesting, yet completely inexplicable, was happening. His 2017 YA novel, *They Both Die at the End*, had suddenly reemerged on the *New York Times* Best Seller list for young adult paperback fiction. Silvera had caught wind of this earlier when his agent notified him of the mysterious jump in sales and asked if Silvera had any clue what prompted the book to suddenly sell at a rate the book had never seen before, not even when it was first published. As the fall continued and 2020 turned into 2021, *They Both Die at the End* continued to climb higher and higher on the coveted best seller list, finally reaching the desired number one spot the week of April 9, 2021. In spring 2021, the novel became the second best-selling YA book in the United Kingdom, number five on the National Indie Bestseller list, and made *USA Today*'s Best-Selling Booklist for the first time. And, as the book caught interest, it was also difficult to find. The book was even sold out at Amazon for several weeks in January 2021.

Throughout the journey, Silvera took to Twitter to share the book's success and to ask if anyone knew what prompted these sales. The novel's unexpected success was not lost on Silvera, who noted in a January 8, 2021, tweet, "The #2 spot is the highest I've ever been on the New York Times Bestseller List! For a book that came out in 2017! About queer Latinx boys! THANK YOU!"

(Silvera). Throughout 2021, Silvera would offer Twitter updates about the novel's continued and unexpected success across the globe. While popular TV shows (see: *Lost* and *Lancelot* by Walker Percy) and celebrity endorsements (see: Oprah's Book Club) have prompted renewed book sales, nothing and no one could explain why a book about two queer Latinos finding friendship, love, acceptance, and closure on their last day on earth became a best seller three years after it was published. But, as most things seemed to go in 2020, *They Both Die at the End*'s renewed success was firmly tied to one thing: TikTok.[1]

Several replies to Silvera's tweet confirm the TikTok effect. Barnes & Noble employee @EmpireOfEmily claims, "The amount of teens coming into B&N looking for it because 'they saw it on Tik Tok' is frankly amazing & heartwarming!" As Silvera recognized the love for TikTok—not to mention his anxiety over posting content on the platform—the Huntington Beach, California, Barnes & Noble confirmed: "We literally can't keep enough in stock!" Replies to Silvera's Tweet reinforce the book's TikTok fame. @TheBagelQueen tweets, "I discovered you through Tiktok and I've read almost all your books since! New favorite author!" Other Twitter users acknowledge Silvera's popularity on TikTok, where videos using the hashtag #TheyBothDieAtTheEnd have amassed over 75 million views. These videos, created almost entirely by teenagers and other members of Generation Z, largely speak to the emotional impact Silvera's novel had on them while reading it. Popular TikToks discussed how devastating the book was, with some even noting that they were never going to be able to get over Mateo and Rufus's final day on earth. As these videos went viral, accumulating hundreds of thousands of views and shares, so too did the comment sections grow. Silvera fans took to TikTok to engage in a virtual book club in which teens shared their feelings on the novel, discussed queerness, asked each other questions about the work and their connection to the material, and, of course, made inside jokes. All the while, onlookers and avid readers could only do one thing to truly engage with this corner of BookTok (also known as Book TikTok)—buy and read *They Both Die at the End*.

With *They Both Die at the End*'s renaissance, Adam Silvera had firmly situated himself as one of the leading voices in contemporary YA literature. Coming off critical and commercial successes with *More Happy Than Not* (2015), *History Is All You Left Me* (2017), *What If It's Us* (coauthored with Becky Albertalli, 2018), *Infinity Son* (2020), and *Infinity Reaper* (2021), Silvera was riding a wave of momentum that saw his body of work suddenly sparking interest in TV and film producers who vowed to bring his stories to the silver and small screens. That Silvera achieved these feats as a gay Latino writer whose stories are explicitly entrenched in queer Latinidad is no small feat. Aside from *What If It's Us* Silvera's body of work offers nuanced depictions of queer Latino boyhood that portray the highs and lows, the good and the bad, of growing up Brown and queer in the twenty-first century.[2]

In this chapter, I unpack the origins and culture of BookTok, especially as it pertains to Latinx YA literature. After theorizing BookTok and connecting it to a lineage of queer digital spaces and queer Latinx worldmaking, I shift my focus to how teenagers specifically use TikTok to interact with Silvera's *They Both Die at the End*. As the COVID-19 pandemic disrupted traditional modes of discussing literature, Gen Z used TikTok to stage digital book clubs that enabled Silvera's novel to cement itself on BookTok, gain readership, and become a best seller in the process. With this TikTok fame, *They Both Die at the End* became part of Gen Z culture, joining the likes of Sarah J. Maas's series Throne of Glass and Crescent City and Tahereh Mafi's *Shatter Me* as integral parts of the Zoomer YA canon. Although I privilege Latinx teens who engage with Silvera's novels, BookTok engagement with the novel is not limited to Latinx teenagers. As such, I instead focus on how a general youth readership engages with queer Latinx YA literature, which, in this case, works as a double agent. It serves as a valuable mirror and space of representation while also being a space to educate non-Latinxs about (queer) Latinidad. My argument is that BookTok provides a digital space to engage with queer Latinx YA in a way that traditional book clubs do not. BookTok enables "book talk" in an inclusive, digital space for teens that makes reading more equitable and representative of the type of communities Zoomers wish to forge. That is, BookTok establishes a world in which literature about queer teens of color doesn't exist on the fringes. Rather, queer Latinx teens such as *They Both Die at the End*'s Mateo and Rufus are the norm. They are the mainstream.

BOOKTOK AND THE ROLE OF QUEER DIGITAL SPACES IN THE TIKTOK AGE

BookTok—a portmanteau of "book" and "TikTok"—represents the subset of TikTok dedicated to all things literary. BookTok features short videos in which teens talk about their favorite books, recommend books, tell us who their favorite characters are, and make inside jokes. Teen readers use general hashtags (#BookTok) as well as more specific hashtags using book titles and author names to find a reading community. From there, TikTok bookworms use the platform to make public their feelings and responses to a text for a largely anonymous audience to engage with. BookTokers then respond to questions in the comment section, creating a digital discussion group. BookTok's import in teen reading circles has not been lost on the publishing industry. In fact, BookTok was the subject of a much-circulated March 20, 2021, *New York Times* profile that detailed how TikTok videos are selling books and changing best-seller lists, something that has been a surprise to everyone involved (Harris). Although the article touches on various aspects of the relationship between TikTok and publishing, one fact remains—this is a definitively teenage space.

In many ways BookTok is a digital book club for teens by teens. Digital spaces afford access in ways that traditional book clubs don't. This space is the antithesis to the classroom in which an adult (their teacher) tells them what to read, gives them homework on the reading, and then tests them on their reading, not to mention that, as Laura Alamillo and Rosie Arenas propose, classrooms are lacking in authentic Latinx texts, which does little, if anything, to address (in)equity in education (53). Moreover, book clubs often mirror in-school literacy practices (reading assignments, answering questions, hierarchies, etc.). In Paulo Freire's germinal *Pedagogy of the Oppressed*, he introduces the concept of the "banking of knowledge" to refer to these educational practices, which reinforce systems of oppression. Freire claims, "The teacher issues communiqués and makes deposits which the students patiently receive, memorize, and repeat. This is the 'banking' concept of education, in which the scope of action allowed to students extends only as far as receiving, filing, and storing the deposits" (58). In this model, there is no communication. Teachers take on an active role in education and students take on a passive one. Digital literacy communities such as BookTok flip these scripts.[3]

We often think of reading as a solitary act, but it doesn't have to be. It can be one that is marked by community. And, while casual onlookers may not view TikTok as a viable space to build community, the app fits into a lineage of online spaces that have been crucial to the teenage experience, from Live Journal and Xanga to MySpace and Tumblr. Like BookTube and BookStagram, BookTok is a digital way for teen readers to meet and connect with fellow bookworms and build community based on a shared interest that isn't always seen as "cool." As a queer play on "Book Talk," BookTok is a space for queer teens and allies to build community through literature. Yet its queerness is not relegated to clever word play. BookTok quite literally queers the way we discuss literature. Discussions via BookTok re-shift how we think of book clubs, democratizing shared reading experiences and blurring the boundaries of discussion. The community leans into the TikTok form and makes YA literature meme-able, fun, engaging, and socioculturally relevant. TikTok reading communities, like other social media book clubs, are appealing to Zoomers because they take place on their apps of choice. Rather than encouraging teen readers to join a new space, BookTok takes place on a platform that most teens already regularly interact with, which makes the space inherently more welcoming to teen bookworms. In this space, BookTok projects, like other digital projects, inherently queer traditional in-school literacy assessments, which Jon Wargo proposes is fundamental to creating inclusive learning spaces ("Lights! Cameras! Genders?" 5–6).

BookTok draws new readers to reading and, most importantly, makes reading cool by introducing potential readers to culturally relevant YA texts. Reading the likes of *All the Bright Places* by Jennifer Niven and *We Were Liars* by E. Lockhart is exciting for teen readers. Reading, therefore, isn't boring like it is in their high school classrooms. No shade to *The Scarlet Letter*, *Paradise Lost*, and *Moby Dick*, but these were books I struggled—and didn't finish (thank you, CliffsNotes)—reading in high school even though I was an avid reader who devoured books at the time. In my work as a high school teacher now, I see the same dynamics play out. Zoomers want their literature to reflect the world they live in. That is, as with most things in their lives, Gen Z pushes for more diversity in literature. BookTok is primarily filled with YA literature, which should come as no surprise given how TikTok skews toward Gen Z even if the app has users from all ages and walks of life. It should come as no surprise then that the most popular books on TikTok are *Harry Potter*, *Twilight*, *The Hunger Games*, and *Divergent*. These series have dominated the YA literary scene throughout the 2000s and, even as new authors and titles have gained popularity, these series remain pivotal literature for teen readers. These series also go far beyond the realm typically occupied by young adult literature. They all have massively popular film franchises, recognizable branding, pop culture relevance, and, in the case of Harry Potter, a theme park. That said, beyond the overwhelming interest in these titles, the second tier of BookTok popularity lies firmly in YA literature and, in many cases, YA that privileges stories by and about communities of color.

With this in mind, media studies scholar Andrea Ruehlicke proposes that TikTok "represents a new development in how we think and talk about personalization in virtual spaces." The level of personalization is precisely what separates TikTok from its competitors and enables subcategories to emerge and flourish.[4] In the case of TikTok's subcategories, as these TikTokers know, they do not belong to the so-called Straight TikTok, the colloquial name given to the app's mainstream where TikTok celebrities such as Charli D'Amelio, Addison Rae, and Noah Beck hit dance challenges with each other in multimillion dollar clout house mansions in Los Angeles. In the case of Straight TikTok, "straight" serves multiple purposes, speaking to the straight-edge nature of these creators and the fact that many of them are heterosexual (or at least not openly queer). In TikTokLandia, any community without a name is considered Straight TikTok. That is, the app's default setting is Straight TikTok, making most subcultures of the app inherently queer. Moreover, because of how the algorithm and FYI page work, members of Straight TikTok might not even realize that there are thriving subcultures on the app.

Straight TikTok and Queer TikTok go far beyond sexuality labels. Rather, the difference lies in how TikTokers approach life on the app. Whereas Straight TikTok is invested in maintaining the popular kids table in the lunchroom, becoming Homecoming King and Queen, and fitting into traditional Western Eurocentric beauty standards, TikTok subcultures are spaces where difference is not only celebrated, but is the norm. As an extension of this work, spaces such as BookTok engage in valuable digital civic work to make things such as reading and nerdiness the mainstream, thus queering traditional reading practices. TikTok is a more democratized space for readers to express their interests and develop a supportive community, something that does not typically occur in schools where we often think of literacy practices taking shape. In this social media subculture, bookworms aren't ostracized or the target of high school bullies and mean girls.[5] Rather, their identities are validated and oftentimes celebrated.

Since digital platforms became the norm, queer communities have found online spaces to be not only valuable, but also critical sites to meet fellow queers and build community (Miles). Digital spaces enable queer youth to educate each other about queerness, something that doesn't typically happen in the institutional spaces that teenagers occupy (i.e. schools). And, of course, online spaces allow queer teens to experiment with their identities in ways that may not be viable or safe off-line. Given that queer youth historically face digital problems that their straight and straight-passing counterparts do not experience, the role of queer-friendly and "safe" spaces is critical for queer teenagers.[6] TikTok content, creation, and spectatorship, therefore, is an extension of queer communities. It becomes a key site for teenagers to construct and perform identity.

In the online space of TikTok, like its predecessors Vine, Tumblr, and Musical.ly, queer teens can more openly perform their identities. Loya and Almeida assert that TikTok's queer community differs from its predecessors, "with its emphasis not only on traditional identity expression online but an embrace of absurd and nonsensical humor." TikTok's preferred aesthetics are silly, over-the-top, camp, which all align with queer humor. Media studies scholar Melanie Kennedy affirms that TikTok privileges "goofiness," "relatability," and ordinariness (re: authenticity) (1071). Moreover, queer teens are even using TikTok as a platform to come out to friends and family, "repurposing and remixing songs to capture the reactions of their loved ones on camera and share the results on the platform" (Leskin).[7] BookTok, therefore, participates in what Mollie Blackburn calls "interrupting hate," a process whereby literacy projects push against homophobia and transphobia that queer students may face (17–18). Wargo adds, "Through imaginative play, creation, pleasure, and subversion, [BookTok] disrupts homophobia, injustice, and other forms of oppression by centering the queer in culture" ("Lights! Cameras! Genders?" 9). That is, BookTok enables teen readers to reimagine a queer present in which queerness is a regular fixture in day-to-day life.

While BookTok has cemented itself on the platform, so too has queer (Latinx) YA literature. The landscape of texts has opened in recent years in such a way that readers can see more diverse characters in primary roles rather than secondary or background characters. Historically these are texts with characters that would be considered "banned" because they challenge the status quo or the conservative agenda. Moreover, despite the growth of Latinx YA publishing, Latinx literature scholar and editor of Arte Público Press Gabriela Baeza Ventura affirms, "We have yet to see this literature at the forefront of awards, curricula, and bookstore displays" (244). BookTok pushes against this. In the TikTok age, subgenres of YA such as queer Latinx YA can thrive, pushing against the erasure of queer communities of color that has historically happened in more institutional spaces that teens occupy such as churches and schools. In the case of schools, they rarely engage students in queer-inclusive curriculum, especially in English classes. Schools prioritize the canon where the perspectives of white, male, heterosexual values and identities are privileged. The failure to include intersectional queer literature, especially about communities of color and working-class peoples, in the curriculum disadvantages Latinx youth. Accordingly, BookTok becomes a corrective that imagines a reading community in which intersectional queer identities can be discussed and celebrated far from the supposed "safe" spaces that most high schools claim to foster. In this space, there is choice. Reading and "membership" are a choice. By making certain choices, relevant discourses can take shape that engage reading and discussing queer Latinx texts such as *They Both Die at the End*.

THEY BOTH DIE AT THE END

They Both Die at the End takes place in what looks and feels just like present-day New York City. But something is different. In this alternate universe, Adam Silvera paints a dystopian world in which people receive a phone call from Death-Cast on the day they are going to die, giving them anywhere from a few seconds to nearly twenty-four hours to live. The phone call doesn't give any details—just that they are going to die. At the start of the book, we meet the two protagonists—Mateo, an eighteen-year-old gay Puerto Rican homebody, and Rufus, a seventeen-year-old bisexual Cuban American who has faced many of life's challenges in recent years, including becoming a foster kid after he witnesses his family die. These two teenage boys are going to die and there is nothing they can do to stop it. Silvera's novel doesn't rely on a single narrator; rather, the point of view frequently flips back and forth between Mateo and Rufus in addition to vignettes from other supporting characters. While some of these brief interludes from other characters may seem unnecessary at first, all the stories converge at some point, influencing Mateo and Rufus's narrative. Once Mateo and Rufus get the infamous call, they become known as "Deckers," join a social media app called "Last Friend," meet each other, and eventually spend their last day filled with the highs and lows that one would expect from such a story. As the two boys become friends throughout the day, they build community. Rufus and Mateo come together through sharing the same problem—they are two queer Latinos who are going to die. Naturally, this leads everyone in their lives to pity the two boys, wishing they could help but ultimately knowing that there is nothing that can be done. The two boys process grief, imagine what could have been, make peace with the past, check off items on their bucket lists, and fall in love. Oh, and they both die at the end.

Latinx YA scholar Marilisa Jiménez García argues that YA literature and Latinx studies intersect in a way that "[functions] as a counter-canon to both US and Latin American tropes and norms. Today's Latinx authors for youth challenge the kind of internal and external racism, sexism, and classism that has rendered Latinxs invisible in US and Latin American literature and society" (117). Novels like *They Both Die at the End* do precisely this, challenging the very systems that have historically oppressed Latinx teens and creating a new canon of YA that imagines a world where queer Brown boys are the norm. That teenagers on TikTok have embraced Silvera's novel should, therefore, come as no surprise. According to Loya and Almeida, "TikTok is designed for this inherent queering that takes place. It calls us to think about this small paradigmatic subversion that queer creators undertake." That is, teens queer BookTok to build community that is centered around identities that are often obfuscated and excluded from high school classrooms. TikTok becomes a corrective in which teen bookworms can engage with their favorite books, constructing new meanings through a mixture of video, images, sound, and texts. And in the case of *They Both Die at the End*, the TikTok archive is vast. Videos using the hashtag #TheyBothDieAtTheEnd have over 75 million views. Despite the robust archive, there are clear patterns and trends.

The most straightforward use of BookTok revolves around using TikTok as a digital book club. TikTokers will create short videos discussing different aspects of the book and/or giving a brief review. They then encourage their followers to discuss the book in the comments section, where, oftentimes, a lively debate will erupt that expands the world of the novel into the purely digital realm. For example, in a video uploaded on January 31, 2021, seventeen-year-old Mexican American teen Erick Reyes (@erey1324) holds up a copy of *They Both Die at the End* while proclaiming, "If you're gay or bi and a teenager then this is your book" before telling viewers about how much he loved the book. His caption adds, "I never liked reading but this book is everything" (Reyes). The video's more than three hundred comments spark discussion about readers' favorite aspects of the book, their shock that Mateo and Rufus actually die at the end, and their recommendations for other Adam Silvera books to read. Reyes's video is just one of thousands that follow the same pattern, offering reactions to the novel and prompting organic discussions. These videos speak to reader response theory and, specifically, the notion that readers want to create a community and discuss the text, which ultimately enhances their understanding of the novel.

Other TikTokers marry the novel's content with popular TikTok trends. These videos embrace Gen Z aesthetics such as idiosyncratic humor, silliness, and self-deprecating jokes to create a new sort of fan fiction riffing off the world of the book. Oftentimes, these videos find a bridge between the creator and the characters of the novel in question. In the case of *They Both Die at the End*, Mateo and Rufus offer a fertile playground to TikTok. For example, popular BookToker @lanjerry's June 14, 2020, video sees him entering the world of Silvera's novel. As his narration explains the premise of the novel, @lanjerry, who is Asian American, reenacts the novel's plot, playing Mateo opposite Rufus, who is played by a massive teddy bear. The video, engaging with the popular TikTok POV aesthetic, sees the BookToker become an embodied part of Silvera's universe, drawing parallels between himself and the fictional Mateo. His more than 158,000 followers fill the comment section discussing their love for the novel's dual protagonists. Not surprisingly, for queer teens of color drawing parallels between themselves and fictional queer teens of color can be empowering. This is especially true if we consider the dearth of representation that queer Latinx youth face in mainstream media. This is only exacerbated by traditional reading communities like English classrooms, where queerness is deemed taboo or controversial and is thus excluded from the space, replicating systems of oppression that queer students face in their day-to-day lives. Although speaking of Harry Potter, Latinx studies scholar Domino Pérez claims that YA literature serves an important role in teen identity formation: "By aligning their own experiences with favorite characters, readers' efforts are an attempt to see themselves represented in the literature, or to write themselves into the stories they love" (75). We see these same dynamics play out in the *They Both Die at the End* BookTok archive where queer teens of color quite literally embody Mateo and Rufus in their BookTok videos.

Another common trend on *They Both Die at the End* BookTok revolves around how devastating teen readers find Silvera's novel. These TikToks engage in teenage culture that embraces the feeling of being devastated. TikTokers engaging with this trend are being emotional in such a way as to fit into group and generational culture. For example, a November 10, 2020, video by Latino teen @earth2mateo begins with him holding up a copy of the book. Text on the video reads, "Record yourself before and after you read They Both Die at the End." We see Mateo before he begins Silvera's novel; all is well. The video immediately transitions to after finishing the novel: Mateo cries uncontrollably, covering his mouth with his hand and moving back-and-forth. Although having an emotional breakdown in public would have been "social suicide" before, for teenage Zoomers, this is acceptable. The comment section affirms this, with most readers sharing how the book also devastated them. Comments include, @kermitlover420, "I WENT INTO MY LIVING ROOM AND CRIED INTO MY MOTHERS ARMS SHE THOUGHT I WAS DYING OR SUM"; @zerooheroo, "You don't recover from this book you just learn to live with the pain"; and @eviolois, "Book pain hurts way more than movies will ever do." Shannon DeVito, director of books at Barnes & Nobles, acknowledges, "These creators are unafraid to be open and emotional about the books that make them cry and sob or scream or become so angry they throw it across the room, and it becomes this very emotional 45-second video that people immediately connect with" (quoted in Harris). In this digital reading community, being devastated and emotionally vulnerable on TikTok creates a sense of belonging. It means not only did you read the book, but you *got* the book. Teens then use TikTok to profess and perform their bookworm identities. This process also sees TikTokers competing with each other over who can cry the most and who can, therefore, be the most devastated by the book. This is not to say that teens like Mateo are not genuinely emotionally affected by the novel, but that there is a certain performance at play in the BookTok archive.

Performing devastation on BookTok exemplifies TikTok messiness, vulnerability, and camp aesthetics which have come to define Gen Z aesthetics and generational culture. This is especially relevant for queer teens who use TikTok as a space to actualize their identity through queer Latinx YA such as *They Both Die at the End*. In speaking on queer TikTok culture(s), Loya and Almeida propose, "As creators, a queer enacted identity is able to contextualize the relationship not only between the creator and the sound, but the viewer and the queer digital space." That is, producing BookToks on queer Latinx YA literature and engaging with this digital community reinforce the value in queer Latinx identities and how literature and digital media can be a critical site to unpack these intersections.

The aforementioned trends exemplify only a fraction of how teenagers have used TikTok to play with *They Both Die at the End*. Throughout this expansive archive, we can begin to understand how BookTok offers a fertile playground for young readers to not only engage with queer Latinx YA literature in a definitively teenage space, but also how TikTok trends become identity scripts in which queer Latinx teens have a safe(r) space to unpack their identities. Within this queer digital space, queer Latinidades are normalized and celebrated, something not often seen in institutionalized spaces such as schools and churches. On TikTok, queer Latinx teen readers can be themselves, more openly expressing their identities and offering a possibility of what a queer Latinx future might hold.

CONCLUSION

In *Good Reception: Teens, Teachers, and Mobile Media in a Los Angeles High School*, education scholar Antero García questions how cell phones can transform the way that students learn, both in school and out of school. García poses a series of questions: "How are these new devices shifting the culture of school campuses, creating new forms of social participation, and shaping youth civic practices?" (4). As this chapter reveals, cell phones and apps that fill their screens energize the teenage experience, especially for young readers on TikTok. Teenage TikToking trends have quickly transformed mainstream culture as well. For instance, TikTok has revolutionized the music industry, proving that virality on the app directly corresponds to commercial and mainstream success. Critical media studies scholar Meghan Grosse proposes, TikTok "is uniquely well positioned to connect artists with potential fans." As *They Both Die at the End*'s TikTok archive conveys, the same dynamic is taking place in YA literature, in which TikTok virality can lead to mainstream success. Of course, this hasn't been lost on Adam Silvera. On March 10, 2021, Silvera took the plunge and posted his first TikTok post. Although he had created an account months earlier, Silvera had largely lurked on the platform, seeing what was out there, following BookTok conversations, but largely keeping his distance. Inspired by *They Both Die at the End*'s continued commercial success largely thanks to TikTok, Silvera's video thanks BookTokers for making his book popular. "You all have really given this book a second life and put me in the position to expand the Death-Cast Universe in ways that I've always wanted to" (Silvera, TikTok). Silvera then introduces viewers to the rest of his oeuvre, showing that there is something for everyone on Adam Silvera TikTok. Indeed, although Silvera's novel has influenced teen readers, it is also abundantly clear that the relationship is reciprocal. Even though the BookTok archive is still in motion, *They Both Die at the End*'s TikTok community speaks to the power of queer Latinx YA literature. It is not just an empowering space for queer teens of color or for writers such as Adam Silvera. Rather, on TikTok, queer Latinx YA is for everyone.

NOTES

1. During the COVID-19 pandemic, TikTok became the most popular social media platform in the United States. It became a critical space for entertainment, political organizing, and civic engagement. For example, virtually every popular song from 2020 made its mark on TikTok, from The Weeknd's "Blinding Light" to Megan Thee Stallion's "Savage." Moreover, Gen Z made use of TikTok to organize against Donald Trump's presidential campaign, famously reserving over one million tickets for his June 2020 Tulsa rally, which only saw a few thousand in attendance. At the same time, nearly every celebrity and brand joined the platform, which quickly transitioned from a largely Gen Z affinity space to the social media app of choice for much of the United States, regardless of generation.

2. For more on Adam Silvera's work, see Cristina Rhodes, Alyssa Chrisman and Mollie V. Blackburn, and William Orchard.

3. BookTok also engages with what Jon Wargo calls multimodal literacies and what Antero Garcia calls transmedia. Due to space constraints, an analysis of BookTok under these lenses is beyond the scope of this chapter. For more on multimodal literacies, see Jon Wargo, "Between an iPhone and a Safe Space" and "Designing More Just Social Futures or Remixing the Radical Present?"; and Antero Garcia, "A Narrative Across Platforms" and *Good Reception: Teens, Teachers, and Mobile Media in a Los Angeles High School*.

4. For more on TikTok's subcultures, see Trevor Boffone, *TikTok Cultures in the United States*.

5. For a discussion of validating and celebrating Latinx nerds, see Cristina Herrera's *ChicaNerds in Young Adult Literature: Brown and Nerdy*, and Trevor Boffone and Cristina Herrera, eds., *Nerds, Goths, Geeks & Freaks: Outsiders in Chicanx and Latinx Young Adult Literature*.

6. For example, the 2017 Stonewall School Report revealed that "two in five LGBT young people are bullied online," even if the study also found that anti-LGBT bullying had lessened in recent years (Stonewall).

7. Such was the case of mega star Jojo Siwa, who came out on TikTok in January 2021.

WORKS CITED

Alamillo, Laura, and Rosie Arenas. "Chicano Children's Literature: Using Bilingual Children's Books to Promote Equity in the Classroom." *Multicultural Education* 19, no. 4 (2012): 53–62.

Baeza Ventura, Gabriela. "Latino Literature for Children and the Lack of Diversity." *(Re)mapping the Latina/o Literary Landscape: New Works and New Directions*, edited by Cristina Herrera and Larissa M. Mercado-Lopez. Palgrave Macmillan, 2016, 241–54.

Blackburn, Mollie V. *Interrupting Hate: Homophobia in Schools and What Literacy Can Do about It.* Teachers College Press, 2012.

Boffone, Trevor, and Cristina Herrera. *Nerds, Goths, Geeks & Freaks: Outsiders in Chicanx and Latinx Young Adult Literature.* University Press of Mississippi, 2020.

Boffone, Trevor. *Renegades: Digital Dance Cultures from Dubsmash to TikTok.* Oxford University Press, 2021.

Boffone, Trevor. *TikTok Cultures in the United States.* Routledge, 2022.

Chrisman, Alyssa, and Mollie V. Blackburn. "Interrogating Happiness: Unraveling Homophobia in the Lives of Queer Youth of Color with *More Happy than Not*." *Engaging with Multicultural YA Literature in the Secondary Classroom: Critical Approaches for Critical Educators*, edited by Ricki Ginsberg and Wendy J. Glenn. Routledge, 2019, 83–92.

Emily (@EmpireOfEmily). "The amount of teens coming into B&N looking for it because 'they saw it on Tik Tok' is frankly amazing & heartwarming!" Twitter, 4 January 2021, 9:48 p.m., https://twitter.com/EmpireOfEmily/status/1346302503567163392?s=20. Accessed 8 October 2021.

Freire, Paulo. *Pedagogy of the Oppressed.* Herder and Herder, 1970.

García, Antero. *Good Reception: Teens, Teachers, and Mobile Media in a Los Angeles High School.* MIT Press, 2017.

García, Antero. "A Narrative Across Platforms." *Literacy Today*, September/October 2017, 34–5.

Grosse, Meghan. "Self-Promotion in 15 Seconds: Finding Mainstream Success through Memeable Sound Clips on TikTok." *Flow Journal* 27, no. 1 (2020).

Harris, Elizabeth A. "How Crying on TikTok Sells Books." *New York Times*, 20 March 2021. https://www.nytimes.com/2021/03/20/books/booktok-tiktok-video.html.

Herrera, Cristina. *ChicaNerds in Young Adult Literature: Brown and Nerdy.* Routledge, 2020.

Huntington Beach Barnes & Noble (@BNEvents_HB). "We literally can't keep enough in stock! 💀 Twitter, 4 January 2021, 11:30 p.m., https://twitter.com/BNEvents_HB/status/1346328261584801793?s=20. Accessed 8 Oct. 2021.

Jerry (@lanjerry). "They Both Die at the End by Adam Silvera." *TikTok*, 14 June 2020. https://vm.tiktok.com/ZMekjNNVs/. Accessed 12 March 2020.

Jimenez García, Marilisa. "Side-by-Side: At the Intersections of Latinx Studies and ChYALit." *The Lion and the Unicorn* 41, no. 1 (January 2017): 113–22.

Kant, Tanya. *Making it Personal: Algorithmic Personalization, Identity, and Everyday Life.* Oxford University Press, 2020.

Kennedy, Melanie. "'If the Rise of the TikTok Dance and E-Girl Aesthetic Has Taught Us Anything, It's That Teenage Girls Rule the Internet Right Now': TikTok Celebrity, Girls and the Coronavirus Crisis." *European Journal of Cultural Studies* 23, no. 6 (2020): 1069–1076.

Leskin, Paige. "Teens Are Using TikTok as a New Way to Come Out to Friends and Family, and It Shows How Vital the App Is Becoming to Gen Z's LGBTQ Community." *Insider*, 19 November 2019. https://www.businessinsider.com/tiktok-lgbtq-teens-coming-out-online-2019-11. Accessed 24 Sept. 2021.

Loya, Luis, and Elaine Almeida. "Things That Shouldn't Have Gay Energy but Do Anyways: CTI, Remixes, and TikTok Duets." *Flow Journal* 27, no. 1 (2020).

Miles, Sam. "Still Getting It on Online: Thirty Years of Queer Male Spaces Brokered through Digital Technologies." *Geography Compass* 12, no.11 (2018).

Orchard, William. "Endless Happy Beginnings: Forms of Speculation in Adam Silvera's *More Happy Than Not*." *ASAP Journal*, 2 December 2019, http://asapjournal.com/endless-happy-beginnings-forms-of-speculation-in-adam-silveras-more-happy-than-not-william-orchard/.

Pérez, Domino. "Afuerx and Cultural Practice in *Shadowshaper* and *Labrynth Lost*." *Nerds, Goths, Geeks, and Freaks: Outsiders in Chicanx and Latinx Young Adult Literature*, edited by Trevor Boffone and Cristina Herrera. University Press of Mississippi, 2020, 74–87.

Reyes, Erick (@ereyes1324). "Thank you Adam Silvera for this amazing book. I never liked reading but this book is everything." *TikTok*, 31 Jan. 2021, https://vm.tiktok.com/ZMek2tpNW/. Accessed 12 March 2021.

Rhodes, Cristina. "Imagining the Future: The (Im)Possibilities of Queerness in Two Latinx Speculative Young Adult Novels." *Label Me Latina/o* 11 (2021), 1–10.

Ruehlicke, Andrea. "All the Content, Just for You: TikTok and Personalization." *Flow Journal* 27, no. 1 (2020).

Silvera, Adam (@AdamSilvera). "The #2 spot is the highest I've ever been on the New York Times Bestseller List! For a book that came out in 2017! About queer Latinx boys! THANK YOU!" Twitter, 8 January 2021, 12:33 p.m. https://twitter.com/AdamSilvera/status/1347612444357652480?s=20. Accessed 8 Oct. 2021.

Silvera, Adam (@adamSilvera). "Infinite thanks to everyone on #BookTok for supporting #TheyBothDieAtTheEnd!!" *TikTok*, 10 March 2021. https://vm.tiktok.com/ZMek2PEAm/. Accessed 12 March 2021.

Stonewall. "Stonewall School Report 2017: Anti-LGBT Bullying Down but LGBT Young People Still at Risk." 27 June 2017. https://www.stonewall.org.uk/news/stonewall-school-report-2017-anti-lgbt-bullying-down-lgbt-young-people-still-risk. Accessed 24 Sept. 2021.

@TheBagelQueenn. "I discovered you through Tiktok and I've read almost all your books since! New favorite author!" Twitter, 5 January 2021, 8:33 a.m. https://twitter.com/TheBagelQueennn/status/1346464805180338177?s=20. Accessed 8 Oct. 2021.

Wargo, Jon M. "Between an iPhone and a Safe Space: Tracing Desire in Connective (Auto) Ethnographic Research with LGBTQ Youth." *International Journal of Qualitative Studies in Education* 33, no. 5 (2019): 508–23.

Wargo, Jon W. "Lights! Cameras! Genders? Interrupting Hate through Classroom Tinkering, Digital Media Production and [Q]ulturally Sustaining Arts-Based Inquiry." *Theory Into Practice* 58, no. 1 (2018): 18–28.

Wargo, Jon W. "Designing More Just Social Futures or Remixing the Radical Present?: Queer Rhetorics, Multimodal (Counter)Storytelling, and the Politics of LGBTQ Youth Activism." *English Teaching: Practice and Critique* 16, no. 2 (2017): 145–60.

Chapter Nine

SIDEWAYS LATINX QUEERNESS IN YOUNG ADULT VIDEO GAMES

Life Is Strange 2 and *Gone Home*

Regina Marie Mills

To be a Latinx teenager willing to question and explore sexual and romantic love challenges assumptions of both queerness and Latinidad. In Trevor Boffone and Cristina Herrera's introduction to *Nerds, Goths, Geeks, and Freaks*, they write that Latinx outsiders "must navigate their communities as outsiders within an already marginalized community," and they "[insist] that to understand Latinx youth identities, it is necessary to shed light on outsiders within an already marginalized ethnic group . . . who might not fit within Latinx popular cultural paradigms such as the chola and cholo" (4, 7). In examining queer Latinx youth in video games, I go beyond not only the popular paradigms and stereotypes in YA literature but also beyond the print text. YA and children's literature scholars in the realm of queer studies and Latinx studies, such as Derritt Mason and Marilisa Jiménez García, respectively, argue that we examine a variety of trans-media texts, such as comics and video games, in addition to traditional print media (Mason 6, 16; Jiménez García 6). According to the Entertainment Software Association (ESA), 20 percent of those who play games are under the age of eighteen (2).[1] And of course, it is well-known how popular YA literature is among adults, with YA books and series from *The Hunger Games* (2008–2010) to *The Hate U Give* (2017) being adapted as big-budget Hollywood films. Games scholar Ian Bogost, in his review of the game *Gone Home* for the *Los Angeles Review of Books*, in fact, laments this fact as a form of "media degeneracy": "What if games haven't failed to mature so much as all other media have degenerated, such that the model of the young adult novel is really the highest (and most commercially viable) success one can achieve in narrative?" As scholarship on children's literature and young adult literature have shown, YA literature and media reveal a great deal about how we imagine childhood, adulthood, and the world will live in. Unlike Bogost, I argue that games that focus on young characters and their struggles are not less thoughtful or critical but rather meaningful and interactive ways of exploring how ideas of citizenship are colored by ethno-race and queer possibility. As Jiménez García emphasizes, "Much of what we know as pop culture exists in unexplored, interrelated notions of race, youth, childhood, and the nation" (6). In the twenty-first century, video games have presented queer Latinx young adult stories about romance, friendship, and coming of age that are rarely represented in traditional media. In this essay, I consider queer Latinidad in games about adolescence and childhood that feature queer Latinx teenagers, examining not only issues of representation but also how these games queer common Latinx narratives. I analyze two games—*Gone Home* (2013) and *Life Is Strange 2* (*LIS2*, 2018–19)—by drawing from Kathryn Bond Stockton's notion of sideways queerness. These games' walking simulator structure—winding, exploratory, encouraging dead ends and backwards movement—force the character to confront queer Latinidad and refuse one-dimensional readings of these characters as merely queer *or* Latinx. Though their queerness or Latinidad may sometimes have to enter the narrative in a sideways manner, *Gone Home* and *LIS2* provide a queer Latinx critique of citizenship, criminality, and the migration narrative.

    Both games lay claim to the genre of so-called "walking simulators," which eschew competitive or violent gameplay. As Bonnie Ruberg writes, "The term 'walking simulators' describes a category of games that tell stories through player movement and environmental exploration" and has historically been used as a pejorative term (*Video Games*, 200–1). Ruberg notes that, "Rather than speeding players along from challenge to challenge, they invite a slower, more contemplative relationship with the games' rich visual and material environments" (201). While frequently maligned by certain gamers (e.g. white cisgender male) as not really games, game journalists and game studies scholars write about how the genre challenges masculinized conceptions of games.[2] For example, Matthew Payne and Jeff Vanderhoef argue that "the walking simulator engenders a unique protagonist: the intersectional digital flaneuse," whose wandering "[evokes] crises of narrative, politics, and identity" (51). Walking simulators provide the perfect space to reflect and contemplate the worlds we inhabit and the worlds we would like to create. While *Gone Home* fits more squarely into the walking simulator category, as it is often named as a representative example, *Life Is Strange 2*'s primary mechanic is walking and interacting with objects and documents as well. However, the game also includes cutscenes interspersed throughout the story, as well as a choice mechanic not available in *Gone Home*. In fact, *LIS2* has a complex choice system that influences what happens in later episodes and even how the game ends, while *Gone Home* ultimately tells one story, though the path you take to get there and how much of the side stories you read depend on how long you linger and explore.

Gaming journalism and particularly game studies scholarship have struggled to fully engage the queer Latinx teenagers that are key to both games. In *Gone Home*, the fact that the queer relationship is between a Mexican American girl and a white Protestant girl is simplified to a "queer narrative" rather than a queer interracial narrative.[3] No peer-reviewed scholarship names or discusses Lonnie's Mexican American identity. In *LIS2*, Sean's ability to be played as a queer character is usually discussed separately from its Trump-era political critique.[4] I contend that, despite these erasures in games scholarship and journalism, neither game actually presents these queer Latinx youth in one dimension or tries to hide their queer Latinidad. In *Gone Home*, Lonnie's Mexican Americanness is asserted frequently, but recognizing this would problematize how scholarship approaches the game's 1990s setting.

GONE HOME: SIDEWAYS MEXICAN-AMERICANNESS

Gone Home has the player take on the role of white teenager Katie Greenbriar, who has recently arrived home to the Pacific Northwest after a year in Europe. The house is empty, and there are a few cryptic phone messages that create an anxious environment. Because the Greenbriars moved to the house in which the game takes place while Katie was gone, the environment is unfamiliar to her (as it is to the player). As Katie, you walk around the house and piece together the major events that have rocked her family during the year she's been gone, the most significant of which is that her younger sister Sam has fallen in love with a girl at school, Lonnie. By reading letters, zines, listening to cassette tapes, and interacting with every object you can, the player can see how Sam's parents react to her sexual awakening. Since the game takes places in the mid-1990s (primarily 1994), your inability to contact anyone is easily explained. This mid-1990s context also places you squarely in the Riot Grrrl moment. The game appears at first to be a horror survival game, both because it depends on a game engine used for such terrifying games as *Amnesia: The Dark Descent* and because the house creaks, lights flicker, thunder booms, and you always have the feeling that something is waiting for you around the corner. The horror tropes eventually fall away though, and despite being a game about two lesbian high schoolers in love, there is actually a somewhat-happy ending: Sam and Lonnie run away to be together, rejecting boot camp (for Lonnie) and college (for Sam).

Gone Home has substantial scholarship and yet none mentions the fact that Lonnie's full name is Yolanda DeSoto and that she is Mexican American.[5] In fact, Tulloch, Hoad, and Young critique *Gone Home* as a game that reinscribes white hegemony,[6] and while Lonnie can certainly be read as white-presenting, I argue that the game does not characterize her as attempting to pass for white. While many celebrate the game for its queer narrative structure, such as its refusal to provide a pleasurable (narrative) climax (Chess 91), the refusal to see Lonnie's Latinidad suggests that scholars do not see her Latinidad as meaningfully incorporated. In analyzing the documents and pictures in which Lonnie takes center stage, I assert that Lonnie's Mexican Americanness is in fact quite meaningful to her character and pushes against a homogenous queerness in the game, though it must enter sideways into the narrative to do so. *Gone Home* resists presenting Latinidad as no different from Anglo whiteness. The game, cowritten by Latina game writer Karla Zimonja—cofounder of the studio that made *Gone Home* and who also worked on *Life Is Strange 2*—welcomes a demographic often denied space in video games, the Riot Grrrl movement, and LGBTQ history.

Lonnie's Mexican American identity is showcased in a several ways for the player right from the beginning.[7] One is a letter that Sam receives from Lonnie while she is (likely) visiting her family in Mexico.[8] The player can find this letter in the basement of the house, and it pairs with the calavera that the player can find on the bookshelf in the foyer of the house near the start of the game, as Lonnie sent the painted skull as a gift. In fact, the skull is later a required object to interact with to progress in the story. In addition, as a brightly decorated Mexican decoration, it stands out from the décor of the old stately manor. The skull is a clue to the changes and exploration that Sam has experienced since Katie left. In addition to the skull, Lonnie's voice is also one of the first voices we hear in the game. She has left two voice messages on the answering machine; Lonnie is in fact voiced by Zimonja.[9] The anxiety and fear in her voice help set the tone for the game.

In addition to the ways that Lonnie frames how we enter into playing *Gone Home*, the letter she sends from Mexico demonstrates how her Mexican heritage continues to influence her identity and dreams for the future. The letter includes a Spanish vocabulary lesson at the top, including the Spanish way of saying "your love." She begins by gushing about the Mexican landscape and believing that Sam would love it there, showing that she would like to bring Sam to see her family's homeland. While some might read Lonnie's choice to go by a less clearly "Latina" name (Lonnie) over her legal name (Yolanda) as an attempt to whiten or Americanize herself, nicknames are a strong tradition in Latinx and Latin American cultures. It is not clear where her nickname originates, but it is not proof itself that Lonnie rejects her roots. In fact, Lonnie's ability to incorporate Mexico into the fantasy of her future with Sam shows that her Mexicanidad is far from rejected. Indeed, when Lonnie connects the nature she sees in Mexico to Sam's Allegra tales, she finds meaningful ground to attach the lovers' fantasies. The Allegra tales are stories that Sam has written since she was little, and as the player, you can find them throughout the house. The tales trace Sam's sexual exploration as the pirate Allegra and begin by following a fairly standard heteronormative fairy tale of falling in love and adventuring with her female first mate. In this case, Lonnie places herself in the role of Sam's first mate, imagining them traveling the world together and ending up in Mexico, a paradise. While it is certainly a romantic vison of that nation, Lonnie is telling a romantic tale. In fact, emphasizing Mexico's beauty, she pushes against negative portrayals of Mexico.

The most striking evidence of Lonnie's queer Latinidad comes through a picture of Lonnie in her JROTC uniform, with "DESOTO" on her nametag, which can be found in the downstairs hallway on the way to the basement. One of only two pictures of Lonnie in the game,[10] the choice to depict her in the cadet uniform while also having dyed pink hair embodies the conflict that Lonnie faces as well as the ways in which Lonnie presents a commentary on the relationship between queerness, Latinidad, and citizenship. As noted, *Gone Home* is set in the mid-1990s in the heyday of the Riot Grrrl movement, as scholars are quick to note, but this was also the heyday of JROTC expansion (Pérez 8).[11] As Gina M. Pérez writes, "Since its inception in 1916, JROTC has been promoted as a vital program for developing in young people the moral and physical discipline necessary for good citizenship" (5). One important part of the JROTC experience is wearing and maintaining the uniform. Pérez, in fact, spends an entire chapter on the cadet uniform, an "object of fascination, derision, respect, and pride" (60). The uniform is a powerful symbol that particularly influences how Latinx bodies are read:

> For young Latinas/os and working-class youth who are often regarded as dangerous, unworthy, and/or unwilling to be respectable members of society, membership in JROTC and wearing the cadet

uniform offers an alternative narrative that highlights their positive social contributions, as well as their ability to develop the kind of self-discipline required to fulfill their aspirations for economically secure lives." (Pérez 61)

Lonnie's father is a military man, and her choice to join JROTC reflects her desire to make her family proud but also to embody a citizenship not automatically extended to Latinas. However, her pink hair (which certainly breaks uniform code) also reflects her resistant spirit, as she makes a zine with Sam (Grrrl Justice Now!) and listens to bands like Bratmobile and Heavens to Betsy. Her disciplinary referral also indicates that she is not the stereotypical rule follower that one expects from JROTC. The common depiction of "seriousness" that Pérez illustrates in her book on JROTC is challenged. The cadet uniform, as described by Pérez's interviewees, encourages Latinxs to be "serious" and well-behaved, both due to the gravitas attributed to the uniform and because it physically encumbers and limits the movements of the wearer (87). Lonnie is not a perfect cadet, and the uniform does not seem to weigh on her, literally or figuratively, in a way that dampens her resistance to norms that define citizenship through Anglo identity and heteronormativity.

The game invites the player to think about Sam's love interest as more than a love interest. In fact, Lonnie's Mexican Americanness is a key facet of her identity. Through the pictures we see of her, the letters she sends, her voicemails, and other fragments, Lonnie is made into a character, too, and we can see how her queerness faces obstacles that differ from Sam's. The antiqueerness of the military is well-documented, so she must fear what her career military father thinks. The JROTC uniform symbolizes these struggles; but her pink hair also shows her resistance to the pigeonholing that her uniform might encourage. By thinking about Lonnie as a queer Mexican American teenager and cadet, navigating an Anglo-centered Pacific Northwest culture, the feminist Riot Grrrl movement, and JROTC expansion, the game provides insight into a queer Latina experience of the 1990s.

LIFE IS STRANGE 2: SIDEWAYS LATINX QUEERNESS

The Life Is Strange series, by Don't Nod Entertainment, is well-known for its representation of queer characters and storylines. The queerness of the first *Life is Strange* (2015) has been discussed, celebrated, and critiqued extensively by game bloggers, game journalists, and some scholars.[12] This first entry in what is now a three-game series also appears eminently comparable to the previously discussed *Gone Home* both for its exploration of queer teenaged romances and for its status as a YA game.[13] In fact, one review for the original *Life Is Strange* lamented that despite the popularity of teenage drama shows and YA literature, similar YA experiences have been lacking in gaming: "You'd think the huge YA audience would get a little love. But with the exception of *Gone Home* in 2013, pickings are slim to none for players looking for some juicy teen drama in interactive format" (Morganti).[14] While the first *Life Is Strange* told the story of two white girls in the town of Arcadia Bay, *Life Is Strange 2* (*LIS2*) begins in Seattle and explores the US West Coast. Like *Gone Home*, *LIS2* represents a queer Mexican American teen who must navigate ideas of family and the ways in which Latinxs are seen as threats in the US—what Leo Chávez calls the narrative of the "Latino threat." I analyze *LIS2*'s choice-based mechanics and cutscenes with attention to how Sean's sideways queerness interacts with expectations of queer and Latina/o/x criminality and the pressures of family and brotherhood. In addition, I argue that the game queers the US immigration narrative, by presenting a migration story where escaping to Mexico is presented as the only option for freedom from persecution.

In *Life Is Strange 2*—a five-part, episodic adventure game—Sean and Daniel Díaz (sixteen and nine years old, respectively) are the sons of a Mexican immigrant father and white American mother. After he watches his father get murdered by a police officer, powerful telekinetic powers awaken in the younger of the two, Daniel. The brothers become fugitives from the law, running south with the goal of finding refuge in their father's hometown of Puerto Lobos, Mexico. Each episode of the game traces their journey southward, allowing the player to learn more about the Diaz family and giving the characters a chance to grow and change (or stubbornly stay the same). However, rather than play as the superpowered Daniel, the player takes the role of the older brother Sean. Like *Gone Home*, the player is put at a remove from the focal character, refusing to make us the "main character" of the story. Because we are not the character with the most power, the limits of our agency and influence are made clear. By placing us in the periphery, however, the game does not make us powerless and, in fact, encourages us to see the power that comes from our past actions or how we have (or have not) modeled honesty, integrity, kindness, or other key values to those around us. The game's choice-based narrative design provides the player with the ability to pursue a relationship with either a boy (Finn), a girl (Cassidy), or even to state a lack of romantic interest (which some read as the choice to be asexual). If one pursues a relationship with Finn, Sean becomes a queer Latinx character, though as I will argue, Sean's queer potential is baked into the game.[15]

The representation of Sean's sexual exploration as well as the game's larger narrative framing, which posits the US as a land of oppression and Mexico a land of freedom and possibility, queers the migrant narrative. As Bo Ruberg argues, "Queerness in video games means more than the representation of LGBTQ characters or same-sex romance. Queerness and video games have a common ethos: the longing to imagine alternative ways of being and to make space within structures of power for resistance through play" (*Video Games* 1). Angel Daniel Matos has also highlighted, in his examination of the Legend of Zelda series, how exploration-based games "challenge universalizing approaches toward being" and "disrupt monolithic narratives on growth, identity, and the body" (36). The combination of walking simulator and choice-based mechanics in *LIS2* provides players the opportunity to choose queer exploration and resist the ubiquitous American Dream narrative. While Daniel's sexuality is not so explicitly explored (because of his age),[16] he of course is a "freak," a super-powered Mexican American whose powers manifest in a time of great stress and who gradually learns to use and amplify his powers. Daniel makes choices about how and when to use his powers based on the choices you, the player, make as Sean. Thus, the game presents a character through which the player can choose to explore queer relationships (Sean) and a child-monster (Daniel). Monsters and freaks have been read as metaphors of queerness in the tradition of monster theory. Queerness's lack of rigidity, its experimentation and "shiftiness," make it monstrous in a Puritanical American culture, as Jeffrey Cohen asserts (5). In addition, monsters "are disturbing hybrids whose externally incoherent bodies resist attempts to include them in any systematic structuration" (Cohen 6). In this case, Daniel's nine-year-old body suggests a powerlessness and innocence that is belied by both his superpowers and his Brown Latinidad. Similarly, Sean is a sixteen-year-old who should be viewed as a child but whose Brownness marks him as threat. Thus, the game provides representations of queerness but also critiques and queers foundational American beliefs such as notions of childhood and the American Dream.

By having the player take the role of the big brother Sean, *LIS2* explores concepts of family duty but from a brotherly perspective, rather than from the far more represented and stereotypical position of the strict Mexican American patriarch or the self-effacing Mexican American mother. With his father dead and his mother gone (having abandoned the family), Sean must balance his own fears and sadness with his new caretaking responsibilities as Daniel's parental figure. Through Sean's "wolf brothers" tales—told to Daniel during cutscenes and used as a recap before each new episode—the game represents the brothers as a loyal pack, committed first and foremost to each other. The game's final destination, Puerto Lobos, also connects the wolf (lobo) to the boys' refuge. Sean's commitment to his brother is not negotiable; the player is required to stay with his brother, and despite being provided wide-ranging choices, the dialogue for these choices are couched in a concern for keeping his brother safe.

The complex choice mechanics in the game control many aspects of future narratives across episodes, but one of the most important is the brothers' relationship. How you talk to Daniel, what he sees you do when the chips are down, and what you ask Daniel to do or not do (particularly with his powers) ultimately determine whether or not Sean lives, dies, escapes the cops, or ends up in jail, as well as whether or not the brothers are separated, stay in the US, or make it to Mexico. By requring the player to think about what kind of man we want our brother to be, the game asks us to consider our duty to family. While familial duty is a frequent topic of concern in YA and Latinx literature, the interactive nature of *LIS2* demonstrates how difficult it is to be the perfect brother or father figure. Whether or not you shame Daniel for using his powers determines whether he'll listen to you when it comes to future choices only he can make. And sometimes, a choice that might seem to make Daniel upset is actually the best one for him (and counts positively towards your relationship building stat).

Of course, Sean is still a child himself, but as a Latino teenager, he is viewed as an adult and a threat in ways that white non-Latino teenagers (and even some adults) are not. In the first two episodes of the game, the conflict comes from the fact that Washington and Oregon are incredibly white states, and as they leave Seattle, their Brownness stands out, which some people use as an excuse to target the brothers. In Episode 1, a white gas station owner (who, based on a chamber-of-commerce letter players can find, is seen as a pillar of the community) assaults Sean and Daniel. While Daniel escapes, the owner kidnaps Sean, handcuffing him to a pipe after falsely accusing the brothers of stealing.[17] Despite knowing what her husband is doing, the gas station owner's wife does not interfere with the kidnapping and decides to trust her husband's (criminal) decision. In Episode 2, the boys' white maternal grandparents will not send the brothers to school and tell them not to go outside so as not to raise suspicions. The one outing that the brothers take ultimately leads them to need to run again. In the first two episodes of the game, there are no other nonwhite characters other than the brothers.

After the events of Episode 2, the Diaz brothers must escape the police again, so they decide to freight-hop southward. This decision to illegally ride cargo trains immediately brings to mind La Bestia, the infamous train that Central American immigrants often use on their way through Mexico to the United States.[18] In this case, this south-bound train is also used to flee to safety, but not al norte, rather to Mexico, away from the US criminal justice system that pursues two children as cop killers.[19] As the player, you are rooting for the Diaz brothers to make it to Mexico and find freedom, a feeling that most games rarely elicit, considering the violent and desolate depiction of Mexico. Mexican game designer Augusto Quijano (*Guacamelee!*), in fact, came to this conclusion when he saw media representations of his homeland in Canada: "Mexicans are no heroes." He asks the reader, "How can we stop putting migrant children in cages if we don't believe they deserve heroic roles in video games? . . . When I say 'hero' I don't only mean do-gooders—I mean people through whom we see the world" (Quijano). By making Mexican Americans the heroes of *LIS2*, the developers ask players to reconsider the American Dream and what it entails. Furthermore, the game questions the definition of criminality, which bodies are seen as criminal, and which countries supposedly "breed" criminals.

Episodes 1–2 and 4–5 rely heavily on discussions of racial politics and prejudice, and the game's commentary on anti-immigrant attitudes in the Trump era has sometimes overshadowed Sean's queerness. The game provides opportunities for the player to characterize Sean as queer, particularly in Episode 3: Wastelands; but even if the player chooses a heterosexual romance, Sean's queerness is narratively built into the game. During their train journey south, the brothers meet up with two drifter teenagers they met in Episode 2, Cassidy and Finn. The two help get Sean and Daniel jobs on an illegal marijuana farm. Sean decides that they should work there until they get enough money to get to Puerto Lobos. During their stay with these misfits and runaways, Sean meets people from around the world and can explore aspects of his identity. While players are not required to play Sean as a queer character,[20] the game provides plenty of clues that he is interested in Finn. For example, the player can choose to sketch a detailed picture of Finn or Cassidy. If Cassidy sees the sketch of Finn, Sean gets very embarrassed and protective of the picture. In addition, there is friction with Sean's brother regarding Finn. Daniel appears to see Finn as a role model, someone he looks up to, even though Finn has a tendency towards trouble. Sean can discourage Daniel's closeness with Finn, but sometimes that discouragement seems more like jealousy and a desire for Finn's attention than concern for Daniel. For example, near the beginning of the episode, Sean finds Daniel practicing knife throwing with Finn. Daniel excels since he is clearly using his telekinesis. When Sean tries, he also excels until Daniel uses his powers to mess up one of the player's throws. Sean gets angry, but it appears to be less about Daniel using his powers to cheat and more about being embarrassed in front of Finn. There are other small signs that Finn and Sean have chemistry—the two frequently touch each other, and Finn compliments Sean's looks more than once, calling him "hot" and telling him that any scars he gets from cutting the marijuana buds would make him "sexier." While the player can choose not to pursue this chemistry, the chemistry is there nonetheless.[21]

A limitation of the queer relationship represented in *LIS2* is that if the player wants to pursue Finn, the game treats that romantic relationship differently from a similar relationship with Cassidy. In fact, because of the choices you must make to kiss Finn, there has been debate about whether the game provides a healthy view of queerness. One critique is that if the player chooses to romance Cassidy, Sean and Cassidy can have sex. The depiction of this scene is quite thoughtful and realistic, as the encounter is awkward and quite short.[22] However, if one chooses to pursue Finn, the two do not go any further than a kiss, which suggests that the representation of gay sexual experience is less acceptable in a YA game. In addition, to pursue the Finn relationship, the character must agree to a dangerous plan to rob the farm supervisor using Daniel's powers. That is, the player needs to make a reckless decision that puts Daniel in danger.[23] If I had not been writing this essay on Sean's queer Latinidad, I would not have made such a decision, as I had avoided stealing and other possibly criminal choices in earlier episodes. I worried that choosing Finn tied queerness to criminality.

However, the game encourages players to consider questions of criminality and who decides what is criminal. Sean is already a fugitive under suspicion of what is usually considered a capital crime. His boss at the farm—which is a criminal enterprise—has fired him for dubious reasons and refused to give him his pay. Discrimination has often been baked into the law, and people with enough money, power, or status can evade the label of criminal. Racialized people have often been associated with criminality no matter their choices; queerness has historically been treated as a crime. And of course, even Sean's goal to get him and Daniel to Mexico is a crime, as getting into Mexico in Episode 5 requires using Daniel's powers to destroy a blockade at the border. In fact, anti-immigrant militias target Sean and Daniel, assuming that he is an undocumented immigrant trying to *enter* the US.

Beyond the game's commentary on criminality in relation to queerness and Mexican Americanness, the game also shows what teenaged love can lead to: stupid choices. Just as straight couples can be Romeo and Juliet or Bonnie and Clyde, queer teenagers can allow their lust to lead to bad decisions. By representing a same-sex relationship as just as desperate and reckless as straight ones, the game simulates the reality of teenage whirlwind romances.

CONCLUSION

In a world in which Don't Say Gay bills barrage LGBTQ youth and claim that sexuality is only an adult experience, *Gone Home* and *Life Is Strange 2* affirm that sexuality is part of childhood. Kathryn Bond Stockton's examination of the image of "the gay child" seems to be ever more relevant to our political moment. When Stockton asks, "Is there a notion of a child lingering in the vicinity of the word gay, having a ghostly, terrifying, complicated, energizing, chosen, forced, or future connection to this word?" (2), she pinpoints the fear of children's sexuality and particularly the queer potentiality of children.[24] "For this queer child, whatever its conscious grasp of itself, has not been able to present itself according to the category "gay" or "homosexual"—categories culturally deemed too adult, since they are sexual, though we do presume every child to be straight." (Stockton 6). Queer children are made to fear that they may not grow out of their queerness. In the games discussed, the queer Mexican American characters navigate this fear alongside the anti-immigrant and anti-Latino prejudices of the 1990s and Trump era. Through exploration, documentary fragments, and character interactions, both games refuse stereotypical characterizations of Mexican American queerness and encourage thoughtful reflection on notions of citizenship in a queer context.

NOTES

1. Overall, 58 percent are under the age of thirty-five.

2. In addition to the two scholars discussed in this paragraph, see Kagen.

3. For examples of this erasure of Lonnie's Latinidad in games journalism and blogs, see Bogost and Kunzelman (who has a collection of *Gone Home* criticism).

4. For an example of the erasure of Sean's queerness in games journalism, see Martens. One piece of games journalism brings up the queer erasure issue explicitly; see Henly. Queer Latina game journalist Natalie Flores ("*Life Is Strange 2*"), also discusses seeing herself in the game: There is not yet any peer-reviewed scholarship on *Life Is Strange 2*.

5. For example, see Ruberg Chess ("Straight Paths"), and Tulloch, Hoad, and Young.

6. The Riot Grrrl movement and memorialization of the movement have indeed privileged whiteness, as Nguyen argues. The YA novel *Moxie* by Jennifer Mathieu attempts to remind readers of these problematic racial politics but also to show how modern-day Riot Grrrls of color can adapt and reinvent their strategies.

7. Developer Steve Gaynor also reiterates Lonnie's Mexican American identity in a podcast interview (Chick).

8. Note that some of these screenshots come from my own playthroughs, though a few come from a Steam Community guide that attempts to place all the documents in the game in chronological order (Saraneth).

9. Zimonja's voice acting is uncredited but has been verified. This information can be found on the *Gone Home* Wiki entry for Yolanda DeSoto, though I have gone to the original citations to ensure its accuracy.

10. In the picture of Lonnie that Sam hides in her bedroom locker, Lonnie's religious background, represented by her cross necklace, also suggests a possible conflict with her faith.

11. Lonnie's characterization as a JROTC cadet also welcomes discussion of the Don't Ask, Don't Tell policy enacted in 1993. Under this policy, LGBTQ members could serve in the military but only if they were closeted. See Burrelli and Huffman and Schultz (eds.).

12. For some representative games journalism, see Morganti and Shepard. For a recent scholarly work, see de Miranda.

13. In addition to prequel games that expand the story of the original *Life Is Strange*, Deck Nine and Square Enix recently released the third game in the series: *Life Is Strange: True Colors* (2021), which focuses on Alex Chen, an Asian American bisexual protagonist.

14. For scholarship that compares *Gone Home* and *Life Is Strange*, see Drouin.

15. His earlier interest in Lyla, an Asian American girl, during the prologue then casts him as bisexual or at least willing to experiment.

16. Players of *Life Is Strange 2*, however, do speculate as to whether Daniel may also subtly explore his romantic and sexual interests, believing that he may have had a crush on Chris in episode 2 or even on Finn. See https://gamefaqs.gamespot.com/boards/241940-life-is-strange-2/78238477.

17. In my May 2022 playthrough, I did not take any of the opportunities to steal and still received this narrative result. According to the *LIS2* wikis, the gas station owner does this no matter if you try to steal or not.

18. For one account of immigrants riding La Bestia, see Martínez.

19. In the postcredits frame of Episode 3, an ominous voice of authority says, "We got a lot of room in jail for cop murderers like you."

20. And in fact, most players pursue Cassidy, the teenaged girl option. As of my last playthrough in May 2022, the statistics presented after the game told me that only 14 percent of players had kissed Finn, while 86 percent had kissed Cassidy.

21. Interestingly, spending extra time with Finn or Cassidy is often antithetical to building a relationship with your brother. However, staying up late also allows a conversation with the other teenagers about whether or not you prefer boys or girl or nobody.

22. For developer discussion of the choice to show a less idealized first sexual experience, see Hernandez.

23. For critiques of the Finn path, see Wright and Flores.

24. See also Muñoz.

WORKS CITED

Boffone, Trevor, and Cristina Herrera, editors. *Nerds, Goths, Geeks, and Freaks: Outsiders in Chicanx and Latinx Young Adult Literature*. University Press of Mississippi, 2020.

Bogost, Ian. "Perpetual Adolescence: The Fullbright Company's 'Gone Home.'" *Los Angeles Review of Books*, 28 September 2013. https://lareviewofbooks.org/article/perpetual-adolescence-the-fullbright-companys-gone-home/

Burrelli, David F. *"Don't Ask, Don't Tell": The Law and Military Policy on Same-Sex Behavior.* Report for Congress, R40782, Congressional Research Service, 14 October 2010.

Chávez, Leo R. *The Latino Threat: Constructing Immigrants, Citizens, and the Nation.* 2nd ed. Stanford University Press, 2013.

Chess, Shira. "The Queer Case of Video Games: Orgasms, Heteronormativity, and Video Game Narrative." *Critical Studies in Media Communication* 33, no. 1 (January 2016): 84–94.

Chick, Tom. "Gone Homecast with Developer Steve Gaynor." *Quarter to Three* (podcast), August 21, 2013. https://www.quartertothree.com/fp/2013/08/21/qt3-games-podcast-gone-homecast-with-developer-steve-gaynor/. Accessed 14 Feb. 2022.

Cohen, Jeffrey Jerome. "Monster Culture (Seven Theses)." *Monster Theory: Reading Culture*, edited by Jeffrey Jerome Cohen. University of Minnesota Press, 1996, 3–25.

De Miranda, Luis. "*Life Is Strange* and 'Games Are Made': A Philosophical Interpretation of a Multiple-Choice Existential Simulator with Copilot Sartre." *Games and Culture* 13, no. 8 (December 2018): 825–42.

Drouin, Renee Ann. "Games of Archiving Queerly: Artefact Collection and Defining Queer Romance in *Gone Home* and *Life Is Strange.*" *Alphaville: Journal of Film and Screen Media* 16 (Winter 2018): 24–37. https://doi.org/10.33178/alpha.

Entertainment Software Association. "2021 Essential Facts about the Video Game Industry." Report. July 2021. https://www.theesa.com/resource/2021-essential-facts-about-the-video-game-industry/

Flores, Natalie. "*Life Is Strange 2* Humanizes Latinx People in Ways No Other Game Has Done Before." *Paste Magazine*, 2 October 2018. https://www.pastemagazine.com/games/life-is-strange-2/life-is-strange-2-humanizes-latinx-people-in-ways/.

Flores, Natalie. "Why *Life Is Strange 2*'s Ungraceful Depiction of Queerness Is Important." *Paste Magazine*, 16 May 2019. https://www.pastemagazine.com/games/life-is-strange-2/why-life-is-strange-2s-ungraceful-depiction-of-que/.

Gone Home. The Fullbright Company, 2013.

Henly, Stacey. "We Should Talk about *Life Is Strange 2* More." *The Gamer*, 19 March 2021. https://www.thegamer.com/life-is-strange-2-talk-more/.

Hernandez, Patricia. "*Life Is Strange 2* Writer Explains the Game's Surprising Sex Scene." *Polygon*, 2 July 2019. https://www.polygon.com/2019/7/2/20679924/life-is-strange-2-sex-scene-cassidy-sean-dontnod.

Huffman, J. Ford, and Tammy S. Schultz, eds. *The End of Don't Ask Don't Tell: The Impact in Studies and Personal Essays by Service Members and Veterans.* Marine Corps University Press, 2012.

Jiménez García, Marilisa. *Side by Side: US Empire, Puerto Rico, and the Roots of American Youth Literature and Culture.* University Press of Mississippi, 2021.

Kagen, Melissa. "Walking Simulators, #Gamergate, and the Gender of Wandering." *The Year's Work in Nerds, Wonks, and Neocons,* edited by Jonathan P. Eburne and Benjamin Schreier. Indiana University Press, 2017, 275–300.

Kunzelman, Cameron. "A Collection of Criticism About Gone Home." *This Cage Is Worms*, 19 August 2013. https://thiscageisworms.com/2013/08/19/a-collection-of-criticism-about-gone-home/.

Life Is Strange 2. Dontnod Entertainment and Square Enix, 2018–19.

Martens, Todd. "'Life Is Strange 2,' a Video Game Saga That Reflects the Trump Era." *Los Angeles Times*, 9 January 2020. https://www.latimes.com/entertainment-arts/story/2020-01-09/life-is-strange-2-video-game-trump-era.

Martínez, Óscar. *The Beast: Riding the Rails and Dodging Narcos on the Migrant Trail*. Verso, 2013.

Mason, Derritt. *Queer Anxieties of Young Adult Literature and Culture*. University Press of Mississippi, 2021.

Mathieu, Jennifer. *Moxie*. Roaring Book Press, 2017.

Matos, Angel Daniel. "The Queerness of Space and the Body in Nintendo's The Legend of Zelda Series." *Media Crossroads: Intersections of Space and Identity in Screen Cultures*, edited by Paula J. Massood et al. Duke University Press, 2021, 34–49.

Morganti, Emily. "Review for *Life Is Strange*." *Adventure Gamers*, 20 November 2015. https://adventuregamers.com/articles/view/28237.

Muñoz, José Esteban. *Cruising Utopia: The Then and There of Queer Futurity*. NYU Press, 2009.

Pérez, Gina M. *Citizen, Student, Soldier: Latina/o Youth, JROTC, and the American Dream*. NYU Press, 2015.

Nguyen, Mimi Thi. "Riot Grrrl, Race, and Revival." *Women and Performance: A Journal of Feminist Theory* 22, no. 2–3 (July 2012): 173–96.

Payne, Matthew Thomas, and John Vanderhoef. "The Digital Flâneuse: Exploring Intersectional Identities and Spaces through Walking Simulators." *Media Crossroads: Intersections of Space and Identity in Screen Cultures*, edited by Paula J. Massood et al. Duke University Press, 2021, 50–64.

Ruberg, Bonnie. "Straight Paths Through Queer Walking Simulators: Wandering on Rails and Speedrunning in *Gone Home*." *Games and Culture* 15, no. 6 (September 2020): 632–52.

Ruberg, Bonnie. *Video Games Have Always Been Queer*. NYU Press, 2019.

Saraneth. "The Chronological Order of Events in 'Gone Home.'" *Steam Community: Gone Home*, 21 October 2015. https://steamcommunity.com/sharedfiles/filedetails/?id=516046372.

Shepard, Kenneth. "*Life Is Strange* Has Yet to Portray a Healthy Queer Relationship." *Gayming*, 12 August 2019. https://gaymingmag.com/2019/08/life-is-strange-has-yet-to-portray-a-healthy-queer-relationship/.

Stockton, Kathryn Bond. *The Queer Child, or Growing Sideways in the Twentieth Century*. Duke University Press, 2009.

Wright, Steve. "*Life Is Strange 2* Has a Disappointing Same-Sex Relationship." *Stevivor*, 12 May 2019. https://stevivor.com/features/opinion/life-strange-2-disappointing-sex-relationship/.

Chapter Ten

ATRAVESANDO NEPANTLA

Queer Familia in Chicanx and Mexican Young Adult Novels

Jesus Montaño and Regan Postma-Montaño

Queer Chicanx and Mexican youth need caring, accepting familias. They need familias that not only provide support but also culturally sustaining sabidurías and vital connections to Chicanx and Mexican[1] communities and their resources. Even as we note the importance of familia to counter the deleterious anti-LGBTQIA+ practices and policies that permeate cultural and social spaces, in this chapter we call for a more expansive understanding of familia that disavows its heteropatriarchal value systems. In particular, we seek to show how literary representations in contemporary Chicanx and Mexican young adult novels help us to envision such familias. Indeed, as Cherríe Moraga persuasively argues in "Queer Aztlán," familia traditionally has been deployed in the service of maintaining normative kinship arrangements. However, as she goes on to add, familia, specifically if it can be reconfigured in more just and equitable ways, has the potential for collective empowerment and social change. This is significant for queer Chicanidades, as Richard T. Rodríguez posits in *Next of Kin*, because it is in the best interest of LGBTQIA+ individuals and the Chicanx community; in place of conventional notions of family, we can imagine and then construct an alternate understanding of family, a "queer familia" (Rodríguez's term) that provides comfort and support as well as the resources inherently important to a sense of cultural identity (168). In this, we believe that queer familia can both critique the adverse effects of heteronormative family structures and provide the comfort, security, and cultural values necessary for a strong sense of Chicanx/Mexican identity. At play in our chapter is a search for what this revised vision of familia might look like—this is to say, how literary representations of queer familias in Chicanx and Mexican young adult literature invite us to envision familial relationships that provide all members, including LGBTQIA+, comfort and support. These progressive representations counter pernicious and stereotypical depictions of Chicanx/Mexican families with representations of queer familia in which parents are loving and caring, siblings of queer youth are supporting and attentive, and the community of family and friends who stand in solidarity can make all the difference. These representations of queer familia in Chicanx and Mexican young adult literature, we believe, can serve as a source of inspiration, voice, and lucha for many LGBTQIA+ young people.

With this intention in mind, we examine Benjamin Alire Sáenz's coming-of-age Chicanx novel, *Aristotle and Dante Discover the Secrets of the Universe* (2012), alongside two Mexican young adult novels, Mónica B. Brozon's *Sombras en el arcoíris* (translated *Shadows in the Rainbow*, 2017) and Esteban Hinojosa Rebolledo's *De día gaviotas, de noche flores blancas* (*Seagulls by Day, White Flowers by Night*, 2017). In each of these novels, young characters begin to share openly about their sexual and/or gender identity and wonder how their families, in particular, will respond to them—if with hatred and violence or with acceptance and love. We argue that these novels model a reconfigured (or at times a reconfiguring of) queer familia, thereby providing young readers a vision of more just and equitable familia and, by extension, of collective empowerment and societal change. In particular, we examine the role of parents in *Aristotle and Dante*, the role of siblings in *Sombras en el arcoíris*, and the role of the queer village (parents, siblings, friends, and mentors together) in *De día gaviotas* as they offer a fresh understanding of what is possible for queer Mexican familias.

Further, through our chapter, we show that much can be gained by examining the continuities and differences between US Chicanx YA literature and Literatura Juvenil from Mexico as they concern queer coming of age. In this way, our work advances the approach of Ramón Saldívar who envisions Chicana/o studies not in isolation, but rather as "contextually valuable" to adjacent fields including hemispheric studies (Orchard and Padilla 191, 186). In terms of hemispheric binational readership, *Aristotle and Dante* has been translated into Spanish and made available to readers as *Aristóteles y Dante descubren los secretos del universo* in 2019. Along with many other novels by Sáenz in translation, *Aristóteles y Dante* is widely available in Mexican bookstores in both digital and print versions. Further, the translated novel has received multiple BookTube reviews by Mexican (as well as other Latin

American) young people.[2] The 2023 film based on *Aristotle and Dante* (directed by Aitch Alberto) is also drawing interest from Mexican viewers with its Latinx and Mexican cast (Solis). Concerning the two Mexican YA novels, both *Sombras* and *De día* are available to US readers through US booksellers in print and digital form (as well as in audiobook form in the case of *Sombras*). Since the novels have not been translated into English, they are most accessible to Spanish speakers. We hope that hemispheric comparative scholarship like ours will only increase readership (and translation) of such titles from Mexico and Latin America in the US. Further, to our present study, we believe that Mexican and Chicanx cultures, held together by familia as well as history and heritage, add to our understanding of what it means to be queer in our Americas. In other words, our work points to the possibilities of resistance and solidarity across a shared nepantla.

REPARATIVE REPRESENTATIONS OF MADRES AND PADRES IN *ARISTOTLE AND DANTE DISCOVER THE SECRETS OF THE UNIVERSE*

We begin with Benjamin Alire Sáenz's novel, *Aristotle and Dante Discover the Secrets of the Universe*, to consider the role of parents in supporting gay children as a key part of queer familia. Set in the 1980s in the border city of El Paso, Texas, *Aristotle and Dante* details the often-bewildering assortment of intersectional ties, including race, ethnicity, class, language, gender, and sexuality, that confront Dante, who is fair skinned and who grows up in an affluent family, and Ari, whose complexion is darker and whose family is working-class. Further, Dante is open about his sexuality as a gay teenager while Ari initially is not. These questions often leave Ari and Dante feeling lost and alone, as represented in one of Ari's dreams in which Ari stands on the Juárez side of the border, unable to communicate with Dante, his dad,[3] or his brother Beto on the El Paso side (78).[4] And yet, Ari's later exhilaration as he and Dante grow closer together in the borderlands desert allows readers to see the disentangling of various facets of identity, including queerness in Chicanidad. By offering a reparative take on queer familia, we suggest *Aristotle and Dante* foregrounds the significant role of family, in particular parents, as young people disentangle intersectional identities.

Ari and Dante indeed need help processing some of their greatest insecurities, especially those that emerge at the intersections of ethnicity and sexuality. Beyond worrying if he is a "real Mexican" (88), for example, Dante struggles with the impossibility of conforming to Chicanx male gender expectations to reproduce biologically as a gay man: "The thing is I love my dad. My mom too. And I keep wondering what they're going to say when I tell them that someday I want to marry a boy. I'm the only son. What's going to happen with the grandchildren thing? I hate that I'm going to disappoint them" (227). Ari has questions about how his sexuality will be received as well. For him the situation is more dire, as he fears violence and rejection by certain homophobic family members. His brother Bernardo, as Ari comes to find out, is in prison for beating a transgender sex worker to death, and his Aunt Ophelia was ostracized for her romantic relationship with another woman. Violence and rejection, as it often does in queer coming-of-age novels, lurks throughout. As these examples show, ethnicity and sexuality intersect in challenging and oppressive ways.

Yet, to leave their biological families and find solidarity as gay men with a "chosen family" would mean letting go of the support they need as young Chicanx men.[5] The course followed in this novel involves what Richard T. Rodríguez, in his article "Making Queer Familia," observes is the near impossible task of disengaging from one's given biological Chicanx family "given the comfort and security family offers in a dominant, and often hostile, white culture" (324). In other words, along with a growing understating of their sexual identity, Ari and Dante face perplexing questions involving ethnicity, race, language, and belonging. They need their (queer) familia to support them as they confront these questions. Thankfully, as Angel Daniel Matos suggests, the novel offers "an alternative, more reparative take on the limits and possibilities of queer Latinx life in Texas in the late 1980s" (49). This is to say that the novel is recuperative in the way it "mobilizes a reparative process through its historical representation of queer Latinx adolescence" (33). For the purposes of this chapter, the reparative process involves representations of familia, that is, how Ari and Dante's families, in particular their parents, assist in healing el daño caused by being divided from each other and from familia.

The novel creates a more just vision of familia in several ways. Ari's mother, for example, provides him an alternative epistemology for understanding complex identities by having him observe how ecotones, the geological terms for where two different ecosystems meet, boast higher levels of biodiversity (238). With this way of seeing the world, Ari is better able to understand borderlands, or those places where various identities intersect, as places of richness that thrive because of a kind of natural mestizaje (Postma-Montaño 8). The support of his parents becomes even more pronounced when Ari, as a Chicanx teen on the verge of fully realizing his love for his best friend Dante, is confronted by his father. In this scene, Ari's father tells him to stop running from Dante's love and from his shared feelings. As his father states, "The real problem—for you, anyway—is that you're in love with him" (348). Even as Ari protests, "Dad, no. No. I can't. I can't. Why are you saying these things," his father stops him by stating, "Don't, amor. Te adoro" (348). The scene ends with Ari accepting that for once in his life, he understood his father perfectly and what is more, "*he understood me*" (349).[6]

What is significant about this moment in *Aristotle and Dante* is the positive, supportive interaction between a queer son and his father. As M. Roxana Loza notes, Ari, by learning that his father's previous silence was due to his trauma as a veteran of the Vietnam War, can begin the processes of reciprocation. This moment in which Ari's dad tells Ari that he loves him marks a newfound openness and connection between the two (6). Instead of disidentifying with his father, or trying not to be like him, what Ari discovers is that his father loves him unconditionally and that he loves his father the same way. Because of this reciprocity, Ari feels that they now better understand each other, highlighting the transformative power of queer familia.

In contrast to this scene of mutual love and acceptance between Ari and his dad, fathers are usually represented in negative ways, as the lead enforcer of patriarchy and promulgators of homophobia. Progressive responses and interactions between Chicanx fathers and their queer sons are few, as Daniel Enrique Pérez notes while alluding directly to *Aristotle and Dante* (243–44). And yet, as he continues, the overwhelming depictions using negative stereotypes "underscore the need to present more nuanced and positive portrayals of them" (244). As Adelaida del Castillo informs us, given the scarce positive representations and resultant lack of study of this subject, we "have much to learn about queer Chicano/Mexicano male kin relations in the United States especially with regard to relations with fathers and notions of fatherhood" (5). Our study, we believe, advances this idea. That is, our examination of *Aristotle and Dante* highlights the growing, supportive relationship between Ari and his father in order to better understand the role of familias in queer coming of age. To this point, more progressive representations both highlight a more potent view of Chicanx familias and open a door for young readers to imagine better futures. Reading for queer Latinx futures, Cristina Rhodes notes, "means accepting the necessity for imagination and the promise of a better tomorrow" (8).

SOMBRAS EN EL ARCOÍRIS: THE ROLE OF RAINBOW-LOVING SIBLINGS IN A NOT ALWAYS RAINBOW-LOVING WORLD

We now turn to the role of siblings in creating a queer familia in Mónica B. Brozon's *Sombras en el arcoíris*. The novel begins with Constanza, the ten-year-old protagonist and narrator of the novel, waiting in suspense over whether her sixteen-year-old brother, Jero, has had his anticipated conversation with los jefes, their parents. As it turns out, Jero had, and this confirms Constanza and Jero's notion that their parents are so cool ("son la onda nuestros papás") (19).[7] When Jero comes out of the closet, his mom and dad respond with joyful laughter and much support. As he explains,

> I was so very, very nervous. At first when I tried to speak, my throat snapped shut. It was so strange. But then I took a breath, and then another, and just like that I spit it out: "Dad, mom, I'm gay." Then my dad turned around to look at my mom and said with a big belly laugh, "You see? I told you so!" as if he had won a bet. You should have seen them. It was so funny that I laughed too, and this moment made me feel better about everything. Afterword they told me they loved me and that they supported me with my decisions.

> Yo estaba muy muy nervioso. Cuando intenté hablar la primera vez, hasta se me cerró la garganta. Bien raro. Pero luego respiré, respiré, y así tal cual, les solté: "Papá, mamá, soy gay." Entonces mi papá volteó a ver a mi mamá y le dijo "Ja. ¿ves? ¡Te lo dije!", con una carcajada, como si estuviera ganando una apuesta. Los hubieras visto, fue tan chistoso que también me reí, y eso alivianó mucho las cosas. Al final me dijeron que me querían y me apoyaban en cualquier cosa que yo decidiera. (19)

Much like Ari's parents in *Aristotle and Dante*, Jero's parents support their son's sexuality and personal decisions. Their response indicates radical acceptance of their son; Jero's coming out for the family is something to celebrate.

While many coming out narratives usually refer to disclosure to parents, *Sombras en el arcoíris* explores another lightly treated subject, that is, the role of siblings in the construction of queer familia. Here, in Constanza and Jero's sibling debrief conversation after Jero shares with los jefes, Constanza suggests hosting a party, complete with their favorite enchiladas and a dance party, together with Oscar (Jero's love interest), his family, and their friends. She too is eager to support and celebrate. Concerning siblings, there is a "dearth of information about coming out to our brothers and sisters," Andrew Gottlieb notes, "even though many gay men and lesbian women disclose their sexuality to their siblings before anyone else in their families" (2). To Gottlieb this dearth of information is at odds with the fact that siblings "frequently serve as a testing ground, safe place, or dry run before coming out to parents—an emotionally riskier endeavor . . . thus solidifying their own bond" (3). As Ariana Lee explains in her testimony for Gottlieb's anthology of queer and straight siblings, "Justin's [my brother's] coming out to me was the best thing that ever happened for us as brother and sister, and the best thing that ever happened for us as a family. I'm proud to have been the first to know" (16). For Constanza likewise, Jero's coming out allows for a stronger bond between the two as she supports and celebrates with him.

Siblings are foundational for constructing the kinds of familial structures in which queer youth feel accepted and loved. Further, in the process of advocating for their siblings, *Sombras en el arcoíris* clues us in to the way that finding out about an LGBTQIA+ sibling's experience is life altering, in their own ways, for ally siblings like Constanza. In *Sombras en el arcoíris*, even as Constanza is relieved that her parents are supportive of Jero, the problems are just beginning. For example, when Vane, a friend at school, notices Constanza's new rainbow bracelet and asks her to make another one, Constanza explains that she made it in honor of her brother and that she can only make Vane one if she has a gay sibling, or at least a very best friend. While Vane understands Jero's sexuality as a nonissue, another classmate Anamari responds, "What a nasty bracelet, and what it stands for, and so is having a brother like that" / "qué asco esa pulsera. Y lo que significa. Y tener un hermano así" (24). Here we see that while Jero's family welcomes his newfound sexual identity, not everyone is so enthusiastic. As the chapter title reminds us, "Not everyone likes the rainbow" / "No a todo el mundo le gusta el arco iris" (16).

Much of the novel, in fact, tracks Constanza's response to the emotional violence that her peers enact. As Constanza is only ten years old, we see through her experience how she learns about social oppression and then what she does to propel a more just vision of the world. At one point, for example, she learns about hatred directed at gay people through religion. Sofía, one of her classmates, stops by Constanza's table as she eats lunch and tells her that Jero is going to hell after he dies and that she will be separated from him for all of eternity (31). Sofía goes on to roll out the religious hate speech about the place of gay people in hell, alongside robbers and murderers, and justifies her words with "The Bible says it clearly. Didn't you know?" / "Lo dice clarito la Biblia, ¿no lo sabías?" (31).

Even as the emotional attacks continue, worse awaits in that while Jero has come out to his family, Jero's love interest, Oscar, keeps putting off telling his parents fearing their response. With each passing day, Jero is increasingly inconsolable. Then one night Jero disappears. Friends do not know where he is and even the police have trouble finding him. Their worst fears are confirmed when they get a call from the hospital. To Constanza, Jero looks worse than Rocky after he fought the Russian fighter Drago. Besides the many bruises on his face, he also has broken ribs. Oscar was also assaulted with similar painful results.

When Constanza asks if they know who is responsible, all that Jero and his parents can say is that it will never happen again. Unperturbed, Constanza keeps asking until they finally tell her that the persons responsible for attacking Jero and Oscar were Oscar's father and brother. Much in the same way that familial violence lurks in *Aristotle and Dante*, *Sombras en el arcoíris* underscores the totality of hurt when familia is responsible. As Constanza tells us, "My brother says that he doesn't know what was worse, the punches or everything they yelled at him. He didn't want to tell me what they said and I didn't want to hear it either" / "Dice mi hermano que no sabe qué fue peor, si los golpes o todo lo que les dijeron. No quiso contarme y yo tampoco quiero saberlo" (60). As hard as it is to fathom the physical violence enacted on a queer family member by other members of his family, Constanza's observations allow us to see that the wounds inflicted by words create emotional pain that can seem much worse. Calling the violence (both physical and emotional) into question, the novel ends with Constanza underscoring the unfathomable nature of homophobic hatred by noting how incomprehensible it is that "some people think that falling in love makes someone a bad person" / "por qué algunos piensan que enamorarse de alguien hace mala a una persona" (61). She is comforted, however, by the fact that not all people are like Oscar's parents, that is, that there are people like her parents, her friend Vane, and her teacher who believe "it's perfectly fine to choose whoever makes you happy" / "que lo que cada quien escoja para ser feliz está bien" (61).

To our study, *Sombras en el arcoíris* speaks to the significant role of siblings in coming-of-age queer narratives. Constanza serves as a key player in the creation of a queer familia in what is often a dangerous world for queer youth. This is to say that because violence toward queer youth exists, so too do worlds in which queer youth can feel safe and loved. Furthermore, because homophobic violence, whether physical or emotional, affects all family members to varying degrees, it is important to see the ways in which family members combat harmful beliefs and counter violence with love. In other words, familia means familia: all family members are impacted by homophobia and all stand together to create better worlds in which loyalty is an important component of love. These positive and progressive representations of familia, we argue, are invaluable for young readers as they create their own versions of queer familia.

DE DÍA GAVIOTAS, DE NOCHE FLORES BLANCAS: IT TAKES A QUEER VILLAGE

In *Post-Borderlandia*, T. Jackie Cuevas makes the astute observation that even as queer sexuality brings out the homophobic sexuality "police," it is gender nonconformity that threatens to disrupt the social order. As Cuevas underscores, "It is not necessarily queer sexualities but rather queer genders that threaten a Chicanx cultural or familial sense of unity" (3). To her observation, in this chapter we add that queer genders also pose a threat to Mexican heteronormative gender systems because of the way they disrupt traditional binaries. To illustrate our point, we here turn to Esteban Hinojosa Rebolledo's *De día gaviotas, de noche flores blancas*. Our governing idea, directly impacted by Cuevas's thesis, is that while gender nonconformity and trans identity threaten gender systems that have been naturalized over time, reconfiguring familia into queer familia allows us ways to counter these systems of oppression. Further, our analysis of Rebolledo's novel proposes that a queer village, that is, people from the larger community, can not only offset deleterious practices but also model ways to nurture queer youth. These more positive representations, we believe, go a long way toward reordering gender systems to be more just and equitable.

Set in a coastal town along the Gulf of Mexico, *De día gaviotas, de noche flores blancas* tells the story of nine-year-old Lázaro, a boy who is less interested in soccer, like his older brother, and more interested in dresses, makeup, and dances like the girls in his school (22). As the novel begins, Lárazo is fighting bouts of depression and loneliness. Angry that his family refuses to talk about his mental health or his interests, he takes off running down the street. He thankfully is rescued from being hit by a car by MiauMiau, a new hairstylist in town.

As the novel progresses, MiauMiau and La Traviata, both trans women, open Lázaro's eyes to a world in which his creativity, specifically with fabrics and colors, is welcomed. Further, they expose him to new knowledges about gender. As MiauMiau tells Lázaro when Lázaro is confused about her gender,

"Cutie, I am a woman by choice, and a very, very happy one" / "Yo soy mujer por elección, chulito. Y muy, muy feliz" (50). Showing that he understands what she is teaching, Lázaro asks MiauMiau to color his hair as a way of exploring his identity. When he looks at the green hair in the mirror, Lázaro begins to worry what his parents will say or what his classmates will think. MiauMiau then tells him that the color can simply be washed out and that MiauMiau can do it immediately. Lázaro however responds emphatically, "No—I told her almost yelling—I want to have it like this a bit longer" / "No—le dije casi gritando—Quiero tenerlo así un rato más" (52). Lázaro's newfound gender knowledges, in this way, allow him to normalize trans experiences and resist heteronormative gender binaries.

This richer array of gender knowledges is crucial at the end of the novel. With the support of La Traviata, Lázaro decides to enter the annual competition for elementary-age girls, la Reina del Verano, or the Summer Queen. Under her new name La Sarita, a word play on Lázaro, she enters the competition dressed in a gown that she made. As Sarita is announced the winner, one of her male classmates recognizes Sarita and yells "It's a boy. It's Lázaro" / "Es un niño. Es Lázaro" (157). In a dress of her own making, Sarita, in the words of Cuevas, is an "unreadable, illegible, or ambiguously gendered [body] that stand at center stage" (*Post-Borderlandia* 19). The unreadability of genderqueerness, in turn, poses a great challenge to heteronormative gender expectations. To wit, the classmate can only understand Lázaro as a boy, even as she is standing before them dressed like a girl. In other words, the classmate falls back into rigid binaries even as Sarita's gender expression has shifted the terrain around them. What is more, by his denouncing of Sarita, the classmate shows the ways in which unreadable is also rendered unacceptable. In this regard, his statement reveals a fissure in gender systems. While the classmate "reads" the dress as a mask that hides Lázaro, the dress is meant to reveal and to demand public notice. It is, to quote Sonia Rodríguez, a form of ornamentation useful for "creating epistemologies that challenge hetero-normative ways of thinking. These subversive knowledges ... assert a queer identity through style and style politics" (224). Seen through this lens, Sarita's handmade dress allows her to construct a public queer identity, one more in concert with who she understands herself to be.

Sarita's construction of a public queer identity and the response of the community to it can best be seen in the conflict over Sarita's tiara, the quintessential emblem of female gender in the beauty pageant. When the school principal tries to take the tiara off Sarita, La Traviata admonishes the crowd, "What's wrong with you all? Are you crazy? ... Are sure you want to take this dream from her? Are you sure you are capable of such cruelty?" / "¿Qué les pasa? ¿Están locos? . . . ¿Están seguros de querer quitárselo [su sueño]? ¿Están seguros de que son capaces de tanta crueldad?" (159). Here we see the dream not only of winning the pageant but of Sarita expressing herself in the way that feels most authentic to her.

Thankfully for Sarita others step in to defend her, and she finds affirmation in their actions. Sarita's father, for example, yells at the principal to take her hands off his child. Though her father does not say more, Sarita explains that "the way he defended me made me feel strong" / "su defensa me envalentonó" (160). As she moves to the front of the stage, people start applauding and the rest of the contestants "came up to me and each one gave me a kiss on the cheek" / "se acercaron a mí y me dieron cada una un beso en la mejilla" (160). Even more surprising to Sarita, her brother stands up and begins to whistle and yell out her name and stays behind, after everyone else leaves, to walk her home.

> My brother was the only one who waited there for me. He kept applauding with his hands that looked like mine, only ten years older. He winked at me and cracked a smile for my parents as if to tell me not to worry. We would go home together just as soon as we wrapped up with my duties as queen of the festival. Ever since that moment I knew that everything was alright.

> Sólo mi hermano se quedó allí para esperarme. Seguía aplaudiendo con esas manos parecidas a las mías, pero diez años más viejas. Me guiñó el ojo y torció una sonrisa hacia mis padres como para decirme que no me preocupara. Iríamos juntos a casa apenas se acabaran mis trámites de reina. Pero para entonces yo ya sabía que todo estaba bien. (161)

The novel thus concludes with Sarita's brother, who is a beloved athlete in town, walking back with Sarita to their home in support of her. He even asks her for the full story, "Are you going to tell us everything? How you won the contest? And about your dress?" / "¿Nos vas a contar todo? ¿Cómo ganaste el concurso? ¿Y ese vestido?" (162). Though we are not told of her parents' response, the novel leads us to believe that Sarita's parents too are on their journey to be as fully supportive as her brother. Sarita herself shares this desire "I desired nothing more than to stretch out in the big chair in our living room and rest with my family" / "Nada deseaba con más fuerzas que acostarme en el sillón de la sala a descansar con mi familia" (162).

In the process of describing *De día gaviotas*, author Esteban Hinojosa Rebolledo notes that his young adult novel is a polemic, an uncomfortable one for some people ("es un libro polémico, acaso incómodo para algunos") because of its engagement with LGBTQIA+ gender and sexuality. It is, he insists, at the same time, profoundly necessary, "profundamente necesario" (Catálogo). What Hinojosa Rebolledo hopes is that in the future, it will be only one more story of a young person discovering and going after their dream: "en el futuro, espero, será solo otra historia de un niño que descubre un sueño y lo persigue" (Catálogo). That is to say, in the future queerness and a queer familia will be normalized.

De día gaviotas opens a space in which Mexican queer youth can envision worlds full of potentials in which they will be loved unconditionally, that is, in which they will be full participants in a queer familia, with all the gifts and responsibilities that entails. As José Esteban Muñoz reminds us, "The future is queerness's domain" (1). These future utopias, to Muñoz, "are the hopes of a collective, an emergent group, or even the solitary oddball who is the one who dreams for many" (3). At this moment, these utopias "are the realm of educated hope" (3). Further, as Angel Matos and Jon Michael Wargo explain, the significance of envisioning these future worlds is vital for young readers: "Because children have not been restricted, hampered, or defined by the influences of knowledge and experience, their futures are therefore more open—full of promise, potentiality, and the ability to imagine a place and time different from the present" (2). Approaching futurity as a potentiality lets us read into *De día gaviotas* a future in which Sarita, her brother, and their parents reconfigure familia into queer familia. Moreover, given the importance of MiauMiau and La Traviata to Sarita's well-being and the fact that Sarita's fellow contestants and the townspeople applauded her, a future-oriented reading points us toward a world in which kids like Sarita are nurtured by a queer village and supported in their dreams.

CONCLUSION, OR THE BRIDGES OF CHICANX/MEXICAN QUEER FAMILIA

Bridges, Gloria Anzaldúa informs us, are thresholds to other realities; they are passageways and connectors that connote transitioning and changing perspectives. Anzaldúa explains that they "span liminal (threshold) spaces between worlds, spaces I call nepantla, a Nahuatl word meaning tierra entre medio" (1). *To bridge* is "to attempt community" (3); to bridge "is an act of will, an act of love, an attempt toward compassion and reconciliation, and a promise to be present with the pain of others without losing themselves to it" (4). The title of the chapter, "Atravesando Nepantla" ("Crossing Nepantla"), enlists the idea that while some see borders and abysses, we, together with Anzaldúa, choose to see places to cross, to step across the threshold, and to attempt community. Our contention, with Anzaldúa's directives in mind, is that the world is ready for more comparative studies of US Chicanx YA and Mexican literatura juvenil that bridges the border separating Chicanx from Mexican literary and cultural production.

One reason we chose to examine *Aristotle and Dante* in this study is that the novel is a bridge that connects Chicanx and Mexican YA. Translated into Spanish, the novel finds a reading public in Mexico that is greatly interested in the intersectional issues impacting Ari and Dante, from their newfound love for each other to the ways in which Chicanx youths articulate cultural identities in a country that does not always see them as belonging in the national imaginary. Booktuber Alberto Villareal, for example, notes in his channel AbriendoLibros that while the novel is about "dos chavos que viven en Estados Unidos" ("two young men who live in the United States"), Ari and Dante in fact are two chavos of "ascendencia mexicana" ("Mexican ancestry"). A young adult himself, Villareal goes on to add that while Ari and Dante face similar issues to that of most young adults, of special interest to his audience is the way in which the characters live "en esta línea en medio" (in "the borderlands") in which "no pertenecen a Estados Unidos y no pertenecen a México" ("they do not belong in the US and they do not belong in Mexico"). Young adult booktuber Sam Ponbe likewise mentions this nepantla state of being separated from and connected to various cultures. As she explains, "al vivir en Estados Unidos y tener ascendencia mexicana puede resultar más difícil el que ellos encuentren su identidad" ("living in the US and having Mexican heritage can make it more difficult for them to find their identity"). What these two booktubers tell us is that young readers in Mexico are greatly interested in Ari and Dante's intersectional identity formations. That both booktubers note Ari and Dante's Mexican ancestry provides further evidence that young readers in Mexico not only find links between themselves and the novel's characters but are also creating solidarity and allyship with the characters. In other words Ari and Dante are like them—part of a larger familia that young readers wish to know more about in order to form bridges from which to contest the oppressions they all face.

In our study, atravesando nepantla in Chicanx and Mexican YA literature allows us to see the ways in which these transnational reading spaces have the potential to disrupt the emotional and physical violence of homophobia and antiqueerness. In examining the loving and nurturing forms of queer familia across our shared space of nepantla in these pieces of young adult literature, our study demonstrates that young Chicanx and Mexican readers, when presented a more coherent view of their intertwined transnational lives, can find common ground in these novels. Firmly planted in this shared space of nepantla, these young readers, we believe, can begin tracing the ways in which queer familia can be sustaining and how one can be sustained by queer familia. In this regard, queer familia becomes a strategic site for novel forms of resistance and solidarity that are hemispheric and transnational. Instead of allowing national borders and cultural boundaries to separate them, young readers can begin the artful crafting of queer familias informed by their common goals and aspirations. Much can be gained, therefore, if we move across our shared nepantla.

NOTES

1. We use the term *Chicanx* to refer to people of Mexican descent living primarily in the United States and *Mexican* to refer to people of Mexican descent living in Mexico. One of our hopes in using these terms is to point to the specific points of transnational connection between Chicanxs and Mexicans who share a common history, culture, border, and oftentimes language. The term "Latinx" also appears in our article in moments where scholars speak to Latinx culture (people of Latin American descent, including Mexico, living primarily in the US) more broadly.

2. See for example reviews by Mexican Booktuber Alberto Villareal in his channel AbriendoLibros and Mexican Booktuber Sam Ponbe.

3. M. Roxana Loza's study on familial trauma is especially pertinent here. The stereotype of the silent, emotionally unsupportive father abounds in literature in film. And yet, as Loza persuasively shows about *Aristotle and Dante*, Ari's father's trauma-induced silence was caused by his experiences in the Vietnam War. Seen from Loza's lens, silences and disengaged parenting by Latinx fathers need to be examined at the macro level, that is, how traumatic events such as war, crossing the border, or racism and ethnophobia impact fathers. For more information, see Loza.

4. Carolina Alonso calls for treating this topic of violence and queer coming-of-age narratives with care and attention. In opposition to "bury your gays" tropes commonly found in young adult literature, Alonso calls for more positive representation of Chicanx young adults exploring their burgeoning sexuality, specifically when this means growing up in the midst of societal and familial violence. Considering the violence surrounding queer youth, "Positive representation in literature is not just entertainment; it is a vital source of support and empowerment" (187).

5. Frederick Luis Aldama and Arturo Aldama's introduction to *Decolonizing Latinx Masculinities* offers much on this topic. Part testimonio and part call to action for decolonizing hegemonic masculinity, los Brothers Aldama investigate the colonial, neocolonial, and exploitative capitalist roots of toxic masculinities and then put forth a plan for the dismantling of all things machista. To our study, this is specifically important for queergenders

and queersexualities. As they note, it is time for Chicanx folx to reconfigure the "concept of family to be gender- and queer-inclusive" (6).

6. Loza wisely observes that in moments like these, *Aristotle and Dante* depicts ways in which healing help both father and son deal with the generational trauma that impacts both. In this way, they "are able to move forward and begin to shed some of the painful experiences that weighed them down" (8). For more information, see Loza.

7. All translations are ours.

WORKS CITED

Aldama, Frederick Luis and Arturo J. Aldama. "Decolonizing Latinx Masculinities: An Introduction." *Decolonizing Latinx Masculinities*, edited by Arturo J. Aldama and Frederick Luis Aldama. University of Arizona Press, 2020, 3–19.

Alonso, Carolina. "The Coming-of-Age Experience in Chicanx Queer Novels *What Night Brings* and *Aristotle and Dante Discover the Secrets of the Universe*." *Nerds, Goths, Geeks, and Freaks: Outsiders in Chicanx and Latinx Young Adult Literature*, edited by Trevor Boffone and Cristina Herrera. University Press of Mississippi, 2020, 175–90.

Anzaldúa, Gloria. "Preface: (Un)natural Bridges, (Un)Safe Spaces." *This Bridge We Call Home: Radical Visions for Transformation*, edited by Gloria Anzaldúa and AnaLouise Keating. Routledge, 2002, 1–4.

Brozon, Mónica B. *Sombras en el arcoíris*. Illustrated by Rául Nieto Guridi. Fondo de Cultura Económica, 2017.

Cuevas, T. Jackie. "Fighting the Good Fight: Grappling with Queerness, Masculinities, and Violence in Contemporary Latinx Literature and Film." *Decolonizing Latinx Masculinities*, edited by Arturo J. Aldama and Frederick Luis Aldama. University of Arizona Press, 2020, 131–150.

Cuevas, T. Jackie. *Post-Borderlandia: Chicana Literature and Gender Variant Critique*. Rutgers University Press, 2018.

Del Castillo, Adelaida R. "Introduction: Queer Chicano/Mexicano Accounts of Fathers, Fathering, and Fatherhood." *Fathers, Fathering, and Fatherhood: Queer Chicano/Mexicano Desire and Belonging*, edited by Adelaida R. Del Castillo and Gibrán Güido. Palgrave Macmillan, 2021, 1–20.

Gottlieb, Andrew. "Introduction." *Side By Side: On Having a Gay or Lesbian Sibling*, edited by Andrew Gottlieb. Routledge, 2005, 1–5.

Lee, Ariana. "I Was the First to Know." *Side By Side: On Having a Gay or Lesbian Sibling*, edited by Andrew Gottlieb, Routledge, 2005, 13–16.

Loza, M. Roxana. "He Doesn't Talk:" Silence, Trauma, and Fathers in *Aristotle and Dante Discover the Secrets of the Universe* and *I Am Not Your Perfect Mexican Daughter*." *Label Me Latina/o* 11 (2021). Edited by Trevor Boffone and Cristina Herrera.

Matos, Angel Daniel. "A Narrative of a Future Past: Historical Authenticity, Ethics, and Queer Latinx Futurity in *Aristotle and Dante Discover the Secrets of the Universe*." *Children's Literature* 47, no. 1 (2019): 30–56.

Matos, Angel Daniel, and Jon Michael Wargo. "Editors' Introduction: Queer Futurities in Youth Literature, Media, and Culture," *Research on Diversity in Youth Literature* 2, no. 1 (2019): 1–16.

Moraga, Cherríe. "Queer Aztlán." *The Last Generation*. South End Press, 1993, 145–74.

Muñoz, José Esteban. *Cruising Utopia: The Then and There of Queer Futurity*. NYU Press, 2009.

Orchard, William, and Yolanda Padilla. "'You Choose Your Space and You Fight There': An Interview with Ramón Saldívar." *Bridges, Borders, and Breaks: History, Narrative, and Nation in Twenty-First-Century Chicana/o Literary Criticism*, edited by William Orchard and Yolanda Padilla. University of Pittsburgh Press, 2016, 177–200.

Pérez, Daniel Enrique. "Like Father, Like Queer Son? Gay Chicanx and Latinx Males and Their Fathers." *Fathers, Fathering, and Fatherhood: Queer Chicano/Mexicano Desire and Belonging*, edited by Adelaida R. Del Castillo and Gibrán Güido. Palgrave Macmillan, 2021, 233–54.

Ponbe, Sam. "Reseña: *Aristóteles y Dante descubren los secretos del universo*." *YouTube*, 14 March 2021. https://youtu.be/FBPsNXKU1do, accessed 1 August 2022.

Postma-Montaño, Regan. "Naturalizing the Border: Eco-Justice Poetics in *Aristotle and Dante Discover the Secrets of the Universe* and *All the Stars Denied*." *Research on Diversity in Youth Literature* 4, no. 2 (2022): 1–25.

Rebolledo, Esteban Hinojosa. *De día gaviotas, de noche flores blancas*. Illustrated by Oliver Marino. Punto de Vista Editores, 2017.

Rebolledo, Esteban Hinojosa. "Catálogo: *De día gaviotas, de noche flores blancas*." Punto de Vista Editores. http://puntodevistaeditores.com/catalogo/de-dia-gaviotas/. Accessed 1 March 2022.

Rhodes, Cristina. "Imagining the Future: The (Im)Possibilities of Queerness in Two Latinx Speculative Young Adult Novels." *Label Me Latina/o* 11 (2021): 1–10. Edited by Trevor Boffone and Cristina Herrera.

Rodríguez, Richard T. "Making Queer *Familia*." *Routledge Queer Studies Reader*, edited by Donald E. Hall and Annamarie Jagose. Routledge, 2012, 324–32.

Rodríguez, Richard T. *Next of Kin: The Family in Chicano/a Cultural Politics*. Duke University Press, 2009.

Rodríguez, Sonia Alejandra. "'Fierce and Fearless': Dress and Identity in Rigoberto González's *The Mariposa Club*." *MeXicana Fashions: Politics, Self-Adornment, and Identity Construction*, edited by Aída Hurtado and Norma E. Cantú. University of Texas Press, 2020, 216–34.

Sáenz, Benjamin Alire. *Aristotle and Dante Discover the Secrets of the Universe*. Simon and Schuster, 2012.

Solis, Jared. "Max Pelayo y Reese Gonzales protagonizan 'Aristóteles y Dante' la peli basada en un exitoso libro." *Nación Flix*, 13 October 2021. https://www.nacionflix.com/cine/Max-Pelayo-y-Reese-Gonzales-protagonizan-Aristoteles-y-Dante-la-peli-basada-en-un-exitoso-libro-20211013-0006.html. Accessed 1 August 2022.

Villareal, Alberto. "*Aristótles y Dante descubren los secretos del universo*, Benjamin Alire." *YouTube*, AbriendoLibros, 2 June 2015. https://youtu.be/GPwwHGqfouE, accessed 1 Aug. 2022.

Section Four

Queer Futurities

Chapter Eleven

ROSES AND REMEDIOS

La Llorona's Queer Children in *When the Moon Was Ours*

Domino Renee Pérez

On the book jacket of Anna-Marie McLemore's *When the Moon Was Ours* (2016), the author's biography indicates that they were "born in the foothills of the San Gabriel Mountains . . . and taught by [their] family to hear *la llorona* in the Santa Ana winds."[1] La Llorona, the weeping woman of diasporic Mexican folklore purported to have drowned her children, serves as the subject of countless stories that emphasize sorrow and punishment. Known for haunting the shores of rivers, lakes, and other waterways, she is the woman in white who murdered her children and wanders for eternity, as punishment, in search of their bodies. Such a terrifying tale about a child killer might not seem like a subject that would lend itself to younger audiences. But stories aimed at children, ranging from the board book *La Llorona* (2018) by Patty Rodriguez and Arla Stein to young adult books such as *Summer of the Mariposas* (2012) by Guadalupe Garcia McCall and *Throw* (2018) by Ruben Degollado, prominently feature La Llorona and her story.[2] While some authors portray her simply as a scary villain, over the years Latinx authors have imagined La Llorona in ways that refuse certain elements commonly included in her stories (such as the infanticide or the heterosexism embedded in traditional versions) to reimagine this powerful figure for children of all ages. So instead of a predatory child snatcher, she is a protector, healer, and guide, while also serving as a means of educating young Latinx readers, through folklore, about storytelling traditions and imparting cultural knowledge in ethno-racial communities. McLemore's own family naturalized La

Llorona into the Southern California landscape as a predatory figure looking to steal innocent children and whose voice traveled on the wind.

In *When the Moon Was Ours*, McLemore offers their own fantastical story about La Llorona and the lives of her queer children. Within the context of the story, queer, as defined by Steven Bruhm and Natasha Hurley in *Curiouser: On the Queerness of Children*, is best understood as both "the sense of being odd or peculiar" and "of being outside the usual and accepted parameters of the sexual child" (xiv). The narrative focuses on siblings Miel and Leandro, who both drown in the river. Miel is swept away during her mother's attempts to "cure" her daughter's affliction—the sprouting roses from her wrist—by holding the girl beneath the surface of the water. Leandro jumps into the water to save his sister after the river carries her away, but both succumb to its power. The story indicates that Miel's drowning was accidental, the desperate act of a terrified mother trying to "save" her child from a life of thorns and blood at the insistence of the church priest, other women, and in response to her husband's more brutal methods. Both children find life (and love) after they drown. Reborn with her uncanny ability intact, Miel develops a deepening emotional and eventually physical relationship with Sam, a transgender boy who hangs reflective moons around their town. Leandro, in her true form as a woman, emerges from the river as Aracely, an older gifted curandera with the power to cure people of love sickness.

McLemore's fantastical tale takes its inspiration, in part, from European storytelling traditions. McLemore's novels, such as *The Weight of Feathers* (2015); *Wild Beauty* (2017); *Blanca & Roja* (2018); *Miss Meteor* (cowritten with Tehlor Kay Mejia) (2020); *Dark and Deepest Red* (2020); *The Mirror Season* (2021); and *Lakelore* (2022), often identified as magical realism, sit squarely in young adult fantasy fiction.[3] The author has stated, more specifically, that their work is very much inspired by fairy tales (Richmond, "About"). Garnering the attention and favor of critics, McLemore's novels have appeared on best books lists, including those compiled by *Kirkus* and *Booklist*. In 2016, *When the Moon Was Ours* was longlisted for the National Book Award in Young People's Literature and won the Stonewall Honor Award in 2017. Understanding all too well the impact of young people seeing themselves and/or their experiences represented in the works they consume, McLemore has devoted themselves to writing stories as "queer, Latine, and non-binary as they are" (Richmond, "About").[4] With *When the Moon Was Ours*, however, their goals were much more specific: "At the heart of this book is my belief that transgender characters, queer characters, and characters of color deserve fairy tales" (Joe). The author indicates a lack of presence of or an emphasis on queer people of color (QPOC) and/or transgender characters in fairy tales. Arguably, characters that can be read as queer, though none is explicitly identified as such, appear in fairy tales, as for example the Pied Piper, Rumpelstiltskin, and the Snow Queen. These same figures are presented as antagonists, threats to heterosexual romance and the symbolic futurity of children or youth as represented through the children of Hamlin, the miller's daughter, and Snow White. McLemore flips this script, in part, by having cisgender ostensibly heterosexual young women serve as the antagonists in their fairy tale, while the unambiguously queer couple serve as the central protagonists who persevere together. The resolution of their story affirms both their lives and love within the space of the fairy tale.

McLemore's expressly writing their way into a European storytelling tradition is representative of a process that José Esteban Muñoz calls *disidentification*. To disidentify," according to Muñoz, "is to read oneself and one's own life narrative in a moment, object, or subject that is not culturally coded to 'connect' with the disidentifying subject" (12). Through this process, McLemore transforms from within the white European heteronormative space of the fairy tale and its compulsory heterosexuality with the help of Chicanx folklore. At the same time, the indeterminate past that characterizes the temporality of the fairy tale allows McLemore to write their characters into both a history and a present. In doing so, McLemore creates for their QPOC and transgender characters what Angel Daniel Matos has termed "a future past," one that allows for both an undetermined past and a future present that makes space for a "positive affect" (39). For McLemore's QPOC and transgender characters that means finding love, support, and "the freedom to live outside" strict gender roles (Foulis). So although the author does not identify which kinds of fairy tales Black, Indigenous, people of color (BIPOC), transgender, or queer characters *deserve*, based on the outcome of *When the Moon Was Ours*, presumably they mean ones with happy endings.

The novel draws upon and makes evident the relationality between European and Chicanx storytelling traditions. A brief overview of the relationship between the two forms is necessary to understand how both intersect in McLemore's novel. Folklore and fairy tales are objectively and historically intertwined. Both are stories that teach, often an ideal set of values and behaviors. However, in *Children's Literature: A Reader's History from Aesop to Harry Potter* (2008), Seth Lerer distinguishes the *fairy tale* as an English "translation of the French *conte de fées*, the genre that arose in the salon to narrate social criticism or offer moral instruction under the guise of fantasy" (210). These stories found enthusiastic audiences among courtiers, aristocrats, and in literary salons across Europe. From there, the "fairy tale grew, as a literary genre out of the folk stories of the European past" and, "as we know them now, are really the creation of literature collectors, editors, and authors, working from the late seventeenth until the mid-nineteenth century" (210). The fairy tale genre is often associated with Charles Perrault's French fairy stories, more popularly known as Mother Goose, which are based on older folktales and written to entertain children; Hans Christian Andersen's *Fairy Tales Told for Children*, published in three installments from 1835 to 1837, which include classics such as "Thumbelina," "The Little Mermaid," and "The Emperor's New Clothes"; and most famously, the German brothers Jacob and Wilhelm Grimm, folklorists and philologists known for *Kinder- und Hausmärchen* (*Children's and Household Tales* 1812–22), now more widely known as *Grimm's Fairy Tales*. Across popular culture, these stories endure to this day, from the television series *Once Upon a Time* (2011–2018), set in the fictional town of Storybrooke, Maine, and populated by such personages as Prince Charming, Snow White, the Evil Queen, and Rumpelstiltskin, to the live-action films *Red Riding Hood* (2011), *Cinderella* (2015), and *Beauty and the Beast* (2017).

YA reimaginings of fairy tales, including queer retellings, abound and are incredibly popular with readers. For example, the following represent only a handful of novels that recast *one* fairy tale. *Cinder* (2012), the first book in The Lunar Chronicles series (2012–2015) by Marissa Meyer, takes a science fiction approach to one of the most widely known fairy tales—Cinderella.[5] Malinda Lo's *Ash* (2009) also represents a retelling of a Cinderella story, where the titular heroine is pulled into a queer love triangle involving a fairy and a huntress. Similarly, Kaylynn Bayron's *Cinderella Is Dead* (2022) turns the familiar tale inside out and has the QPOC protagonist seeking out Prince Charming, not to marry, but instead to murder. Rather than a retelling of a familiar story, McLemore takes the folktale about La Llorona and turns it into a dark fairy tale about her children, complete with witches, entombment, glass pumpkins, and magical transformations, to create something new in a familiar form. *When the Moon Was Ours* is clearly not the first book to interpolate QPOC characters into fairy tales, but McLemore's work is distinct for the way they demonstrate the unequivocal connection between folklore and fairy tales, using the former to transform the latter from within.

THERE WAS A WOMAN

La Llorona's story is one that many have told and heard over centuries, resulting in a number of different versions. McLemore's family story about hearing La Llorona voice in the Santa Ana winds represents one such version. Folktales about her can teach, entertain, frighten, or import cultural values, and sometimes do all of these at once. Her stories often begin with the phrase "there was a woman." To speak of this "woman" in the past tense creates distance between the event narrated in the story about her and the present. In other words, she is located at a far enough distance to not be an immediate threat, though she might be according to traditional versions that figure her as a predator.[6] McLemore also locates La Llorona's story in the past and uses it as the basis for their fairy tale in unexpected ways.

In the late twentieth century, Chicanx writers took up La Llorona's story and revised her traditional position in the lore "as a despairing figure who has lost both her man and her children" (Perez 23). Reimagined and reconfigured, writers draw upon La Llorona to critique the patriarchy and heterosexism at the center of the story, and more widely to comment on such issues as environmental pollution, immigration, domestic abuse, and war in Central America, to name but a few. Cordelia Candelaria in her 1993 poetic triptych ("La Llorona at Sixteen"; "La Llorona: Portrait by the River"; "Go 'Way from My Window, La Llorona") offers an unusual perspective on the woman of legend, one that imagines her before the tragedy that marks her life of weeping and wandering for the children she has lost. The shift in the temporal locus emphasizes that prior to an eternity of searching for her lost children, the woman who would become La Llorona was an innocent young person who was marked by tragedy. Monica Palacios's short story "La Llorona Loca: The Other Side" (1991) revises the darkness of the tale by infusing it with humor, centrally featuring a lesbian romance, and not including children in her story. The latter shifts the narrative violence away from the children and onto other sites. Though neither Candelaria nor Palacios's works is aimed at children, their versions of La Llorona represent significant revisions to the traditional stories that feature La Llorona, a quality both share with, for example, Gloria Anzaldúa's picture book *Prietita and the Ghost Woman* (2001) and Garcia McCall's young adult novel *Summer of the Mariposas*, which includes such figures as the lechuza, chupacabra, and La Llorona.[7] Anzaldúa's Llorona serves as a teacher who silently guides the protagonist to the curative plant she needs to help heal her mother. Prietita learns through her encounter that La Llorona is not the sinister figure described in stories. Similarly, in Garcia McCall's novel, La Llorona acts as guide and protector for the five sisters at the center of the novel.[8] Moreover, La Llorona tells "her side of the story which she has never been able to tell on her own terms," thereby using her voice to teach the protagonist, as Cristina Herrera asserts, how "to refute patriarchy" so that the sisters can exercise more authority over their futures, ones not dependent on men like their wayward father (103). In *When the Moon Was Ours*, McLemore offers a fantastical version of a La Llorona story that gives voice to the "lost" children, affirming their presence outside of tragedy and mapping a future direction for their lives.

Historically, the children have no agency, have no voice, and remain innocent. They are narrated pawns in a heteropatriarchal, heterosexist power struggle, plunged beneath the surface of the water to drown. In the aftermath, it is the mother we hear weeping and wailing for her lost children. McLemore retains a portion of this narrative. Miel recalls her mother holding her down in the water, moments before they are swept away: "The memory of her mother's screaming rang through her head. It splintered into each trembling note, and then resolved into a clear, haunted sound" (*When the Moon* 158). Not knowing "that the drought had given what little water was left [in the river] claws," Miel's mother "accidentally" drowns her daughter (158). The older brother Leandro "dies" trying to save his sister and mother. Both children are magically saved by the spirit of the water that protects them and releases them to new lives. Miel is mysteriously reborn from the town's felled water tower. Leandro, however, emerges from the river transformed and takes the name Aracely. When Miel spills out of the water tower alone and afraid, Aracely assumes responsibility for the new orphan without revealing their relationship to each other. The children are reunited, but forever altered by everything they have experienced. As a Llorona figure, the mother disappears from the narrative as easily as she slips beneath the water, though her memory lingers on and impacts her children, who are haunted by what she did. Regardless, the siblings give voice to the circumstances that lead to their mother's horrific choice.

La Llorona's actions make possible the events of the fairy tale. Trying to "save" her daughter in the river creates the conditions for the fairy tale about Miel and Aracely's lives. The river becomes a place of transition and transformation, a borderland, where the siblings cross over from one life into the next, having been rebirthed by the spirit of the water. In this way, the river serves, in place of a fairy godmother, as an intervening figure that does what their mother could not: "That water, that river that did not save their mother, had adopted them. It had found [Miel] and Leandro when their mother couldn't. It had kept them until it decided it was time to let them go" (223). The river understands Miel and Leandro's innocence, as well as their suffering, and gifts the siblings a second chance to be together. It also becomes the place where folklore and fairy tale meet.

ONCE UPON A TIME...

Fairy tales often begin with four familiar words: "once upon a time." The temporal logic of such a phrase locates the story in an ambiguous past while at the same time opening up space, at least narratively, toward a future that may or may not yet have come to pass. *When the Moon Was Ours* does not open with the familiar phrase, but it does create the same temporal distance between the present and the events of the story so that they could have happened "once upon a time" in a distant, or not so distant, past. Undefined, "fictional representations of the past," as Matos's own analysis of *Aristotle and Dante Discover the Secrets of the Universe* (2012) suggests, "enable more egalitarian, open, and emotionally nourishing ways of thinking about the world we inhabit in the present, and the queer futures that have yet to arrive" (Matos 33). Once Miel's roses appear, the siblings are subject to abuse, fear, shame, and intolerance. The fantastical place McLemore creates for Sam, Miel, and Aracely is not without dangers of its own, but it does provide them ultimately a place of safety and belonging where they can be nurtured emotionally and loved.

Certain conventions exist in fairy tales. They have familiar beginnings, magic, and most have morals. *When the Moon Was Ours* offers "true love conquers all" as its moral. While that lesson may seem trite, it is one delivered to powerful effect through fantasy and McLemore's own pointed social criticism regarding the exclusionary practices and heteronormativity of fairy tales. McLemore's work pushes back against the prescriptive moralizing of conventional fairy tales, namely the obedient adherence to community belonging often achieved through self-sacrifice. At the same time, McLemore mindfully refuses any single experience for their transgender characters so that each emerges as a subject rather than a trope or "figuration."[9] The latter distinction contradicts Roberta Trites's observations about "gay and lesbian YA novels" and "the limits of queer discourse at work in adolescent literature . . . as a group they show how a genre can become more self-aware of a social issue without necessarily providing the reader with progressively transformative experiences" (104). And yet, transformation is at the heart of *When the Moon was Ours*.

The interpolation of QPOC and transgender characters into the heteronormative fairy tale form draws attention to their previous absence, while at the same time transforming it from within and giving audiences who identify with the characters a point of connection. In an effort to give BIPOC and queer characters the fairy tales "they deserve," the author engages in a process of disidentification by centralizing QPOC and transgender characters in a fairy tale of their own making. As a strategy for dealing with dominant ideologies, such as fairy tales and the messages contained therein, disidentification "works on and against dominant ideology" (11). Muñoz further elucidates this process:

> Instead of buckling under the pressures of dominant ideology (identification, assimilation) or attempting to break free of its inescapable sphere (counter-identification, utopianism), this "working on and against" is a strategy that tries to transform a cultural logic from within, always laboring to enact permanent structural change while at the same time valuing the importance of local or everyday struggles of resistance. (11–12)

The alterity of Sam, Miel, and Areceli cause each to struggle against community values and ideas of belonging. They are aware of their differences and actively working, through different strategies, to carve out a space of belonging for themselves without compromising who they are individually. Almost two decades have passed since Trites's work on white queer YA novels. Queer YA fiction has changed substantially to represent a wide range of LGBTQIA+ experiences, including those of BIPOC youth. By placing a queer romance front and center, McLemore transforms the heterosexual cultural logic embedded in fairy tales to make space for and align with her QPOC and transgender characters who find love, acceptance, and a place (or someone) to call home.

The author crafts a fairy tale romance between Sam (Pakistani American) and Miel (Latine), who are initially drawn together as children, a transgender immigrant boy and a girl who tumbled out of a water tower. The two fortify their bond further through their alterity: Sam for the beautiful moons he paints and hangs from the trees around town; Miel for the hem of her dress that always drips water; and together for the love they share. Their romance is one filled with longing, tenderness, an understanding of "each other's bodies," and is consummated in detail "on the page" (McLemore, "Everything We Are"). Indicative of most fairy tale romances, the path to Miel and Sam's happy ending is filled with everyday struggles, as well as profound hardship. McLemore embraces the more terrifying aspects often present in fairy tales to demonstrate the violence visited on and used against Sam and Miel to keep them apart. They do so most effectively through the Bonner sisters.

McLemore turns to unsettling themes such as violence, death, and disfigurement in their fairy tale. Miel suffers profoundly at the hands of the Bonner sisters, known throughout town as las gringas bonitas (the beautiful white girls). Whiteness is often associated with La Llorona through the tattered dress she wears as she weeps and wails. It also visibly marks her and makes her legible as a threat to others, though primarily to children and men. McLemore disarticulates the whiteness associated with La Llorona and, instead, visually associates it with the Bonner sisters, thereby marking *them* as the threat in the novel. The red-haired sisters, who are rarely seen apart and often act as a single unit, like a pack, serve as the principal antagonists, terrorizing and repeatedly violating Miel for the blooms on her wrist. The Bonner girls (believed by some townspeople to be witches) have the ability to secure the romantic attention of any man they desire, but their powers are waning. Las gringas bonitas believe that Miel's magical roses are the key to restoring their potency and swear to possess them by any means possible. In an effort to coerce Miel into willingly relinquishing her roses, the sisters threaten to reveal the secrets about Miel's flowers and her mother's death, both of which she keeps hidden. One of the Bonner girls claims to have "heard a story from a woman a few towns up the river . . . about a woman who tried to kill her children and then herself" (42). The details convey the elements of a Llorona story, but the sisters are not as interested in the particulars of what happened as they are in the shame the details will cause Miel if revealed publicly. Another sister later accuses Miel of not caring about her dead mother. Still, these threats are not enough for Miel to submit. So when she refuses, the sisters take the roses by force: "The sideboard drawer slid shut, the wood rasping against a worn track. But Miel didn't see the scissors until Ivy was peeling back her sweater sleeve. Tarnish dulled the brass of the blades, the handle rubbed shiny by the oils of the Bonner's hands. . . . Ivy snipped the stem. The cut bit into Miel, like thorns waited under her skin. She cried out just a second before biting back the sound" (44). The violation of Miel's body by cutting the rose from her wrist is reminiscent of a sexual assault. This association is made more substantial by the symbolic association between flowers and sexuality, menstruation, and virginity. Stealing the rose is an act of power exercised by the beautiful sisters, who hold sway over the town, to bend Miel to their will. The Bonner sisters escalate their menacing of Miel, first by imprisoning her in a glass coffin and then by threatening to show the town Sam's birth certificate indicating that he had been assigned female at birth. The latter motivates Miel to compromise by providing one rose for each of the sisters. At this point, she *chooses* to give up her roses to protect Sam's secret from the town.

Sam and Miel's romance is central to the novel, but a secondary, equally powerful love story also emerges: a love between siblings so great that one dies trying to save the other. After, Leandro jumps into the water to rescue his sister and is swept away, the two do not again cross paths until Miel tumbles from the water tower. Aracely steps forward and becomes her sister's guardian, all while keeping her past identity and actual relationship to Miel a secret. Rather than from feelings of shame or a desire to deceive, Aracely withholds the story of her transformation from Miel as a form of protection. The curandera believes that disclosing the truth in full will cause her sister to remember the abuse their parents inflicted or the circumstances around events at the river that altered both their lives. Additionally, Aracely worries that Miel will not understand the change her older sibling has undergone. Indeed, later when Miel initially learns the truth, she accuses Aracely of "hiding" in a new form to escape the shame of their mother's actions. Aracely explains to her sister: "Miel, . . . [this] isn't me hiding. Me trying to be her son, that was hiding" (225). Miel's reaction is derived from not knowing the desire her sibling harbored in secret. In her former life, Aracely never revealed a need to express a gender identity different from Leandro's, though she later confesses that such a longing would have gone unfulfilled due to familial and cultural expectation, largely because "the boundaries constructed by . . . culture to define and contain gender" would have made such a desire an impossibility (Stryker 1). But the river sees the selflessness of Leandro's actions and fulfills his wish.

The river, however, changes the brother Miel knew in a number of unexpected ways, too: "But the water took Leandro, folded him into its current, brought him back as the girl he'd always wished he could grow into. Not a girl. A woman, finished and grown" (102). Aracely's desired, biological, and expressed gender are brought into alignment, but the process also ages her. As a guardian for the siblings, "The water had felt [Aracely's] sorrow, her broken heart because she had failed to save her sister. That sorrow had aged her heart, made her grown instead of a child. So the water made the outside of her show the truth in all ways, not just by making her a woman, but by making her old enough to match her bitter heart" (102). The river delivers Aracely to a future-present, one that affirms her identity not as a child, but as a transgender Latine woman. "There is tremendous damage," according to Julian Gill-Peterson in *Histories of the Transgender Child* (2018), "in the figurative separation of racialized trans negativity and white trans childhood futurity" (2). More specifically, in *Brown Trans Figurations: Rethinking Race, Gender, and Sexuality in Chicanx/Latinx Studies*, Francisco J. Galarte expresses concerns about "what kind of future brown trans folks are imagined as looking toward and how their narratives are imagined" (7). Galarte surmises that the "answers to both questions appear to be characterized by solitude and pain" (7). McLemore refuses this particular figuration for their transgender characters. Sam and Meil find happiness together, and Aracely's life is an affirmation of Latine queer futurity through her family with Miel and. by extension, Sam and his mother. Together they make their own version of happily ever after.

The bridging of folklore and fairy tale through *When the Moon Was Ours* reflects McLemore's own childhood fears about "la llorona [sic], the mythical spirit-woman who had drowned her children and now wailed through the night, looking to steal [mestizo children] . . . from our parents" (271). Those fears directly informed their project to "reimagine the legend of la llorona [sic] in a book about a girl who fears pumpkins and a boy who paints moons." McLemore goes on to add: "All I knew as a child was that my fear of her was evidence that I'd been born between two worlds" (271). And in that in-betweenness, that borderland, like the river in their story, McLemore makes for themselves what they always wanted and imagined but never had.

AND THEY LIVED . . .

When the Moon Was Ours attempts to present a sympathetic version of La Llorona's story within a fairy tale landscape complete with a moral, magic, obstacles, and an ever-after. The book does not revise the figure of La Llorona in any significant way: she is still responsible for the deaths of her children. But it does give voice to the weeping woman's children, who live beyond the events in the river. The book addresses a major absence in La Llorona lore, while also raising a series of troubling issues. While Miel and Aracely's survival and voicing of the trauma caused by their mother's actions represent a notable departure from traditional versions of the lore, they also further entrench La Llorona's position as an instrument of the heteropatriarchy.

When the Moon Was Ours offers a complicated, and troubling, view of the power of normativity and how it motivates a mother to drown the difference out of her daughter in order to "save" her. The mother believes her husband's reading and interpretations of the roses that sprout from their daughter's wrist—they are an abomination that auger doom for the family. She defers to his authority and believes that something must be done to help her daughter, which initially includes binding Miel's wrist. But when the father presses the hot butter knife against his daughter's skin, this is a step too far: "The mother had never disagreed with their father that their daughter needed to be cured. She's just disagreed on the method. . . . Her mother held to her conviction that she could cure Miel without hurting her" (221). In other words, the mother believes that Miel's physical alterity, her queerness, is a problem that needs to be "fixed," an idea at the heart of "reparative" or "conversion therapy" that purports to "cure," most often through physical or spiritual methods, LGBTQ folx. The father is so fearful of Miel's determined future that he abandons the family. Miel's mother also worries about her daughter's roses destroying their family, so much so that that she cannot see that her efforts accomplish what the roses alone could not.

The mother accidentally kills her daughter to save her and is motivated to do so by those around her, including her husband, the priest, and the other women in the community. They all convince her that Miel needs healing, and she succumbs to their fear mongering: "What woman could ignore the warnings of señoras and priests who said they knew how to save her child? How could she not bring her daughter down to the river when they promised the current would take this curse from her?" (254). She sees her methods, which include sealing Miel in a pumpkin shell overnight, as less violent than those of her husband. The possibility of seeing Miel's roses as something other than negative does not occur to the mother. Instead, she sees her daughter and the roses separately: one as good and the other as unquestionably bad. The distinction calls to mind the Christian cliché, "love the sinner, hate the sin." Watching her daughter fight for air beneath the surface of the water, the mother sees "it as proof that these roses had cursed her, that her daughter was pure and good and just needed to be saved" (158). In order to make her daughter normal, the mother sees her actions as justified and, even more troubling, as an expression of the love she has for her daughter.

The novel also places the burden of explaining (and rationalizing) the mother's abusive actions on the children. After revealing her true identity to Miel, Aracely tries to soothe her sister's feelings of guilt about and responsibility for their mother's death: "She loved you. . . . But she got lost thinking that your roses were something outside of you. . . . She never wanted to hurt you" (223). However, this kind of thinking, especially about queer children, reinscribes and apologizes for the violence done to them in the name of "love" or "protection." Even more unsettling is the idea that "love" gave their mother permission to do bad things that were *perceived* as less harmful than those done by her husband. But pumpkins, water, and the memory of her father's hot knife are all equally terrifying to Miel. There is no distinction in the trauma those experiences caused for her. Still, Miel eventually comes around to Aracely's way of thinking to believe that her mother had, in fact, loved her: "Her mother hadn't hated her. She knew that. She'd feared for her. She'd loved Miel, seen her as a daughter she could lose to petals and thorns. She'd been a young mother little older than Aracely, panicked and desperate to hold on to the children she's made" (254). Miel even goes so far as to rationalize her father's abuse as acts of love: "Maybe her father had [loved her] too. Maybe all he did—the bandages so tight her fingers turned numb, the end of the butter knife in the gas flame—was the form his love had taken. Maybe fear had twisted it, leaving it threadbare" (254). Regardless, both parents deny Miel's bodily autonomy and refuse to accept her difference. Love conquers all may be the moral of this fairy tale, yet it does not excuse or justify abuse done in the service of normativity. To be sure, the magic of the river delivers the siblings from familial history of violence and into new lives. But it does not disentangle them from their alterity. Rather, it delivers them more fully into it, and therein lies how McLemore's fairy tale works against the dominant ideology about queer and transgender bodies both in and outside of the novel. One need not look further than the sports, bathroom, healthcare, and education bans targeting transgender youth in more than ten states across the US. Fantasy and magic serve as tools McLemore uses to narrate queer and transgender characters into an aspirational future.

The future present of the fairy tale in which the siblings find themselves is not any less fearful of queerness than the one they knew. But the narrative removes Miel and Aracely from the most immediate threat—their parents. Through their made family, the siblings find love, acceptance, and community that can elude children, especially Brown transgender and queer children. Melissa Ames and Sarah Burcon in *How Pop Culture Shapes the Stages of a Woman's Life* (2016)—an analysis of popular cultural forms and their influences—remind us: the original purpose of the fairy tale was always (in part) to do the work of cultural training. Such tales, which are continuously revised and repackaged for different generations, reveal much about both history and the contemporary time period they are being repurposed to serve" (26). McLemore's purpose could not be clearer. Through McLemore's fairy tale, they write their transgendered and queer characters into a past to create a narrative history that extends into a future present "where those desires will not have been" and that has yet to arrive (Bruhm and Hurley xxx). In this way, McLemore illustrates that, as Muñoz states in different context, queerness is "a temporal arrangement in which the past is a field of possibility in which subjects can act in the present in the service of a new futurity" (*Cruising Utopia* 16). As Miel observes at the conclusion of the novel, she and Sam "would become what they could not yet imagine" (270). More importantly they will live to imagine and make that future together.

NOTES

1. The pronouns in the biography on the 2016 book jacket no longer reflect McLemore's identity. Their website was updated to reflect the change. http://author.annamariemclemore.com/ p/about_10.html.

2. The following is a brief list of children's books that feature La Llorona or her story: *Maya's Children: The Story of La Llorona* (1997, picture book) by Rudolfo Anaya; *Prietita and the Ghost Woman* (2001, picture book) by Gloria Anzaldua; *In My Family* (2001, picture book) by Carmen de la Garza; *Summerland* (2006, young adult novel) by Michael Chabon; *Secrets in the Hills: A Josefina Mystery* (2006, chapter book) by Kathleen Ernst; and *La Llorona Can't Scare Me* (2021, chapter book) by Javier Garza.

3. Racialization and cultural or national geographies are frequently tied to determining works as belonging to the category of magical realism. However, seen another way, the category also excludes particular groups of writers from the larger fantasy genre, one most often associated with works such as J. R. R. Tolkein's *Lord of the Rings* (1954–1955) trilogy or, more recently, J. K. Rowling's *Harry Potter* series (1997–2007). As such, I eschew the term in favor of fantasy.

4. In alignment with the author, I use "Latine" when discussing Latinx identities of the characters in *When the Moon Was Ours*.

5. Each subsequent book reimagines different fairy tales, including Little Red Riding Hood, Rapunzel, and Snow White.

6. La Llorona can be used as a behavioral deterrent; disobedient children are told that La Llorona will "get them" if they do not obey adults.

7. Garcia McCall introduces La Llorona at the end of the first chapter after the protagonist Odilia and her sisters find the body of the dead man in the river and argue about whether or not to take him home to his family in Mexico. Amidst the discord, Odilia sees a woman standing on the other side of the Rio Grande: "One minute her long, white dress was billowing against her legs, and the next she was gone. Disappeared." Odilia immediately thinks of La Llorona, "the legendary Weeping Woman said to have drowned her own children. Mamá says she roams the rivers of the world in search of them" (22). Their mother is the source of cultural knowledge about La Llorona.

8. La Llorona reveals that she is from Tenochtitlan, the capital city of the Aztec Empire, and the night her children died, she and her husband Hernán were arguing about his decision to leave, thus revealing her original identity as La Malinche. Although Garcia McCall conflates the two figures, they symbolize two very different and distinct versions of motherhood in the Greater Mexican cultural imaginary.

9. Francisco J. Galarte uses "figuration" to "refer to the multiple ways narratives about trans people, specifically brown trans people, are mobilized through tropes" (13).

WORKS CITED

Ames, Melissa, and Sarah Burcon. *How Pop Culture Shapes the Stages of a Woman's Life: From Toddlers-in-Tiars to Cougars-on-the-Prowl*. Palgrave, 2016.

Bruhm, Steven, and Natasha Hurley, eds. *Curiouser: On the Queerness of Children.* University of Minnesota Press, 2004.
Foulis, Elena. "Book Review: *When the Moon Was Ours* by Anna-Marie McLemore." *Latinxs in Kid Lit,* 26 January 2017. https://latinosinkidlit.com/2017/01/26/book-review-when-the-moon-was-ours-by-anna-marie-mclemore/.
Herrera, Cristina. "Cinco Hermanitas: Myth and Sisterhood in Guadalupe García McCall's *Summer of the Mariposas.*" *Children's Literature* 44 (2016): 96–294.
Galarte, Francisco J. *Brown Trans Figurations: Rethinking Race, Gender, and Sexuality in Chicanx/Latinx Studies.* University of Texas Press, 2021.
Gil-Peterson, Julian. *Histories of the Transgender Child.* University of Minnesota Press, 2018.
Joe, Ryan. "Gender Expressions: Transgender Books, 2016." *Publisher's Weekly,* 27 May 2016. www.publishersweekly.com/pw/by-topic/new-titles/adult-announcements/article/70501-gender-expressions-transgender-books-2016.html.
Lerer, Seth. *Children's Literature: A Reader's History from Aesop to Harry Potter.* University of Chicago Press, 2008.
Mason, Derritt. *Queer Anxieties of Young Adult Literature and Culture.* University of Mississippi Press, 2021.
Matos, Angel Daniel. "A Narrative of a Future Past: Historical Authenticity, Ethics, and Queer Latinx Futurity in *Aristotle and Dante Discover the Secrets of the Universe.*" *Children's Literature* 47, 2019, 30–56.
McLemore, Anna-Marie. "Everything We Are." *Diversity in YA,* 9 October 2016. http://www.diversityinya.com/tag/anna-marie-mclemore/.
McLemore, Anna-Marie. *When the Moon Was Ours.* Thomas Dunne Book, 2016.
McCall, Guadalupe Garcia. *Summer of the Mariposas.* Tu Books, 2012.
Muñoz, José Esteban. *Cruising Utopia: The Then and There of Queer Futurity.* NYU Press, 2009.
Muñoz, José Esteban. *Disidentification: Queers of Color and the Performance of Politics.* University of Minnesota Press, 1999.
Pérez, Domino Renee. *There Was a Woman: La Llorona from Folklore to Popular Culture.* University of Texas Press, 2008.
Richmond, Caroline. "About, Anna-Marie." *anna-marie,* 2022, http://author.annamariemclemore.com/p/about_10.html
Stryker, Susan. *Transgender History: The Root of Today's Revolution.* Seal, 2017.
Trites, Roberta. *Disturbing the Universe: Power and Repression in Children's Literature.* University of Iowa Press, 2004.

Chapter Twelve

"SILENCE, AT LEAST RIGHT NOW, EQUALS MY SURVIVAL"

The Absence of AIDS in the *Aristotle and Dante* Series

Angel Daniel Matos

Benjamin Alire Sáenz's *Aristotle and Dante Discover the Secrets of the Universe* (2011, henceforth *Secrets of the Universe*) and its sequel, *Aristotle and Dante Dive into the Waters of the World* (2021, henceforth *Waters of the World*) are two of the most well-known and celebrated young adult (YA) novels to explore the intersections between queerness, class, and Latinidad. *Secrets of the Universe* has been the recipient of numerous accolades—including the 2013 Pura Belpré Narrative Medal for Latino Fiction and the 2013 Lambda Literary Award for LGBTQ Children's and Young Adult Literature. Both books have been placed on various bestselling lists, a testament to their enduring popularity since the first volume was published over a decade ago. In spite of the praise attributed to *Secrets of the Universe* in its representation of the overlap between queerness and Latinidad, Sáenz had to consider all of the content that he excluded from this book—in particular, the sidelining of any discourse on HIV or AIDS in a YA novel set during the 1980s. As he discloses in an interview published in 2021 by *Publisher's Weekly*, "I couldn't quite forgive myself for not having included the AIDS pandemic. It was personal.... I wanted very much for the novel to turn outward, for Ari and Dante to turn toward the world in which they lived to make sense of their lives" (Schulman). Sáenz's disappointment was also driven by critiques that circulated in scholarly circles regarding the lack of any content pertaining to HIV and AIDS in the first novel, especially considering that it was set in El Paso, Texas, during the late 1980s—and that HIV and AIDS had significant effects on the ways in which queer people framed their lives and practices during this time.

Discourse on the omission of AIDS in the first novel reached its peak with the publication of Michelle Ann Abate's article "Out of the Past" in 2019, which addresses the issue of a major LGBTQ+ YA novel set in the 1980s failing to acknowledge the epidemic, and goes as far as to interrogate whether the novel "could be viewed as a positive portrayal of queer identity when it fails to engage with one of the biggest challenges to, as well as catalysts for, the LGBTQ community" (2). While the first half of her critique is situated in suspicion, in that she addresses the historical and political implications of this omission and its effects on how we interpret the novel, the later part of her reading pivots to reparative critique to redeem the novel from its faults. To accomplish this, Abate completely rethinks *Secrets of the Universe*'s generic categorization and approaches it not as a form of historically oriented queer teen fiction but as a form of speculative and utopian literature that tries to rewrite and reimagine the past: "The YA novel revisits one of the most tragic periods in LGBTQ[+] history... the novel returns to this era to depict the wonder that was denied, the splendor that was stifled, and the joy that was missed" (18). Abate approaches the first novel as an exercise in utopian and ahistorical thought in its attempts to imagine what queer boyhood would look like in the 1980s without dealing with the deathly connotations associated with the AIDS pandemic.

While this seemingly utopian approach pushes us to reimagine the scope of the novel and view it in a new light, matters of history and cultural context push us to acknowledge the limitations of such a reparative approach. To what extent do queer novels set in the 1980s have an obligation to address the AIDS crisis? Why do some readers feel hurt by the first novel's omission of the epidemic, and why do they go to such great lengths to salvage the book from negative critique? These questions become even more loaded when we consider the state of queer Latine literature in the early 2010s and the ways in which *Secrets of the Universe* needed to carve out representational space to circulate the intersection of queerness and Latinidad on a mainstream scale. In my previous work on the first novel, I discussed how *Secrets of the Universe* deliberately focused on subverting tropes often found in queer Latine YA, not only in its implementation of future oriented logics but even more in its "attempts to imagine a historical moment in which [Latine] parents cultivate, rather than encumber, their child's queerness" (Matos 45). The novel has a clear aim at disrupting some of the ties between machismo, patriarchal values, and queerness, not to mention that it was also attempting to disrupt monolithic approaches toward Chicane communities and practices—it was not written or framed as an AIDS novel.

To further compound issues, note that a utopian approach towards *Secrets of the Universe* is incompatible with the ideological scope of new-wave YA novels focused on AIDS, which Gabriel Duckels describes as texts focused on the politics of memorialization—texts that synergize queer *cultural history* and the representation of queer sexual futures (436). Indeed, there is a sense of ahistoricism necessary when approaching *Secrets of the Universe* as an aesthetic attempt to envision a queer coming of age void of the pressures pertaining to AIDS. This approach to the text does carve a sense of sexual futurity, but it does so at the cost of a cultural, and more specifically, queer Latine history that stands in opposition to the grand narratives of queerness commonly circulated in the United States. Through this approach, we witness a utopic coming-of-age narrative that prevents opportunities for memorialization and for readers to come to terms with the strategies of survival our queer Latine ancestors used.

The stakes of these issues have been amplified with the publications of *Waters of the World*, its meaningful focus on the AIDS crisis, and its impact on the protagonists' psyches and sense of wellbeing as young queer Latine[1] men. *Waters of the World* is a book that's clearly couched in the new wave of AIDS YA literature in its attempts to offer a historically oriented sense of futurism that attempts to "retrospectively remedy the otherization of stigmatized people" (Duckels 436). Approaching the first novel's omission of the epidemic as a utopic opportunity to revisit, rewrite, and redeem the past becomes increasingly untenable when considering the content of the sequel, which serves as a text that reminds young readers of the effects of the AIDS crisis and its lasting effects on contemporary queer life. The remainder of this chapter explores how *Waters of the World* informs and transforms our understanding of the absence of HIV and AIDS in the *Secrets of the Universe*, while simultaneously addressing how the sequel uses the motif of silence to disrupt the politics of legibility and visibility present in many YA texts. Afterwards, I will show how a utopian approach to the first novel's treatment of HIV and AIDS is only viable when completely stripping the novel from the ideological and historical frameworks of Latinidad that are central to the author's reparative aims and the cultural context he represents. Ultimately, I highlight the issues with reparative readings that rely on processes of whitewashing that disregard how the conditions of Latine life have major impacts over what can (or cannot) be represented.

SILENCE = DEATH?

The utopian drive to redeem texts despite their glaring issues, gaps, and ideological tensions is informed by the tenets of reparative reading, an interpretive method that pushes people to acknowledge the ways in which texts can still be useful, important, and emotionally sustaining for certain reading communities in spite of their issues. Largely influenced by the work of Eve Kosofsky Sedgwick within the field of queer studies in the 1990s, reparative approaches historically focused on redeeming texts with heteronormative and antiqueer elements by showing how readers drew comfort and solace from them in spite of these elements—and it arose in part due to the severe issues of queer representation that haunted our culture. As Sedgwick herself puts it, reparative interpretations often rest on the energy of hope "to organize the arguments and part-objects she encounters or creates" in an effort to provide a sense of relief from the hardships of contemporary life (146). Later nuanced and developed by prominent theorists such as the late José Esteban Muñoz within the realm of queer Latine studies and Rita Felski within literary criticism at large, reparative engagement can broadly be approached as a counterpoint to the hermeneutics of suspicion that has dominated literary criticism, one in which "selves and communities succeed in extracting sustenance from the objects of a culture—even a culture whose avowed desire has often been not to sustain them" (Sedgwick 150–151).

In the fields of children's and YA literary studies, reparative approaches have slowly but surely surfaced in research that explores the intersections between youth literature, theory, and activism in queer contexts—with said approaches implemented heavily in my own work, and in the work of other queer scholars such as Jon M. Wargo, Joshua Coleman, Cristina Rhodes, and Abate. While such approaches have been crucial in highlighting strategies that readers implement to develop relationships with texts generated and distributed in oppressive, violent, and capitalist contexts, such approaches, when handled irresponsibly, can come off as ahistorical, apolitical, and contribute little to disrupt the very powers that limit our bodies, practices, and desires.

A reparative approach to *Secrets of the Universe* focusing on reading the text through a utopic, ahistorical lens becomes increasingly unsustainable once we politicize and historicize the text, and even more so, once we interpret it through an intersectional lens that considers notions of ethnicity and culture that are frequently ignored in these analyses. *Waters of the World*, for instance, contains guidance that pushes readers to understand the difficulties and challenges of discussing AIDS in Latine youth contexts, and how many of the ideas upheld by activist groups at the time were antithetical to the normative demands present in Latine, particularly Chicane communities. In critiquing the absence of AIDS discourse in *Secrets of the Universe*, Abate invokes the fact that ACT-UP, a radical group of activists focused on publicly demystifying the stigma of AIDS and of addressing issues of inequality in healthcare—was formed in 1987, months before the first novel takes place. Known mostly for their slogan "Silence = Death," Abate claims that the first novel "does not heed this advice" and that it ultimately "disregards this well-known slogan from the history of the LGBTQ[+] movement," in addition to potentially reinstating the silence that the activist group attempted to disrupt (11). This reading, while highlighting a disjuncture between mainstream AIDS discourse and Latine contexts, unfortunately ignores the exceptional ways in which silences, absences, and omissions operate within Latine families with queer children, and even more so, the extent to which members within ACT UP were aligned with practices that are antithetical to minoritarian being.

Deborah B. Gould has pointed out that racism was quite palpable in the internal conflicts that arose in ACT UP during the late 1980s and early 1990s. Although the rhetoric of the organization was constructed to advocate for all people with AIDS, a handful of participants considered that "ACT UP should fight the epidemic from that perspective alone, effectively privileging the concerns of white, middle class, gay men over those of others with HIV/AIDS" (57). ACT UP's internal conflicts and its tense relationship with nonwhite communities became increasingly complex as many participants sidelined the political dimensions of ACT UP's activist agenda to focus exclusively on financial concerns, especially when it came to expediting AIDS drug research. A significant number of ACT UP's early members considered that a focus on other issues such as race or gender would derail focus from their overarching goals (Gould 57). Other critics such as Alexandra Juhasz have pointed out how logics of whiteness are partially responsible for the visibility of ACT UP's activist agenda, and that for the most part, ACT UP was "thought to be the home of white men," and thus, the activist labor of queer people of color was often overshadowed or made invisible by the more confrontational methods implemented by white members (71–72). Furthermore, we must also recognize that many people—including undocumented people and people of color—oftentimes could not afford to engage with the visible and public activism typically practiced by the affluent and white members of ACT UP. Given that the organization was so focused on concerns that affected the lives of primarily upper-class, white gay men, it becomes questionable whether their activist practices would have been at the forefront of the consciousness of many Latine contexts and communities, and particularly the consciousness of queer Latine *teenagers* in the 1980s, who were still coming to varied and diverging understandings of their sexualities, identities, and sense of national belonging.

Silences, gaps, and omissions are often approached with suspicion when present in young adult texts, especially since they are viewed as detrimental to minoritarian being. Critics such as M. Roxana Loza have pointed out that YA novels, even when centered on Latine experiences, approach silence as oppressive, and these texts ultimately achieve a sense of narrative closure through a dismantling of different forms of trauma induced by the breaking of silence (7). But when looking at the role of silence within a larger tradition of queer Latine and Latin American writing, matters are anything but simple—and the silences present in this literary strand are anything but a matter of unknowing of ignorance, nor do they always lead to violence and oppression. As Ben Sifuentes-Jáuregui suggests, silence in these texts is generated from "a conscious position of unspoken knowledge, an assertive refusal to name that desire—and to link it with an identity" (5). He approaches silence as a trope that can "make certain sexualities possible" and to think critically about how certain identifications manifest even when they are not explicitly voiced (133). Furthermore, we can also heed the advice of Derritt Mason, who has highlighted how "invisible, subtle, latent, and sideways queernesses are at least as worthy of attention as visible manifestations of nonheterosexual desires and identities" (6).

The stakes of these claims become increasingly palpable when applied toward *Waters of the World* as Ari grapples with the implications behind ACT UP's "Silence = Death" slogan and how it is in many ways contradictory to his being: "The men who are dying of AIDS have a poster that says *SILENCE = DEATH*. I think I know what that means. But for a guy like me, silence can be a place where I am free of words. Do you understand that, Dante?" (Sáenz, *Waters* 153). Here, Ari reflects on the self-determination that silence grants him, in that it allows him to think and feel beyond the parameters of language and to acknowledge how words can lock us into certain ways of being and feeling. Silence is imperative in pushing Ari to process his identification with Dante without resorting to the use of predetermined concepts and approaches to the world, and it is equally important in his grappling with the repercussions of being a queer teen coming of age during the peak of the AIDS crisis. Even more so, this process of disidentification with this slogan becomes imperative not only for Aristotle's positionality as a queer Latine teen, but for his very survival and being.

Throughout the novel, the consistent invocation of ACT UP's slogan becomes a motif within the text, and Ari continues to negotiate his own positionality vis-à-vis the disruption of silence prompted by mainstream, white, and visible forms of activism. During a particularly poignant moment in the novel in which Ari comes out to his friend Cassandra, he reveals that he has only disclosed his sexuality to a very small group of people: "I know that all the gay activists are saying that silence equals death, but my silence, at least right now, equals my survival" (184). Ari's contemplation of silence vis-à-vis the declaration of ACT UP's slogan is multilayered and complex. First and foremost, we can approach Ari's engagement with the slogan as a process of disidentification with mainstream forms of queer activism. José Esteban Muñoz approaches disidentification as the "survival strategies the minority subject practices in order to negotiate a phobic majoritarian public sphere that continuously elides or punishes the existence of subjects who do not conform to the phantasm of normative citizenship" (4). Ari's disidentification with the slogan highlights the additional forms of oppression and violence that his embodiment as a Brown, Latine teenager invokes within a majoritarian culture—and it also serves as a way of addressing how ACT UP's claims were aligned with dimensions of class and race that excluded people like him and Dante from their political aims.

Ari understands the weight of silence and the oppressive practices it can mobilize, but he does not let this create a totalizing narrative about silence and its effects on queer life. Ari contemplates the importance of speaking out, but he also basks in the queer potentialities induced by the absence of sound. Near the conclusion of *Waters of the World*, Ari and Dante are walking through the deserts of El Paso, and Ari takes a moment to show appreciation for the geography's lack of sound: "A walk in the desert in the quiet. Sometimes the silence of the desert was a kind of music. Dante and I, we shared a silence between us that was a kind of music too. The desert didn't condemn Dante and me for holding hands" (435). Toward the novel's ending, Ari goes as far as to characterize silence as "rare and so sacred" (514). Silences, gaps, and omissions are not always represented as sources of anxiety for these characters, but rather, as moments of queer potentiality and moments of identification and filiation that elude words and the oppressiveness of language. But even more so, I argue that silence is vital in constructing a fictional Latine world inhabited by queer youth, one in which queer Latine teens had little language, experience, and knowledge to articulate their queerness, much less their fears and anxieties regarding HIV and the proliferation of the AIDS epidemic in the 1980s. Ari acknowledges how he and Dante are engaging in new and difficult worldbuilding processes with few tools or assistance from other people or from their culture: "It seemed that we *had* actually become cartographers of a new world, had mapped out a country of our own, and it was ours and only ours, and though we both knew that country would disappear, almost as soon as it had appeared, we had full citizenship in that country and we were free to love each other" (101, emphasis in original). Wherein lies the stakes of holding Latine teen characters accountable for articulating their relationship with HIV and AIDS discourse as they are attempting to chart out their lives with little knowledge or experience with the queer world—an attempt at charting that is frequently disrupted by heteronormative and supremacist forces? Even more so, what does it say of us as critics when we attempt to conduct reparative readings that are only justifiable by ignoring elements that are crucial in understanding the text's context?

Sáenz has explained that the COVID-19 pandemic pushed him to realize that his "readers could draw their own parallels between the AIDS epidemic and the pandemic they are living through" (Turner), thus prompting him to pen the sequel. However, we have to acknowledge that Sáenz is well aware of the criticism regarding AIDS and the first *Aristotle and Dante* novel, and it is obvious that the sequel was first and foremost an attempt at repair. The stakes of these reparative aims were quite high for Sáenz, especially since the effects and ramifications of the epidemic led to many losses in his personal and professional life. As he discloses in an interview with Daniel Sanchez Torres, "I lost my mentor Arturo Islas, a writer and professor at Stanford. I lost my older brother Donaciano Sanchez, and I lost one of my closest friends Norman Campbell Robertson. And the US government didn't give a damn. Never has the gay community been more hated, because they were afraid [of us]" (Sanchez Torres). In a sense, *Waters of the Word* was a grieving process for Sáenz, in that he had to reckon with the losses that AIDS has caused in his life. But even more so, it was a way for Sáenz to partially disrupt his own silence and bear witness to a difficult moment in queer Latine history that was incredibly personal to him.

It is uncanny to observe the parallels that exist between Sáenz's work and that of his late mentor, Arturo Islas, a Chicane writer who notably explored themes of queerness and sexuality in his groundbreaking semiautobiographical novel *The Rain God* (1984). In his examination of the themes of sexuality and illness in Islas's novel, Manuel De Jesús Vega discloses how AIDS is central to *The Rain God* even though it is not mentioned by name. He points out, however, that the logics of silence often frame the representation of illness within the text, and Islas had to resort to intricate forms of queer coding and "complex metaphor" to confront the issue of AIDS within the text—one which used the motifs of monstrosity, the desert, and pre-Columbian deities to symbolically discuss AIDS (112). De Jesús Vega highlights how Islas's coded approach toward AIDS in *The Rain God* can be partially attributed to the "social climate of the early 80s, along with the homophobia prevalent in the Chicano community" (117). The significance of Islas's silences and coding gains even more traction when we acknowledge his complicated relationship with AIDS. Not only did Islas lose a lover and friends during the height of the epidemic, but he had openly shared fears about AIDS in diary entries and would disclose how this dread further compounded his "own sense of a deformed body and his already acute sense of his own mortality" (Aldama 120). If Chicane authors had a difficult time in terms of directly articulating the ramifications of AIDS in their lives and communities, wherein lies the narrative and ideological stakes of holding imagined teens accountable for dealing with these pressures? Why is there a desire to read this silence, this absence, as a gap or as a fault rather than reading it as a wound? These silences and absences speak volumes.

The overt presence of AIDS in *Waters of the World* not only pressures the ability to read the first book as a utopian type of speculative fiction that imagines a queer world void of AIDS, but it also pushes us to think more critically about whether the absence of AIDS discourse was a gross oversight in *Secrets of the Universe*. The continued implementation and embrace of motifs of silence and absence in *Waters of the World* seem to go against the trend of Latine AIDS texts, which Alberto Sandoval Sánchez celebrates for their potential to "give voice to experiences" and help us to "bear witness and testimony" in order to break the silence tethered to queerness in Latine contexts (172). Latine texts that focused on queerness and AIDS highlight the ways in which AIDS helped characters to construct a subjectivity and purview "that allows for the questioning of sexual taboos and the breaking of silence at home on homosexuality and AIDS" (Sandoval Sánchez 172). And while I do not want to underplay the importance of breaking these silences and the work that early Latine AIDS novels accomplished in making queer Latine subjectivity visible, we must also recall that the impulse to make things transparent, visible, and palpable is very much couched in Western thought.

In his discussion on the critical value of "opacity," Édouard Glissant argues that in Western cultures, "to understand and thus accept you, I have to measure your solidity with the ideal scale providing me with grounds to make comparisons and, perhaps, judgments. I have to reduce" (190). Glissant is critical of the Western obsession with "understanding" and transparency precisely because of their normalizing and assimilative tendencies, and for their focus on being able to make any experience or feeling readable and decodable to a larger population. What if we were instead to approach the silence and absence of AIDS in *Secrets of the Universe* as a project in opacity, one focused not on providing transparency and illumination, but rather on emphasizing the limits of our knowledge and our limits to fully represent certain ideas? To what extent do queer Latine subjects have a right to opacity, the right to limit how much transparency and access is given to wider, potentially nonqueer and non-Latine audiences to understand the intersections between queerness and Latinidad? Juana María Rodríguez has approached queerness as a practice that refuses explication, in that it pushes readers to "read against your preconceived notions of academic disciplinarity, research, language, and scholarship to reimagine the practice of knowledge production" (3). What if we were to approach *Secrets of the Universe*'s lack of AIDS discourse not as an oversight but as a queer attempt to refuse explication?

Waters of the World can be viewed as a disruption of Sáenz's own silence when it came to the representation of HIV and AIDS in a 1980s Latine context, but it does not entirely reject the disruptive and queer potential that silences can offer. Rather than falling into the trap of universally approaching silence or omission as problematic or ideologically faulty, *Waters of the World* pushes us to bear testimony to the ways in which silence carves out moments of possibility and of resistance, moments in which queer Latine characters do not have to frame their identities according to white, neoliberal, and normative standards of livability, activism, and survival. The absence of AIDS can be approached not as a fault of the novel, but as a form of opacity or as a refusal to explicate—one that attempts to highlight the impossibility of distilling certain feelings, experiences, and cultural practices in a way that can be easily digested and "understood" by readers. By highlighting the historical, political, and sociocultural dimensions of silence in Latine contexts, we are better able to understand why AIDS discourse was absent from the first novel, and what is at stake through this absence, without resorting to abstract versions of utopianism that lack historical grounding and that are fundamentally distanced from the historical realities of queer Latine teens.

RETHINKING REPAIR

Reparative readings are often a compromise: they push us to feel comfortable with a text, but this sense of solace and relief always comes at a cost. As we continue to grapple with different and emerging forms of interpreting youth literature, we must be especially mindful and attuned to the cultural expectations that come along with different modes of critique. If the lack of HIV/AIDS in *Secrets of the Universe* is such a major issue, why is it not sufficient to conduct an examination couched in the hermeneutics of suspicion: one that exposes the problem and brings awareness to the issues imbued within this absence, or one that tries to examine this silence from the perspective of Latinidad? Why do readers and critics go to such lengths to feel comfortable and okay with the texts that we read? Do we feel a responsibility to salvage texts that have won awards, or that are generally beloved by reading publics? Or is it the very popularity of these texts that invites us to poke holes in the narrative and try to expose that deep down, something was wrong with the text all along? These questions, of course, connect to larger conversations on the limits of reparative reading and how this mode of critique sometimes reinforces rather than dismantles hegemonic powers.

Patricia Stuelke argues that most forms of reparation and forms of critique fixated on being generous with problematic texts have "historically been implicated in short-circuiting rather than successfully realizing attempts to break with the world as it is in order to create equality" (29). When applying this train of thought towards criticism surrounding AIDS and the *Secrets of the Universe*, we must be upfront about what a reparative reading ultimately accomplishes and what is at stakes in conducting one in the first place. If we take seriously Marilisa Jiménez García's claim (and we should) that contemporary Latine YA literature "serves as a window into how authors narrate the promises and failures of cultural nationalism" in efforts to destabilize the American canon (231), then we must be wary of interpretations that attempt to offer a reparative approach to a queer Latine text by sidelining the cultural, aesthetic, and ideological elements that prompt these destabilizations. Lázaro Lima has further argued that queer Latine writing serves as "narrative acts against oblivion. It is the name we give to an archive of feelings, traits, desires, urges, behaviors, and aspirations in 'American' literary vernacular that can apprehend our relationship to the worlds we inhabit through our collective agencies" (8–9). One could implement a reparative approach to *Secrets of the Universe* that reconfigures its genre to make it seem more utopian and progressive ("imagine *that*, a world without AIDS"), but to do so requires a relegation of the very traits, feelings, and desires that define queer Latine narrative in the first place. Reframing the absence of AIDS as a site of utopian possibility, after all, undermines the critical value of silence and omission in disrupting the tyranny of words, and even more so, the ways in which Latinidad invites us to interpret silence as a strategy of resistance and survival—especially for queer Latine teens growing up in El Paso, Texas, during the early 1980s. Even more so, it undercuts the logics of opacity that are at work in this book—logics that carry even more weight given the fact that Sáenz experienced personal losses directly connected to AIDS and that open up a series of ethical questions pertaining to what queer Latinx authors "owe" their audiences.

Stripping a novel of its historical and Latine context to make a text fit into a broader utopian narrative of progress not only contradicts the pillars of queer thinking, but it is potentially colonizing in its scope. It does little to *challenge* us to confront the ugly realities of the world we inhabit, and even more so, it imposes a normative, nationalist, and white gaze that keeps current structures of power intact and sacrifices intersectional inquiry in the name of comfort—in the name of stretching a hand toward a paradise that is out of history and out of touch with our sociocultural circumstances. Heather Love has pointed out how contemporary queer politics' focus on notions of forward-driven progress and utopianism has made it "difficult to approach the past as something living," and even more so, how these notions of progress often happen "on the condition that one breaks ties with all those who cannot make it" (9–10). To read the absence of AIDS as a utopian reimagining in *Secrets of the Universe* involves approaching history and the past as dead. Rather than examining the absence of AIDS in *Secrets of the Universe* as an attempt to further explore queer Latine subjectivity and the specific sociocultural circumstances that affected what knowledges on queerness and AIDS could be circulated, the reframing of *Secrets of the Universe* as an exercise in utopian thought focuses more attention on *feeling good* about this absence than on thoroughly thinking it through. I am skeptical, if not fearful, of what occurs when feeling good about the texts we read supersedes the very critical, disruptive, and queer goals of a text.

So much is lost through this sacrifice of intersectional inquiry in favor of a comfortable, progress-ridden reading. Cristina Rhodes, in her exploration of temporality in queer Latine literature, has pointed out how this corpus of texts offers us a space to reflect on impossibilities of queer life in the present, and the unique ways in which queer characters in these stories develop strategies for inhabiting worlds that are adverse to Brown, queer being (7–8). A refusal to consider the historical role of silence in Latine contexts when approaching the *Aristotle and Dante* books thus limits an understanding of the radical potentiality of silence in pushing people to resist normative narratives of nationalism and queerness that the novels attempt to address. As Stuelke argues, history should "have some bearing in our reflexive assessments of what is ethical, not to mention what is radical, in our present" (30). Historical thinking pushes us to engage more deeply with the invisible, the absent, and the latent, and to understand why certain ideas and notions are silenced or absent in the first place. It pushes us to understand the difference between reparative readings of queer Latine YA novels that simply want to suture wounds and those that want us to interrogate and dismantle the very agents, powers, and ideas that continuously wound us and force us to develop different strategies for surviving in the first place.[2]

NOTES

1. I use the term "Latine" as a gender-neutral alternative to terms such as "Latina" and "Latino." Although Latinx has gained much traction in its use over the past couple of years, particularly in academic settings, I use Latine instead because it is much easier for Spanish speakers to pronounce.

2. This essay is a revised version of my chapter "The Limits of Repair" from my book *The Reparative Impulse of Queer YA Literature* (Routledge 2024).

WORKS CITED AND CONSULTED

Abate, Michelle Ann. "Out of the Past: Aristotle and Dante Discover the Secrets of the Universe, the AIDS Crisis, and Queer Retrosity." *Research on Diversity in Youth Literature* 2, no. 1 (2019).

Aldama, Frederick Luis. *Dancing with Ghosts: A Critical Biography of Arturo Islas*. University of California Press, 2004.

De Jesús Vega, Manuel. "Chicano, Gay, and Doomed: AIDS in Arturo Islas's *The Rain God*." *Confluencia* 11, no. 2 (1996): 112–18.

Duckels, Gabriel. "From Heterosexualization to Memorialization: Queer History and Moral Maturation in Young Adult Literature about the AIDS Crisis." *Mortality* 26, no. 4 (2021): 424–38.

Felski, Rita. *The Limits of Critique*. University of Chicago Press, 2015.

Glissant, Édouard. *Poetics of Relation*. Translated by Betsy Wing. University of Michigan Press, 1997.

Gould, Deborah B. "ACT UP, Racism, and the Question of How to Use History." *Quarterly Journal of Speech* 98, no. 1 (2012): 54–62.

Jiménez García, Marilisa. "En(countering) YA: Young Lords, Shadowshapers, and the Longings and Possibilities of Latinx Young Adult Literature." *Latino Studies* 16 (2018): 230–49.

Juhasz, Alexandra. "Forgetting ACT UP." *Quarterly Journal of Speech* 98, no. 1 (2012): 69–74.

Lima, Lázaro. "Introduction: Genealogies of Queer Latino Writing." *Ambientes: New Queer Latino Writing*, edited by Lázaro Lima and Felice Picano. University of Wisconsin Press, 2011.

Love, Heather. *Feeling Backward: Loss and the Politics of Queer History*. Harvard University Press, 2007.

Loza, M. Roxana. "He Doesn't Talk:" Silence, Trauma, and Fathers in *Aristotle and Dante Discover the Secrets of the Universe* and *I Am Not Your Perfect Mexican Daughter*." *Label Me Latina/o* 11 (2021). Edited by Trevor Boffone and Cristina Herrera.

Mason, Derritt. *The Queer Anxieties of Young Adult Literature and Culture*. University of Mississippi Press, 2020.

Matos, Angel Daniel. "A Narrative of a Future Past: Historical Authenticity, Ethics, and Queer Latinx Futurity in *Aristotle and Dante Discover the Secrets of the Universe*." *Children's Literature* 47, no. 1 (2019): 30–56.

Muñoz, José Esteban. *Disidentifications: Queers of Color and the Performance of Politics*. University of Minnesota Press, 1999.

Rhodes, Cristina. "Imagining the Future: The (Im)Possibilities of Queerness in Two Latinx Speculative Young Adult Novels." *Label Me Latina/o* 11 (2021): 1–10.

Rodríguez, Juana María. *Queer Latinidad: Identity, Practices, Discursive Spaces*. NYU Press, 2003.

Sáenz, Benjamin Alire. *Aristotle and Dante Discover the Secrets of the Universe*. Simon and Schuster, 2012.

Sáenz, Benjamin Alire. *Aristotle and Dante Dive into the Waters of the World*. Simon and Schuster, 2021.

Sanchez Torres, Daniel. "Aristotle and Dante Are Back." *Xtra**. 14 October 2021.

Sandoval Sánchez, Alberto. "Breaking the Silence, Dismantling Taboos: Latino Novels on AIDS." *Journal of Homosexuality* 32, no. 3–4 (1998): 155–75.

Schulman, Martha. "Q&A with Benjamin Alire Sáenz." *Publishers Weekly*, 5 October 2021.

Sedgwick, Eve Kosofsky. *Touching Feeling*. Duke University Press, 2002.

Sifuentes-Jáuregui, Ben. *The Avowal of Difference: Queer Latino American Narratives*. SUNY Press, 2014.

Stuelke, Patricia. *The Ruse of Repair*. Duke University Press, 2021.

Turner, Molly Catherine. "Benjamin Alire Sáenz: 'I Am the Luckiest.' On Writing Aristotle and Dante Dive into the Waters of the World." *Lambda Literary*, 15 November 2021.

Wargo, Jon M., and James Joshua Coleman. "Speculating the Queer (In)Human: A Critical, Reparative Reading of Contemporary LGBTQ+ Picturebooks." *Journal of Children's Literature* 47, no. 1 (2021): 84–96.

Chapter Thirteen

IMAGINING THE FUTURE

The (Im)Possibilities of Queerness in
Two Latinx Speculative Young Adult Novels

Cristina Rhodes

Imagining the future engages the promise of possibility. José Esteban Muñoz tells us, "The future is queerness's domain" (1). Queerness is inextricably linked to the ability for us to move forward, away from the normative and restrictive structures by which our current world operates. But in Adam Silvera's *More Happy Than Not* (2015) and Alexandra Villasante's *The Grief Keeper* (2019), main characters Aaron and Marisol's traumatic pasts inhibit their movement toward the promise of that queer future. Both characters are queer themselves, though the reader is unaware of these identities at the beginning of each book. Rather, their queer pasts have been suppressed to combat homophobia and cultural expectations for compulsory heterosexuality—in fact, both characters go to great lengths to submerge their queer identities. Aaron, for example, seeks to erase memories of his queerness via the Leteo procedure, a memory alteration surgery. On the other hand, Marisol agrees to undergo an experimental procedure to make her a surrogate for another's grief, an effort she sees as a gateway to citizenship for her and her young sister, lest they be deported to their native El Salvador, where Marisol fears her sexuality will get them both killed. Leteo and the grief surrogacy procedure put Aaron and Marisol at immense risk, both physically and mentally. Nevertheless, Aaron and Marisol regard these medical interventions as the only way to reach a better future. Neither Aaron nor

Marisol is unaware that these procedures could severely limit or even abort their futures, but they have (to their minds, at least) no other options.

When reading both books, I am compelled by Aaron and Marisol's perilous journeys toward what they hope to be better futures. On the surface, both live in a world I recognize as my own—a world in which queer Latinxs are acknowledged as existing but not allowed to thrive. Making tangible a future in which survival and success are not just possible but accessible is part and parcel of my own activist scholarly agenda. And it is this notion that pushes me to pursue this research on Latinx speculative fiction. But, as these books demonstrate, this possibility is tenuous and easily shattered. The specter of that thriving future is omnipresent in speculative and science fiction like *More Happy Than Not* and *The Grief Keeper*, but it might not even be within Aaron and Marisol's reach. In their introduction to a special issue of *Research on Diversity in Youth Literature* on queer futurity, Angel Daniel Matos and Jon M. Wargo ask, "Which youth have the privilege of tomorrows that are open, utopic, or even possible?" (5). Taken within the context of the two novels I center here, it is clear that neither Aaron nor Marisol is protected or allotted a future—just as Matos and Wargo definitively explain, "Many queer, non-white, . . . lower class youth simply do not have access to the material, aesthetic, practical, and ideological means to exist and thrive in the present—much less to envision realities different from the ones in which they currently live" (5). Within the specific contexts of Latinx populations, Rafael Pérez-Torres asserts, "To think of a future for Latinx and Chicanx studies, let alone to consider a Latinx futurity, may indeed be an exercise in magical thinking at odds with the exigencies of the now" (155). Simply put, Aaron and Marisol are not positioned to have the futures they so desperately try to bring to reality.

As I read and analyze, I grapple with my own concern for Aaron and Marisol's futures, and, more broadly, for the futures of real queer Latinx youth. If, as I discuss later, Latinx studies affirms speculative fiction as the space for imagining a positive future, how can we reconcile the futuristic elements and the ambiguous endings in these two novels? In the following sections, I demonstrate how speculative fiction could be the space for queer futurity. I then examine both Aaron and Marisol's subjection to futuristic medical procedures and the negative outcomes of those procedures. Through both case studies, I find tenuous moments wherein queer young Latinxs have a chance at the future. I ultimately determine that these moments are fleeting yet representative of avenues to imagine the future more queerly. In this way, these books provide us with a call to action. I firmly believe that Latinx studies' emphasis on the efficacy of futurity is not misguided, but it has not yet reached Latinx children's and young adult literature. Thus, I use this analysis as a call to imagine more inclusive futures in Latinx, particularly queer, youth literature.

SPECULATIVE AND SCIENCE FICTION

Speculative and science fiction is often a space that takes our current realities to their logical, if tragic, ends. According to Wendy Gay Pearson, Veronica Hollinger, and Joan Gordon in the introduction to *Queer Universes: Sexualities in Science Fiction*, "Science fiction notoriously reflects contemporary realities back to us through the lens of a particular type of imagination, one associated with the future" (3). With this in mind, we can extrapolate that the current realities facing young Latinxs more generally, and queer young Latinxs in particular, translate to an equally oppressive future. However, studies of speculative fiction squaring on Black, Indigenous, and people of color takes a more ameliorative stance. Writing about Black women's science fiction, Sami Schalk explains "how politically astute speculative fiction can be, how it can comment on our world and make us imagine alternative possibilities" (1). What's more, according to Catherine S. Ramírez, who coined the term "Chicanafuturism," a sibling to Afrofuturism, "By appropriating the imagery of science and technology, Chicanafuturist," and by extension Latinxfuturist, "works to disrupt age-old racist and sexist binaries that exclude Chicanas and Chicanos from visions of the future" (189). Further, in their edited collection *Altermundos: Latin@ Speculative Literature, Film, and Popular Culture*, Cathryn Josefina Merla-Watson and B. V. Olguín assert that "[Latinx] sci-fi and the speculative arts—even the most bleak, terrifying, and dystopic—project a utopian spirit through the genre's capacity for incisive social critique that cuts to the bone of our shared pasts and present" (6). This, of course, isn't to say that all Latinx speculative and science fiction is utopic in nature; rather, it works to disrupt normative systems of oppression that are currently in place.

The speculative notions of *More Happy Than Not* and *The Grief Keeper* suggest that Latinxs exist in the future and have access to cutting-edge procedures, and this *should* imply that Latinxs can thrive in the future. Yet the futuristic components of Aaron's and Marisol's stories seem at odds with the inaccessibility of their future successes I alluded to in the beginning of this chapter. How can Aaron and Marisol exist in futuristic worlds wherein these procedures are easily performed, yet not have access to the queer futures that would provide them with agency and possibilities for growth? This conundrum is one that I grapple with in the following two sections, ultimately asserting that the future is rendered both possible and impossible in these novels, and it is this ambiguity that lays the framework for queer Latinx youth literature in our own future.

ERASED MEMORIES—ERASED FUTURES?

In both books, science and medicine often pathologize queerness. Though homosexuality hasn't been qualified as a mental illness by the American Psychiatric Association since the 1970s, that does not stop homophobia and antiqueer sentiments from persisting and from influencing medical decisions and diagnoses. For example, in *More Happy Than Not*, queerness is something that the Leteo procedures claims to suppress or erase via the annexing of queer memories. Memories are intimate, but ultimately fallible. According to Mark L. Howe and Lauren M. Knott, "Memory does not provide a veridical representation of events as experienced. Rather, what gets *encoded* into memory is determined by what a person attends to, what they already have stored in memory, their expectations, needs and emotional state" (633, emphasis in original). Thus, memories are made up of who we are as people (Giaimo 63; Robillard and Illes 1223). The impact of memory on identity and self-efficacy is significant; past experiences radically impact forward motion. Aaron's desire for Leteo finds root in his internalized homophobia, which disallows him from being fully himself. He seeks out the Leteo procedure, not necessarily to use it to erase traumatic memories, as it's meant to do, but to force himself to forget his queer desire and eliminate the possibility of a queer future.

More Happy Than Not opens with skepticism of the Leteo procedure. Aaron knows little of Leteo itself other than being exposed through a friend who recently received the procedure to erase memories of his dead brother. Aaron misses his friend and is curious about how Leteo works, but he is largely unconcerned. As the novel progresses, Aaron—whose own past traumas make him ponder if the Leteo procedure would help him forget his father's death by suicide and Aaron's own ensuing attempt to end his life[1]— is increasingly exposed to Leteo. Aaron and his new friend-turned-crush, Thomas, pass a protest against Leteo. When the two question people in the crowd, they're informed, "A girl has gone brain dead because of Leteo . . . she's the fourth this week. We're rallying to shut this place down" (Silvera 81). Despite this dire prognosis, Aaron becomes obsessed with the idea of Leteo, grasping at the hope that the procedure can make him forget his burgeoning feelings for Thomas and the ensuing violence he would face as an out queer person in his home in near-future Queens, New York City. In denial, Aaron explains, "Leteo is this place of second chances. I read a lot of the stories provided online through Leteo's site" (Silvera 141). He rationalizes that he's found stories on the Leteo website that recount a young woman who had the procedure and it "straightened her out" (Silvera 142). But the procedure isn't foolproof. From a pamphlet that Aaron procures, he learns "buried memories can resurface. This is known as 'unwinding.' [The memories] are typically triggered by detailed reminders, often care of loved ones, of exact moments of trauma. Specific scents, sounds, or images can also trigger an unwinding" (Silvera 147). These risks of unwinding, along with Leteo's other risks as a type of brain surgery, do not seem to trouble Aaron, who is single-minded in his desire for the procedure.

But under the surface of Aaron's longing for Leteo in *More Happy Than Not* is the reality that Aaron has already undergone the procedure before the book's opening. In fact, his buried memories are unwound during a violent fight with his neighborhood friends over his close and queer-coded friendship with Thomas. Silvera details:

> There's an explosion in the back of my head, a delayed reaction. Blood fills my mouth. This is what death feels like, I think. I scream like someone has turned a hundred knives inside of me, spitting up blood as I do. And I'm not crying because of the attack. I'm crying because there's new noise in my head, and it builds from a couple faded echoes into an uproar of jumbled voices—all memories I once forgot have been unwound. (155)

While the Leteo procedure was ultimately fairly straightforward when first performed, its unwinding has dire consequences. The fight and the aftereffects of the Leteo procedure damage Aaron's brain irreparably, giving him a type of anterograde amnesia wherein he cannot form new memories.

Speaking about the blurred lines between fact and science fiction vis-à-vis memory alteration, Elizabeth A. Phelps and Stefan G. Hofmann explain, "Even when the intention of memory editing is to reduce pain or protect someone, there can be unexpected consequences" (43). "Unexpected consequences" is an understated way to describe what happens to Aaron. Unable to form any new memories, Aaron is relegated to living in the past and relinquishing his future. He "[plays] Remember That Time a lot," a game that he had initially devised to play with romantic partners to rehash their best moments, but now uses to help himself maintain the memories he does have (Silvera 253). The Leteo procedure so damages Aaron's brain that it is beyond repair. He maintains "hope in what . . . Leteo [hopes] for" (Silvera 254). That is, he rests in the possibility of a cure, even as one does not come to fruition by the end of the novel. Rather we are left with the image of Aaron cycling through his existing memories, an action that situates him in the past rather than the future.

That *More Happy Than Not* leaves Aaron still relying on a medical procedure is both alarming and hopeful. We know that Aaron's first procedure did not end well. The idea that Leteo would even attempt an operation to erase someone's sexuality when conversion therapies are largely outlawed is problematic and detrimental to imagining a future in which queerness isn't maligned or rejected. Yet the idea that Leteo is seeking to right their wrongs with Aaron hints that medical science will make significant strides in traumatic brain injuries. Regardless, Aaron's future is left in the balance, and his queerness, that which he sought to destroy, is still present.

It would seem, then, that Aaron's future may be tenuous, but it is one in which his queerness still exists. In this way, *More Happy Than Not* is a cautionary tale about the dangers of rejecting one's self. Through Aaron's tragic life, Silvera tells us that the future is dependent on accepting all memories, even those that are painful and especially those that are deeply about ourselves, such as our sexuality. Yet, the tepid view of Aaron's future we receive is not one that provides any comfort or solace to young queer and/or Latinx readers. While I don't contend that all books need happy endings and that we should sugarcoat the realities of homophobia and prejudice, I do find it alarming that Aaron exists in a near-future world but his own future is all but lost. What queer future does *More Happy Than Not* promise? Despite Aaron's own assertion of his approximate happiness, the prognosis for other queer young Latinxs, based on *More Happy Than Not*, isn't good.

UNDOCUMENTED FUTURES

On the surface, Alexandra Villasante's *The Grief Keeper* has a more inclusive and hopeful ending that belies its horrifying premise. In *The Grief Keeper*, Marisol is forced to participate in an experimental medical trial or else risk deportation. Like Aaron, who has no future unless he trusts in Leteo to undo the damage they inflicted on him, Marisol must trust that her participation in this trial will result in legal citizenship status. Upon escaping a detention center with her younger sister, Gabi, Marisol is picked up by the mysterious Indranie and taken to another government facility. There, she is introduced to Dr. Deng, who explains that Marisol must participate in this trial or else be deported. The trial "is the corticotropin transfer system, or CTS. It allows the chemicals, the stress factors—released into the body of a person suffering trauma—to be transferred to another person, a 'clean' subject without the same trauma burden" (Villasante 41). Unlike Leteo, which covers memories, CTS leaves "the memories of the trauma... intact... but the feelings... are greatly reduced. For the aggrieved person, in a matter of weeks it feels as if the trauma is in the distant past. Painful but vague. Remembered but distant" (Villasante 41). Marisol is told little about CTS itself. In fact, when she goes for surgery to receive the CTS implant, she's not even sure what's happening and wakes from anesthesia confused. When Indranie asks if her neck, where the subdermal implant is located, is sore, Marisol replies, "I didn't know there would be an implant" (Villasante 50). Indranie insists this information was in the paperwork Marisol signed, but this assumes that Marisol has the legal status to sign away these rights. She's a minor, undocumented, and not a native English speaker. She is abused in this system and misused for these medical purposes.

What's more, even though the CTS procedure is meant to soothe soldiers with posttraumatic stress disorder, Marisol isn't assigned to help a soldier, but a teenage girl, Rey, whose father is an influential man in the government. Much like Marisol, Rey doesn't know what's happening with CTS. She is unaware that Marisol is the one serving as her surrogate, taking all of Rey's depression into her own body and living with the very real psychological and physiological consequences. When Rey discovers this, she explodes, "Who the fuck are they to decide who suffers and who doesn't?" (Villasante 262). Rey thinks CTS was meant to be symbiotic, that it "was supposed to help *both* of us" (Villasante 274, emphasis in original). Instead, Rey accuses, "you didn't tell me that Marisol was acting like some kind of grief keeper. Like she was a dump where I could safely throw all of my privileged-ass pain" (Villasante 274). Rey, who is white and affluent, further expounds, "Did you think I'd be okay with this? That because she's an immigrant, I wouldn't care? As long as I got rid of my grief, I'd be okay with ruining another girl's life" (Villasante 275). Indranie then likens Marisol's participation in the CTS trial to immigrants taking the jobs that white people typically do not want, like cleaning and farmwork. Rey rejects this and continues to advocate for Marisol, insisting that her undocumented status should not have been reason to subject her to CTS. In the end, after the one-month CTS trial, neither Rey nor Marisol continues with the procedure. Marisol is given an asylum hearing in which she testifies that she has been "been target to gangs in El Salvador" because "[she is] gay" (Villasante 303). The interview concludes with Marisol unsure if she and Gabi will be granted legal citizenship, but the implication is that Rey will use her father's political clout to sway the decision in Marisol's favor.

Despite Rey's advocacy for Marisol and the abortion of the CTS trial, Marisol is never truly in charge of her own future. The choices she makes give her some feeling of control, but she is always beholden to those with more power and social capital than her. That Marisol is subjected to the horrors of this medical trial due to her undocumented status is in keeping with contemporary medical treatment of detained migrants and other asylum-seekers. According to a report put out by New York Lawyers for the Public Interest,

> ICE . . . routinely: deny vital medical treatment such as dialysis and blood transfusions to people with serious health conditions; subject sick people in need of surgery to unconscionable delays; ignore repeated complaints and requests for care from people with serious symptoms; and refuse basic items such as glasses and dentures to people with medical conditions. (1)

To the government, undocumented immigrants like Marisol are disposable. While she is not deprived of medical care per se, she is certainly not treated well within medical settings. The government doesn't care if Marisol lives or dies during the CTS trial, or even after, because she doesn't officially gain legal citizenship status by the end of the novel. Her future is neither their priority nor their problem. Everything Marisol does, despite barriers, is to seek a better future, but the reader can't even be sure if she gets it. Much like Aaron, who has a hope for the future, all Marisol can do is hope that her and Gabi's application for asylum is accepted and rely on others with more power, like Rey and Indranie, to advocate on her behalf. Marisol and Aaron never have any power over their individual futures.

IMPOSSIBLE PASTS, PRESENTS, AND FUTURES

Though we may long for a concrete resolution, the open-endedness of *More Happy Than Not* and *The Grief Keeper* acts as a blank space on which to inscribe a better future, if not for Aaron and Marisol then for others like them. Much like scholars[2] have theorized that the queer and inclusive "x" in Latinx "offers a unique opportunity to do the work of imagining alternate worlds to those of our terrifying present" (Hudson), the unresolved endings of both novels could open paths to imagine new and more inclusive futures. But it is a task that requires immense power of imagination. Our history and present conditions have taught us that for queer youth, particularly queer youth of color, the future is not ready to unfold before them unfettered.

According to a qualitative study by Toomey et al., "Minority stressors and preparation for bias related to sexual orientation were positively associated with depressive symptoms and negatively associated with self-esteem"

(3597). That is, the co-occurrence of racism and homophobia not only has a deep impact on youth of color's abilities to accept their queered sexualities but also negatively affects their quality of life in general. In keeping with Kimberlé Crenshaw's notion of intersectionality, the concomitant effects of homophobia and racism are what prevent Aaron and Marisol from having any present agency. What's more, another study reveals that "as a result of myriad minority stressors, many LGBTQ youth, particularly youth of color, become detached from supportive and protective institutions, including family and school" (Gamarel et al. 290). These young people feel helpless and, often rightfully, that the adults in their lives will perpetuate the homophobia that is prevalent in the surrounding social structures. Added to this, for characters like Aaron, whose low socioeconomic status, and Marisol, whose undocumented status, already mean they have little access to protective measures, they are even more vulnerable to the abuses of Leteo and CTS.

Interestingly, though, the Leteo procedure and CTS are both carried out by other minoritized individuals. William Orchard highlights that "the procedure is presented as a technology that emerges from the Latinx community rather than as one that is imposed upon it." Likewise, Marisol is selected for the CTS trial by Indranie, who mentions she is the daughter of immigrants, and Dr. Deng, who is coded as an East Asian person. Often, minoritized peoples are complicit in their own oppression. For instance, social structures within Latinx communities, like machismo, code behaviors that reinforce heteropatriarchal ideals (Gattamorta and Quidley-Rodriguez 744). Likewise, Rachel M. Schmitz, Julissa Sanchez, and Bianca Lopez found, "Overall, LGBTQ+ Latinx youth are less likely to disclose their sexual and/or gender identities to parents compared to [white] LGBTQ+ youth, and there is evidence that Latinx families are less accepting of gender and sexual diversity" (19). These harsh realities that preclude Latinx youth from accessing support structure bar them from future efficacy.

And fictional worlds fare no better. Queer fiction for children, according to Thomas Crisp, is often grounded in heteropatriarchal ideals (336). Instead of imagining queer adolescents as proprietors of their own futures, literature for young readers reinforces the centrality of heterosexuality and its continued supremacy into the future. What's more, in her analysis of award-winning queer children's book, Laura M. Jiménez notes that children of color are largely absent (419). Taken together, these factors reinforce my assertion that the future is not (easily) accessible to queer young Latinxs. Aaron and Marisol's futures are tenuous at best. The few moments in which their futures seem accessible are not enough to prove that queer Latinx youth have the future speculative fiction espouses.

THE POWER OF IMAGINED FUTURITY

Yet I don't want to, nor can I, end this article on such a dire prognosis. Recent events, like the Pulse and Parkland massacres and the detention of children at the border, make imagining queer Latinx futures more imperative than ever (cárdenas 26). But, as Lysa Rivera explains, "Writing about the future from the bottom up or from the margin to the center, is itself an act of agency and will" (433). It requires an immense power of imagination, but speculative fiction for young readers may be up to the challenge. In "Science Fiction and Latino Studies Today . . . and in the Future," Fabio Chee explains, "Latina/os and African Americans share similar goals when it comes to science fiction: to counter the injustice of bias, racism, and systematic discrimination that negates them a place in the future, as it did to them in the past" (115). Put another way, speculative fiction is a mechanism by which we can test out theoretical paths to futures with more equitable conditions. It might be out of the realm of possibility to say that our future encompasses medical advances like Leteo or CTS, but right now our future is full of new technologies and present oppression. The new future hypothesized through speculative and science fiction can instead seek to undo our present oppression. In a way, by upsetting the dominant order, these imagined futures are distinctly queer.

Shane T. Moreman, in his analysis of queer youth literature, explains, "The potentiality of the queer future is made manifest within moments of reflection upon the dominant messages queer youth receive. This potentiality becomes discursive change when we devise lessons from the past to negotiate better messages for our present queer selves and queer communities" (187). In other words, we need to understand where queer Latinx youth have been to understand where they could go. I opened this article with a discussion of the trajectory of oppressive present to queer future. For Aaron and Marisol, memories of their traumatic pasts move them toward the futuristic and dangerous endeavors of Leteo and CTS. Their hope that these procedures offer a transformative future is suffused throughout their individual narratives.

Their hope renders that ameliorated future both possible and impossible. Resting in the unspoken stretch of the end of both novels, the future is sort of like Schrödinger's cat—both present and absent, possible and impossible, easily imagined and unimaginable. I feel as if I could squint and see it in the distance, or perhaps it is a mirage. In this way, José Esteban Muñoz's hypothesis that "queerness is not yet here" links to the possibility rendered by these books' open endings (1). Angel Daniel Matos further explains, "According to this approach, queerness is thus a rejection of presentist modes of thinking, a striving for a future with different possibilities and outcomes—even though one recognizes that this future may always be out of reach" (39). I suppose, as I meditate on Aaron's and Marisol's tragic pasts and presents, I have to question: are their futures out of reach? Is the future truly an impossibility for queer Latinx youth?

For nearly the totality of *More Happy Than Not*, Aaron does not want to take his queerness with him. And though Marisol could use the persecution she faces for her sexuality as a valid claim to asylum, she instead initially concocts an entirely different story and buries her queerness. Yet the plot progression of both novels reveals that queerness cannot be concealed. Aaron's unwinding brings back his relationship with one of his neighbors and the CTS trial pairs Marisol with Rey and provides them with the opportunity to forge a queer relationship. In *Cruising Utopia: The Then and There of Queer Futurity*, Muñoz calls us to "think about our lives and time differently" (189). In this way, Muñoz and the absence of an explicitly queer future in *More Happy Than Not* and *The Grief Keeper* provides us with a space for imagination. When we think about time differently, we engage in processes not dissimilar to Aaron and Marisol, who seek to reimagine their pasts to influence their present and future conditions.

Imagining a better future, both in and out of Latinx literature, is no small task. *More Happy Than Not* and *The Grief Keeper* give us glimpses of a future in which queer Latinx youth can seek possibilities, even if those possibilities never fully resolve into positive change. Instead, alongside my urging that we think of time and the linkage between the past and future queerly, I assert we read these two novels as the infancy of a corpus of speculative queer Latinx young adult literature. They are the early drafts of what I hypothesize will be a robust genre that seeks to (re)imagine the possibilities of queerness in a better future. In the end, reading for queer Latinx futures means accepting the necessity for imagination and the promise of a better tomorrow.

NOTES

Thank you to: Pete Kunze for finding that source I lost; and to the Shippensburg faculty/staff writing group for their support as I revised this article.

1. Interestingly, Katelyne R. Browne theorizes that Aaron attempts suicide three times: "once by slitting his wrists, and twice by pursuing a treatment known as 'the Leteo procedure,' which promises to completely erase one memory from a patient's brain" (16). Browne's theory here—that the Leteo procedure is akin to attempting death—reifies my assertion that Aaron is not afforded the possibility of a future.

2. Indeed, Hudson isn't the only scholar to note this. Author and scholar David Bowles has penned a series of popular and sometimes vilified articles on the Indigenous implications of the "x" in Latinx and its origins with queer, US-based Latin Americans. Ricardo L.

Ortiz also explains that "the *x* acts here instead as a suspension in time's unfolding, a pause to consider and to accommodate what might take place next in the place of and as an alternative to gender, especially heteropatriarchal, binary cis-gender" (203). The connections between the queer origins and futuristic implications of Latinx are exigent for my analysis.

WORKS CITED

Bowles, David. "Mexican X Part X: What the Hex a 'Latinx'?" *Medium*, 23 December 2018. blog.usejournal.com/mexican-x-part-x-what-the-hex-a-latinx-706b64dafe22.

Browne, Katelyn R. "Reimagining Queer Death in Young Adult Fiction." *Research on Diversity in Youth Literature* 2, no. 2 (2020): 1–25.

cárdenas, micha. "Monstrous Children of Pregnant Androids: Latinx Futures after Orlando." *GLQ: A Journal of Lesbian and Gay Studies* 24, no. 1 (2018): 26–31.

Chee, Fabio. "Science Fiction and Latino Studies Today . . . and in the Future." *The Routledge Companion to Latina/o Popular Culture*, edited by Frederick Luis Aldama. Routledge, 2016, 110–19.

Crisp, Thomas. "From Romance to Magical Realism: Limits and Possibilities in Gay Adolescent Fiction." *Children's Literature in Education* 40, no. 4 (2009): 333–48.

Gamarel, Kristi E., et al. "Identity Safety and Relational Health in Youth Spaces: A Needs Assessment with LGBTQ Youth of Color." *Journal of LGBT Youth* 11, no. 3 (2014): 289–315.

Gattamorta, Karina, and Narciso Quidley-Rodriguez. "Coming Out Experiences of Hispanic Sexual Minority Young Adults in South Florida." *Journal of Homosexuality* 65, no. 6, (2018): 741–65.

Gay Pearson, Wendy, Veronica Hollinger, and Joan Gordon. "Introduction: Queer Universes," *Queer Universes: Sexualities in Science Fiction*. Liverpool University Press, 2010. 1–13.

Giaimo, Genie Nicole. "Memory, Brains, and Narratives? The Humanities as a Testing-Ground for Bioethical Scenario-Building." *Literature and Medicine* 34, no. 1 (2016): 53–78.

Howe, Mark L, and Lauren M Knott. "The Fallibility of Memory in Judicial Processes: Lessons from the Past and Their Modern Consequences." *Memory* 23, no. 5 (2015): 633–656.

Hudson, Renee. "Imagining the Futures of Latinx Speculative Fictions" *ASAP/Journal*, 2019. asapjournal.com/imagining-the-futures-of-latinx-speculative-fictions-renee-hudson/.

Jiménez, Laura M. "Representations in Award-Winning LGBTQ Young Adult Literature from 2000–2013." *Journal of Lesbian Studies* 19, no. 4 (2015): 406–22.

Matos, Angel Daniel. "A Narrative of a Future Past: Historical Authenticity, Ethics, and Queer Latinx Futurity in *Aristotle and Dante Discover the Secrets of the Universe*." *Children's Literature* 47, no. 1 (2019): 30–56.

Matos, Angel Daniel, and Jon Michael Wargo. "Editors' Introduction: Queer Futurities in Youth Literature, Media, and Culture," *Research on Diversity in Youth Literature* 2, no. 1 (2019): 1–16.

Merla-Watson, Cathryn, and B. V. Olguín. "Altermundos: Reassessing the Past, Present, and Future of the Chican@ and Latin@ Speculative Arts." *Altermundos: Latin@ Speculative Literature, Film, and Popular Culture*, edited by Cathryn Merla-Watson and B. V. Olguín. UCLA Chicano Studies Research Center Press, 2017, 1–38.

Moreman, Shane T. "A Queer Futurity Autofantasía: Contouring Discourses of Latinx through Memory and Queer Youth Literature." *Text and Performance Quarterly* 39, no. 3 (2019): 185–202.

Muñoz, José Esteban. *Cruising Utopia: The Then and There of Queer Futurity*. NYU Press, 2009.

New York Lawyers for the Public Interest. *Detained and Denied: Healthcare Access in Immigration Detention*. 2017. www.nylpi.org/wp-content/uploads/2017/02/HJ-Health-in-Immigration-Detention-Report_2017.pdf.

Orchard, William. "Endless Happy Beginnings: Forms of Speculation in Adam Silvera's *More Happy Than Not*." *ASAP/Journal*, 2019. asapjournal.com/endless-happy-beginnings-forms-of-speculation-in-adam-silveras-more-happy-than-not-william-orchard/.

Ortiz, Ricardo L. "Burning *X*'s: Critical Futurities within Latinx Studies' Disidentifying Present." *Aztlan: A Journal of Chicano Studies* 45, no. 2 (September 2020): 201–11.

Pérez-Torres, Rafael. "Introduction." *Aztlan: A Journal of Chicano Studies* 45, no. 2 (September 2020): 153–60.

Phelps, Elizabeth A., and Stefan G. Hofmann. "Memory Editing from Science Fiction to Clinical Practice." *Nature* 572, no. 7767 (2019): 43–50.

Ramírez, Catherine S. "Afrofuturism/Chicanafuturism Fictive Kin." *Aztlán: A Journal of Chicano Studies* 33, no. 1 (2008): 185–94.

Rivera, Lysa. "Future Histories and Cyborg Labor: Reading Borderlands Science Fiction after NAFTA." *Science Fiction Studies* 39, no. 3 (2012): 415–36.

Robillard, Julie M., and Judy Illes. "Manipulating Memories: The Ethics of Yesterday's Science Fiction and Today's Reality." *AMA J Ethics* 18, no. 12 (2016): 1225–1231.

Schmitz, Rachel M., et al. "LGBTQ+ Latinx Young Adults' Health Autonomy in Resisting Cultural Stigma." *Culture, Health & Sexuality* 21, no. 1 (2019): 16–30.

Schalk, Sami. *Bodyminds Reimagined: (Dis)Ability, Race, and Gender in Black Women's Speculative Fiction*. Duke University Press, 2018.

Silvera, Adam. *More Happy Than Not*. eBook. Soho Press, 2015.

Toomey, Russell B., et al. "Family Socialization for Racism and Heterosexism: Experiences of Latinx Sexual Minority Adolescents and Young Adults." *Journal of Family Issues* 39, no. 13 (2018): 3586–3611.

Villasante, Alexandra. *The Grief Keeper*. eBook. G. P Putnam's Sons, 2019.

Afterword

Daydreams Made Real: New Narrative Maps of Resplendent Queer Latinx Futurities

Frederick Luis Aldama

Gloria Velásquez opens *Tommy Stands Alone* with her protagonist Tommy Montoya on his bed with the latest superhero comic splayed open, and him deep in the creative zone, reveling in the joy of sketching his own Batman. His recreative reverie is suddenly interrupted, however. His machista papá barks: "Tráeme una cerveza." *Tommy Stands Alone* is about the trauma of a teen Latino coming out within deeply homophobic and toxic masculinist environs. At home, school, and town he's crushed with all sorts of epithets of verbal shaming and abuse: *desgraciado joto, maricon,* faggot, among others. Tommy spirals into deep depression, turns to drugs and alcohol—and attempts suicide. His dreams of making comics, going to art college, and *getting out* are dashed to the ground.

I open this afterword with mention of *Tommy Stands Alone* not just because of its monumental importance as our first queer Latinx YA novel. I open with it because of Tommy's emblematic traumatic struggle *and* his joy of comics, both as creator and reader. Indeed, it is this latter aspect of Tommy's identity that powerfully reminds us that in addition to the queer Latinx YA fiction so beautifully examined and explored in this volume, there is today a growing presence of queer Latinx YA comics. It's almost as if our beloved Tommys of yesteryear have today come out and into their full potentialities in and through the making of comics. I think readily of LGBTQ+ Latinx comics creators such as Jacoby Salcedo, Ivan Velez, Terry Blas, Josh Trujillo, Breena Nuñez, Cristy C. Road, Jeanette Arroyo, Mike Curato, Dave Ortega, and Emil Ferris. I think, too, of those who crisscross alphabetic and graphic queer Latinx YA fictional storyworld spaces such as Alex Sanchez, David Bowles, Carmen María Machado, Gabby Rivera, and my own forthcoming work.

The intimate relationship of queer Latinx alphabetic with graphic narrative should come with little surprise—and not only because of shared histories of being maligned by those drawing artificial lines between worthy (highbrow) and unworthy (lowbrow) storytelling art. As Cristina and Trevor and their super crew of scholars demonstrate with QLYA novels, so too with QLYA comics: they reconstruct the very real toxic stressors and traumas experienced by queer Latinx youth, and they invite us to cocreate wish-fulfillment fantasies of overcoming abusers and bullies, and of making real daydreams of queer friendly spaces that model positive forms of vulnerability and love. As Alex Sanchez sums up in an interview with me, yesteryear's queer YA fiction had to feature characters that were "lonely, isolated, and eventually die tragically" (216). This is not the case today. While QLYA alphabetic and graphic narratives importantly recreate the traumatic coming out struggles as queer and Latinx youth, today they also dream up new maps of open and accepting social relationalities. As Benjamin Alire Sáenz reflects of his magisterial *Aristotle and Dante Discover the Secrets of the Universe*, "It's about ethnicity, race, sexual identity—and intimacy. It's not just about sex; it's about love" (211).

I don't mean to imply here that queer Latinx youth today are living some sort of nirvanic postrace, posthomophobic moment. Indeed, arguably today more than ever the social tissue is failing queer Latinx teens. It's failing to provide the everyday conditions for the realization of their full potentialities—for the good life, or *eudaimonia* as Aristotle called it.

It's true, all teens experience physical, cognitive, and emotive stressors during a time of development when they are forming their core sense of self. However, it's also a fact that queer Latinx—and queer youth of color generally—face daily violence fed by misinformation that continues to perpetuate myths of rigid race, sexual, and gender binaries and oppositions. It's a fact, too, that US society is rife with the violence of racial surveillance—and not just by police, but also educators. A great percentage of our Latinx youth attend underfunded and underresourced schools where teachers see them only as deficits, misfits, and problems at best, leading to high percentages of dropouts as well as push-outs (suspensions) and lock-outs (expulsions). Queer Latinx youth continue to be crushed. And this, during a time when everything from family to school to society should be fostering the growing of their full potentialities.

Queer youth of color live in a social world that also continues to prescribe binary gender identities—and this despite advances in research in developmental psychology, neuroscience, behavioral endocrinology, genetics, and epigenetics. Sex and sexuality remain a natural part of our development—yet taboos continue to arm-choke this formative part of Latinx teen development, especially when it comes to same-sex and fluid sexual orientations, behaviors, and attractions. And this during a time when more than ever research confirms what we've known all along: male and female gender identity is not fixed to biology, or birth-assigned gender. However, the social stigmas perpetuated and cemented by family prejudice and mainstream media privileging of gender binaries leads to queer Latinx youth struggling with gender identities that fall outside the binary male and female: transgender, nonbinary, and gender fluid.

Like the phase from birth to six-years-old, teenhood (roughly ages thirteen to eighteen) is a huge moment in our physical, cognitive, emotive development. It's a time of explosive curiosity and great creativity, when queer Latinx youth engage with an abundance of novel experiences, stimulations, sensations, experimentations, and explorations that lead to the formation of massive amounts of new neural pathways that in turn lead to novel, creative thinking. It is also a time of great vulnerability, when adrenal stress, sex, and growth hormones flood the brain. It's a time of physical and emotional awkwardness. It's a time of risk taking. It's a time of heightened self-consciousness. The messiness of this phase of our development should be protected. It's not—especially for queer youth of color.

Let me turn briefly to a couple of my favorite QLYA comics that powerfully recreate much of what I just discussed: a) how the social tissue today violently rejects and crushes queer Latinx youth—and queer youth of color generally; and b) how QLYA creators are also inviting us to shape daydreams of new spaces of intersectional relationalities.

With *The Low, Low Woods* Carmen María Machado (writer) and Dani (artist) choose to worldbuild their queer Latinx and Black comic within the speculative genre of horror. Set in a former mining town called Shudder-to-Think, the storyworld is filled to the brim with marauding skinless, hybrid human/animal creatures, woman-child witches, and evil energy that violently turns women's wombs into interdimensional sinkholes. Machado and Dani use the horror genre to allegorize the plight of queer teens of color in society. The protagonists and dominant filters of the story: queer teens of color and best friends, El (Latina) and Vee (Black). The horror of their lives doesn't stem from, say, being bullied as queer teens of color at school. It revolves around central mysteries like why they suffer from bouts of confusion and forgetfulness and shock-horror encounters with frightening (evil) creatures and forces that target the women of the town. In one instance, Vee's sensual encounter with her love interest, Jessica, turns, with the flip of a page, into a splash-page scene of horror. Dani's graphic shaping of Vee's posture and facial expression, along with the page design that tips everything downward diagonally from left to right, triggers the feeling of shock and confusion. Not only does it act as a signpost in the narrative that we are to read this as an allegory of patriarchal society's misogynistic violence, but it powerfully reminds us that as a queer teen of color, Vee can never take for granted the exploration of the pleasures and curiosities of her body with another's that is so important to the healthy development of her as a young woman. Indeed, a central element of El and Vee's journey—and their formation—is to figure out why they suffer from their collective forgetting. They do figure this out, learning deep histories of the town and how the men used special spring water that would erase memories to abduct, rape, maim, and kill the town's girls and women. Along with this knowledge, El and Vee also discover the antidote: suncap mushrooms. This allows them to remember—or rather to rememory, per Toni Morison—their lived collective trauma; all those horrific acts against them during their blackouts, as well as standing up to, fighting, and vanquishing those violent and violating men of the town.

With *You Brought Me the Ocean*, Alex Sanchez (writer) and Jul Maroh (artist) put queer intersectionality front and center in the superhero narrative. Their protagonist is a Black teen, Jake Hyde (son of Black Manta), who struggles to come to terms with a nascent queer sexuality, and water bending superpowers. He lives with his single mamá in Truth or Consequences, New Mexico, where Spanish and Latinxs are everywhere, including his best friend, Maria. As Jake's journey unfolds and he learns to confront and vanquish queer and transphobic bullies (the villains), so too do Maroh's color palettes shift from muted yellows and browns of the desert to vital turquoise blues and greens of the ocean. Along the way Sanchez and Maroh invite us to experience with Jake self-doubt and depression. At the lowest point in his journey, we experience his self-doubt and spiral into depression. Sanchez and Maroh convey this with a splash page that shows Jake falling back on his bed and staring up at the ceiling trying to come to terms with his sense of being monstrous: physical marks on the body and a social mirror that reflects his same-sex desires as deviant. A third of the way through the graphic novel Maroh presents us with a cascade of images, inviting us to think and feel with Jake as he psychologically and physically tumbles into a deep depression. Sanchez's narrative coupled with Maroh's visuals of Jake's body, posture, and expression tumble us through emotions of shame, when he covers his body as he looks at the mirror's reflection; anger, when he sheds his jacket; and helplessness and loss of hope when he slumps over, falls from his chair, and holds this jacket tight. As the story unfolds, however,

Jake becomes more emboldened to allow himself to express his desire for his love interest, Kenny. Maroh uses a series of panels showing Jake and love-interest Kenny in a swimming pool, moving from hesitation to confidence as they mutually explore one another's bodies and express their love for one another. Sanchez and Maroh invite us to share in Jake and Kenney's daydreaming made real. They invite us to cocreate with Jake as he learns to accept and publicly embrace the integration of the totality of his identity: as Black, queer, *and* superhuman.

For queer youth of color like El, Vee, and Jake, the space of the daydream acts as an important space of creativity; of being able to imagine an empowered and emancipated, integrated self, able to act, engage, and explore in a world that constantly seeks to crush and control nonnormative thoughts, feelings, and actions.

These QLYA comics and others already mentioned above powerfully remind readers that for queer youth of color, the daydreaming brain is the wish-fulfillment brain, and this is the fiction-making brain—all of which seek refuge and quietude from everyday queerphobic and racist assaults and map new positive spaces for teen intersectional identities and experiences. Teens need the time and space for reflection and creativity. They need to be able to daydream queer romances, knocking down xenophobic bullies, and new safe spaces to imagine the agency to act, engage, explore—to be curious—in a world that constantly seeks to control and surveil all their thoughts and actions. As such, they do more than daydream wish-fulfillment fantasies of victory over oppressors. They wake readers to ways that youth of color can freely and powerfully grow fluid, messy, exuberant, complex patterns of thought, behaviors, and experiences.

As the incredible coterie of scholars demonstrate herein, QLYA coming-of-age and coming-out narratives at once speak to past and present xenophobic, homophobic, misogynistic violence and trauma *and* celebrate the tremendous potentialities of the imagination and action of queer Latinx youth. They look to the past and present, to carve new pathways into a future. They point us to new social maps that enrich the ways that queer Latinx youth can exist in all their resplendent colors, orientations, and complexities. They daydream new borderland worlds where social and physical spaces are free of ideological and physical surveillance systems that delimit and cut short the cognitive and emotive development of *los atravesados* in all their fluid, messy, exuberant, complex ways of perceiving, feeling, and thinking—as well as positively transforming our world today and tomorrow.

WORKS CITED AND SUGGESTED FURTHER READING

Aldama, Frederick Luis, Oscar Garza, and Rolando Esquivel. *Through Fences*. Ohio State University Press, 2023.

Aldama, Frederick Luis, ed. *Tales from la Vida: A Latinx Comics Anthology*. Ohio State University Press, 2018.

Aldama, Frederick. "Benjamin Alire Sáenz." *Latino/a Children and Young Adult Writers on the Art of Storytelling*. University of Pittsburgh Press, 2018, 207–213.

Aldama, Frederick. "Alex Sanchez." *Latino/a Children and Young Adult Writers on the Art of Storytelling*. University of Pittsburgh Press, 2018, 214–219.

Andreyko, Marc, Sarah Gaydos, and Jamie S. Rich. *Love Is Love*. IDW, 2016.

Arroyo, Jeanette, and Ren Graham's *Blackwater*. Henry Holt, 2022.

Blas, Terry. "Ghetto Swirl." https://terryblas.tumblr.com/post/144554629659/these-are-the-first-four-pages-of-my-new-comic

Bors, Matt, Matt Lubchansky, Sarah Mairk, and Eleri Harris. *Be Gay, Do Comics*. IDW, 2020.

Bowles, David, and Raul the Third. *Clockwork Curandera Vol 1: The Witchowl Parliament*. Lee and Low, 2021.

Curato, Mike. *Flamer*. Henry Holt, 2020.

Ferris, Emil. *My Favorite Thing Is Monsters*. Fantagraphics, 2017.

Glass, Joe, and Matt Miner. *Young Men in Love: A Queer Romance Anthology*. A Brave New World, 2022.

Machado, Carmen María, and Dani. *The Low, Low Woods*. DC Comics, 2020.

Rivera, Gabby, and Celia Moscote. *Juliet Takes a Breath*. BOOM!, 2020.

Rivera, Gabby. *America Vol. 1: The Life and Times of America Chavez*. Marvel, 2017.

Roché, Angélique, ed. *Marvel Voices: Pride*. Marvel, 2022.

Trujillo, Josh. *Dodge City*. BOOM!, 2018

Vasquez, Kalinda. *America Chavez: Made in America*. Marvel, 2021.

Velez, Ivan. *Tales from the Closet*. Planet Bronx Productions, 2005.

About the Contributors

Frederick Luis Aldama, aka Professor Latinx, is the Jacob and Frances Sanger Mossiker Chair in the Humanities at the University of Texas, Austin, where he is also founder and director of the Latinx Pop Lab and the editor of the *Latinx Pop Magazine*. He is an award-winning author, coauthor, editor, and coeditor of over fifty books, including an Eisner for *Latinx Superheroes in Mainstream Comics*. He is editor and coeditor of ten book series, including Biographix, Latinographix, and Brown Ink. He is the author of children's books, including *The Adventures of Chupacabra Charlie* (published in English and Spanish) and *Con Papá / With Papá*, as well as cocreator of the award-winning animation short *Carlitos Chupacabra*. He is the author of comic books, including *Pyroclast, Through Fences, Labrynths Borne, The Steampunkera Chronicles* (forthcoming), and the illustrated novel *The Absolutely (Almost) True Adventures of Max Rodriguez*. He has been inducted into the National Cartoonists Society, the Texas Institute of Letters, the Ohio State University's Office of Diversity and Inclusion Hall of Fame, and serves on the board of directors for the Academy of American Poets.

Trevor Boffone is a lecturer in the Women's, Gender & Sexuality Studies Program at the University of Houston. His work using TikTok with his students has been featured on *Good Morning America*, *ABC News*, *Inside Edition*, and *Access Hollywood*, among numerous national and local media platforms. He is the author of *Renegades: Digital Dance Cultures from Dubsmash to TikTok*, *TikTok Broadway: Musical Theatre Fandom in the Digital Age*, and the coauthor of *Latinx Teens: U.S. Popular Culture on the Page, Stage, and Screen*. He is the coeditor of *Encuentro: Latinx Performance for the New American Theater*; *Nerds, Goths, Geeks, and Freaks: Outsiders in Chicanx and Latinx Young Adult Literature*; and *Shakespeare and Latinidad*, among other collections.

T. Jackie Cuevas is associate professor of English at the University of Texas. She is the author of *Post-Borderlandia: Chicana Literature and Gender*

Variant Critique (Rutgers University Press, 2018), which received Honorable Mention for the National Women's Studies Association's Gloria Anzaldúa Book Prize in 2018 and was a 2019 finalist for a Lambda Literary Award. With Sonia Saldívar-Hull and Larissa Mercado-López, Cuevas coedited *El Mundo Zurdo 4: Selected Works from the 2013 Meeting of the Society for the Study of Gloria Anzaldúa* (Aunt Lute Books, 2015). Cuevas is interim director of the UT Center for women's and Gender Studies and is a member of the Macondo Writers Workshop.

Cristina Herrera is professor and director of Chicanx/Latinx Studies at Portland State University. She is coauthor of *Latinx Teens: U.S. Popular Culture on the Page, Stage, and Screen* and coeditor of *Nerds, Goths, Geeks, and Freaks: Outsiders in Chicanx and Latinx Young Adult Literature*. Cristina's book, *Welcome to Oxnard: Race, Place, and Chicana Adolescence in Michele Serros's Writings* (University of Pittsburgh Press, 2024), is the first monograph to explore Michele Serros's work.

Alexander Lalama is an assistant professor of English at Bradley University in Peoria, Illinois. His research is in Latinx literature of the US, exploring Latinxs in literature and popular culture who affiliate themselves with outsider-music subcultures and practices, such as punks, goths, and metalheads. He is currently working on a project that investigates how the American Gothic is transformed and mutated in Latinx Literature. His work has appeared in *Latina Outsiders: Remaking Latina Identity* (Routledge, 2019). He is currently completing an article on Celia C. Pérez's novel *The First Rule of Punk* for *Contemporary Young Adult Literature and the Fashioning of Black and Brown Youth* (University Press of Mississippi, forthcoming).

Angel Daniel Matos is an assistant professor of gender, sexuality, and women's studies at Bowdoin College who specializes in YA literature and media, queer Latinidades, and screen cultures. His work has been published in *Children's Literature, Research on Diversity in Youth Literature,* the *ALAN Review*, and various other journals and edited volumes. Along with Pamela Robertson Wojcik and Paula Massood, he is one of the coeditors of *Media Crossroads: Intersections of Space and Identity in Screen Cultures*, which was published in 2021 by Duke University Press. His monograph, *The Reparative Impulse of Queer Young Adult Literature and Culture* (Routledge, 2024) explores how queer young adult literature, media, and culture creates a sense of historicity and futurity for contemporary teen readers and viewers, focusing extensively on queer Latinx works.

Regina Marie Mills is assistant professor of Latinx and US multiethnic literature in the Department of English at Texas A&M University. Her research focuses on Latinx, AfroLatinx, and African diaspora literature and media, as well as life-writing studies and critical game studies. Her first book, *Invisibility and Influence: A Literary History of AfroLatinidades* (University of Texas Press, 2024) is part of the "Latinx: The Future Is Now" series. Her research is published or forthcoming in venues such as *Latino Studies*; *The Black Scholar*; *The Lion & the Unicorn*; *Oxford Bibliographies in Latino Studies*; *The Routledge Handbook on Latinx Life Writing*; *Teaching Games and Game Studies in the Literature Classroom*; and *Latinx Literature and Critical Futurities, 1992–2020*. Her second book examines how video games structure societal conceptions of Latinx and AfroLatinx communities.

Joseph Isaac Miranda is an assistant professor of English at Yale University. His research and teaching interests converge at the intersection of Latinx Literature, queer of color critique, and legal and political theory. His first monograph, *Laws of Emplotment: The Suspended States of Latinx Literature*, argues that the Supreme Court's constraint of Puerto Rican sovereignty is a foundational hermeneutic for thinking about Latinx Literature in the long durée of the Insular Cases. His work also appears in *MELUS Journal* and *American Literature* and has been supported by the Ford Foundation.

Jesus Montaño is a teacher/scholar of Latinx literatures and cultures, with special interest in children's and young adult literary and cultural production in Our Americas. His teaching and research, in this way, examine the transformative and reparative power of writing and reading on young minds and spirits. Along with his coauthored book *Tactics of Hope in Latinx Children's and Young Adult Literature* (University of New Mexico Press, 2022), Montaño's program of study also includes articles and book chapters in *The Lion and the Unicorn*, *Children's Literature Quarterly*, and *Liberating Shakespeare* (Arden Shakespeare). His current project, *Young Latinx Shakespeares: Race, Justice, and Literary Appropriation* (Palgrave Macmillan, forthcoming), examines how contemporary Latinx young adult novels utilize Shakespeare as a locus for cultural and literary production to willfully open and create new terrains. He is Assistant Professor of English at Baylor University; he has a PhD from the Ohio State University and a BA from the University of Texas at Austin.

Domino Renee Pérez is a professor in the Department of English and the Center for Mexican American Studies at the University of Texas at Austin, where she regularly teaches courses in young adult fictions and American literature. Dr. Pérez has published numerous book chapters and articles on topics ranging from film and Indigeneity in Mexican American studies to young adult literature and folklore. Her recent book *Fatherhood in the Borderlands: A Daughter's Slow Approach* (2022), which concerns itself with the legibility of Mexican American fathers, sits at the intersection of slow research, personal narrative, and literature, film, cultural, ethnic, and gender studies. The book emphasizes not only the epistemic value of creative inquiry, but also the role such an approach can play in academic research practices.

Regan Postma-Montaño serves as senior academic writing consultant and associate graduate faculty with the School of Education at Baylor University. Her scholarly work focuses on issues of justice in contemporary Latin American and Latinx youth literatures and cultures. In addition to publishing articles with *International Research in Children's Literature, Research on Diversity in Youth Literature*, and *Women's Studies,* among other journals, she coauthored *Tactics of Hope in Latinx Children's and Young Adult Literature* (University of New Mexico Press, 2022). Regan is currently at work on her next monograph on resistance and activism in Latin(x) American youth literature and culture.

Cristina Rhodes is an associate professor of multiethnic American literature at Shippensburg University of Pennsylvania. Her research on Latinx children's and young adult literature can be found in *Children's Literature Association Quarterly, Label Me Latin*, and other journals. She is currently working on a book-length manuscript on speculative fiction, magical realism, and Latinx youth in literature, tentatively titled *Facing Uncertain Futures: The Transformative Possibilities of Latinx Youth Literatures* (under advance contract with the University Press of Mississippi).

Sonia Alejandra Rodríguez (they/she) is a professor in the English Department at LaGuardia Community College (CUNY) where they teach composition, literature, and creative writing. Their research introduces "conocimiento narratives" as a way to read realist fiction within Latinx children's and young adult literature. Rodríguez is coeditor of *Ethnic Studies and Youth Literature*: *A Critical Reader* forthcoming from SUNY Press.

Index

Abate, Michelle Ann, 12–13, 14, 196, 198–99
Abject Performances (Alvarado), 59
AbriendoLibros (Booktube channel), 175
Acevedo, Elizabeth, 20–21n4, 25
Aceves, Aaron H., 11
ACT-UP activist group, 199–201
Ahmed, Sara, 126–27
AIDS crisis, 6, 9; absence in *Aristotle and Dante* series, 195–207
Alamillo, Laura, 136
Albertalli, Becky, 44, 134
Alberto, Aitch, 165
Aldama, Arturo J., 15, 176–77n5
Aldama, Frederick Luis, 15, 20, 66–67, 176–77n5, 222–26
alienation, theme of, 31–32, 119–23, 125, 127, 129
All the Bright Places (Niven), 137
Almeida, Elaine, 138, 143
Alonso, Carolina, 6, 43, 81, 176n4
Altermundos (Merla-Watson and Olguín), 211
Alvarado, Leticia, 59
Alvarez, Eddy, 15
Ambientes: New Queer Latino Writing (Lima), 51
"ambivalent belonging," 59
American Dream, 155, 157
Ames, Melissa, 192
Amnesia: The Dark Descent (video game), 151
Andersen, Hans Christian, 90, 183
Anger Is a Gift (Oshiro), 10
animal metaphors, 58–59, 96, 121
Anthony, Adelina, 57, 62

anti-immigrant attitudes, 157–58. See also deportation, threats of
Antonio's Card (González), 71, 73–74
Anzaldúa, Gloria: "atravesados" concept, 4, 17–18; bridges and thresholds, 174–75; influence of, 5, 15, 57, 127; "la naguala" figure, 87; Nepantla, 47, 96; picture books, 72; *Prietita and the Ghost Woman*, 184
Aragón, Cecilia J., 43
Araujo, Gwen, 8
Arenas, Rosie, 136
Aristotle and Dante Discover the Secrets of the Universe (Sáenz), 8, 21n6, 25, 41, 79, 164–67, 186
Aristotle and Dante Dive into the Waters of the World (Sáenz), 9, 197, 198–99
Aristotle and Dante series (Saénz): absence of AIDS crisis in, 195–207
Arroyo, Jeanette, 222
Arte Público Press, 5–6, 11–12, 139
Ash (Lo), 183
asthma, metaphor of, 123–28
"atravesados" figures: characters, 4; within normative cultures, 17–18; queer kinship networks, 174–76
Aunt Lute Press, 5–6
authors' methodology, 18–20
autofantasía, 64–65, 70, 72–73
Aviles, Gwen, 41, 42

Baeza Ventura, Gabriela, 11–12, 139
"banking of knowledge," 136
banned books, 69, 139
"Barrio Gothic," 18, 26–31

233

barrios in Latinx culture, 27, 31–32
Bayron, Kaylynn, 183
Beauty and the Beast (film), 183
Beck, Noah, 137
Beyond Borders (Linville and Carlson), 14
bildungsromans. *See* coming-of-age narratives
binary frameworks, 16–17, 48, 223–24
binding/binders, 33
bisexuality: characters on television, 52n4; erasure of, 43–44; in *They Both Die at the End*, 41–52
Blackburn, Mollie, 139
Black communities: comics/graphic novels, 224–26; Haitian brujx, 29; intersectionality with Latinx identity, 52n2; and speculative fiction, 211; trans people, 21n5
Blanca y Roja (McLemore), 86, 89, 181
Blanco, María del Pilar, 30
Blas, Terry, 222
Boffone, Trevor, 18, 19, 41–52, 78–79, 118, 133–44, 148, 223
Bogost, Ian, 148–49
Bond, The (Garza), 43
BookTok, 11, 19, 51, 135–44
Borderlands/La Frontera (Anzaldúa), 5
Bost, Suzanne, 101
Bowles, David, 219–20n2, 222
Boyfriends with Girlfriends (Sánchez), 42, 43
Boy Meets Boy (Levithan), 42
Boys of the Beast (Zepeda), 11
Brady, Mary Pat, 125
breathing, metaphor of, 123–28
bridges, metaphor of, 174–75
Brown common, 125–27
Browne, Katelyne R., 219n1
Brown Trans Figurations (Galarte), 16, 189
Brozon, Mónica B., 164, 168–71
Bruhm, Steven, 181
Bruja Born (Córdova), 10
"brujx" community, 26; in *Cemetery Boys*, 26, 28–30; Santa Muerte, 34–36
Burcon, Sarah, 192

B Word, The (San Filippo), 47
Byrd, James, Jr., 7

Café con Lychee (Lee), 11
Call Me Tree (González), 71
Calvo, Luz, 16
Candelaria, Cordelia, 184
Cart, Michael, 3, 14
Castañeda, Claudia, 87
Castillo, Ana, 5
Catholic Church, 34–36
Cavarero, Adriana, 130n5
Cemetery Boys (Thomas), 10–11, 25–38
Chabelita's Heart (Millán), 19, 70, 71–75
Chabram-Dernersesian, Angie, 15
Chávez, Leo, 154
Chee, Fabio, 218
Chicanafuturism, 211
Chicana Lesbians (Trujillo), 15
Chicana/o Cultural Studies Reader, The (Chabram-Dernersesian), 15
Chicano Male Recollections of Consciousness and Coming Out (Güido and Del Castillo), 15
Chicanx community, 163–64, 175–76; Chicanx folklore, 182, 184; use of terms, 176n1. *See also* Latinx culture
childhood: children's literature, 73; contrasted with adulthood, 121; and innocence, 74, 117; "lost" children and futures, 184–85; for queer children, 117–18, 149, 181; as time of transformation, 87
Children's Literature (Lerer), 182
Chulito (Rice-González), 4, 42
Cinder (Meyer), 183
Cinderella (film), 183
Cinderella Is Dead (Bayron), 183
Clare, Stephanie, 119
Clinton, Bill, 6
Cohen, Jeffrey, 155
Coleman, Joshua, 198
Coles, Jay, 10
colonialism, 5, 14, 27–28, 80–81, 118, 176–77n5

comic books/graphic novels, 222–26
coming-of-age fiction, 116–29, 130n2; counternarratives to, 124–25; and violence, 176n4
coming-out narratives, 119–20, 168–69; *Juliet Takes a Breath*, 120–21
Compañeras (Ramos), 15
"comunidad," 45
Córdova, Zoraida, 10, 43
Courage to Imagine, The (Natov), 73
COVID-19 pandemic, 144n1; parallels with AIDS, 202
Crenshaw, Kimberlé, 217
Crip Theory, 105
Crisp, Thomas, 14, 21n13, 217
Crucet, Jennie Capó, 129
Cruising Utopia (Muñoz), 87, 96, 219
Cuando amamos cantamos (Martínez), 62–65, 71
Cuevas, T. Jackie, 18, 56–67, 171
Curato, Mike, 222
Curiouser: On the Queerness of Children (Bruhm and Hurley), 181
Cut Both Ways (Mesrobian), 42

D'Amelio, Charli, 137
Dani (comic book artist), 224–25
Danielson, Marivel, 15, 57
Dark and Deepest Red (McLemore), 86, 90–91, 181
Dear Martin (Stone), 10
Decena, Carlos, 119
Decolonizing Latinx Masculinities (Aldama and Aldama), 15, 176–77n5
De dia gaviotas, de noche flores blancas (Hinojosa Rebolledo), 164, 171–74
Defense of Marriage Act, 7
Degollado, Ruben, 180
De Jesús Vega, Manuel, 202–3
de la Peña, Terri, 6
Del Castillo, Adelaida R., 15, 167
"density of connection," 125
deportation, threats of, 11, 26, 27, 214. *See also* anti-immigrant attitudes

Deposing Nathan (Smedley), 42
DeVito, Shannon, 142
digital book clubs. *See* BookTok
Dinshaw, Carolyn, 66
disability: and intersectionality, 99–112; and Latinx teen identities, 106–11; narrative prosthesis theory, 111–12; and sexuality, 107; studies, 101–5
Disabling Characters (Dunn), 103–4
disidentification, 16, 38, 47, 182, 186–87, 200–201. *See also* identity formation
Dolan-Sandrino, Sage Grace, 10
Dole, Mayra Lazara, 42, 69
"Don't Ask, Don't Tell," 6, 7, 160n11
Don't Say Gay, 159
Double Feature (Hartinger), 42
Down to the Bone (Dole), 42, 69
Dragonlinked (Garza), 43
Duckels, Gabriel, 197
Dunn, Patricia A., 103–4

@earth2mateo, 142
Elman, Julie Passanante, 105, 113n11
Eng, David, 122
Entertainment Software Association (ESA), 148
Epstein, B. J., 42
erasure: in games scholarship, 150; by generic Latinidad, 36, 52n2; and heteropatriarchal traditions, 15–16, 32, 43–44, 70, 111; memory and future, 212–14; white supremacy and, 8, 14, 18. *See also* marginalized identities
Esquibel, Catrióna Rueda, 15, 16, 72

fairy tales, 181–83; elements, 95; and heteronormativity, 186–87; retellings, 87, 90–91; temporal conventions, 186
Fairy Tales Told for Children (Anderson), 183
family structures: "chosen" families, 46–47, 166; and gay coming of age novels, 79, 116, 119; Latinx models, 19, 57–59, 70, 79–80, 122–23, 154; queer kinship,

125–28, 170–71; responses to queer identity, 163–76; sibling relationships, 155, 169; "traditional" family trope, 8, 163–64
fantasy fiction, 9–10, 19, 38n2, 72, 181, 192, 193n3. *See also* speculative fiction
Faris, Wendy B., 86
Faults (de la Peña), 6
Felski, Rita, 198
Femeniños Project, 62
feminism, 77–78; feminist disability studies, 102–4
Ferguson, Roderick, 130n3
Fernández-Garcia, Andrea, 129–30n2
Ferris, Emil, 222
Fifteen Hundred Miles from the Sun (Garza Villa), 11
Figurations (Castañeda), 87
Flores, Juan, 45
flowers, symbolism of, 92–94, 95, 188
Foucault, Michel, 30
Freire, Paulo, 136
Friends from the Other Side (Anzaldúa), 72
futurities, 20, 38; Chicanafuturism, 211; Muñoz's frameworks, 209; power of, 218–19; in speculative fiction, 209–19

Galarte, Francisco J., 16, 32, 33–34, 189, 193n9
gaming. *See* video games
García, Antero, 143, 144n3
García, Magda, 15
García, Mia, 19, 43, 99–112
García Bedolla, Lisa, 28
Garcia McCall, Guadalupe, 180, 193n7
Garland-Thompson, Rosemarie, 102–3, 111
Garza, Adolfo, Jr., 43
Garza Villa, Jonny, 11
Gay Latino Studies (Martínez and Hames-García eds.), 15, 16, 62
Gaynor, Steve, 159n7
Generation Z: perspectives on reading, 137; and TikTok, 134
Gentleman's Guide to Getting Lucky, The (Lee), 42
Gentleman's Guide to Vice and Virtue, The (Lee), 42
ghosts in *Cemetery Boys*, 26, 31–34, 36–38

Gill-Peterson, Julian, 189
Giving Up the Ghost (Moraga), 46
Glissant, Édouard, 61, 203–4
Goin, Keara, 29
Gone Home (video game), 19–20, 148–53, 159
Gonzales, Rodolfo "Corky," 66
González, Christopher, 66–67
González, Emma, 10
González, Maya Christina, 57, 62, 71
González, Rigoberto, 7, 42, 71, 73
González, Tanya, 27
Good Reception (García), 143
Gordon, Joan, 211
Gottlieb, Andrew, 169
Gould, Deborah B., 199
graphic novels/comic books, 222–26; *Juliet Takes a Breath*, 70, 75–81
Grasshopper Jungle (Smith), 42
Grief Keeper, The (Villasante), 209–19
Grimm, Jacob and Wilhelm, 183
Grimm's Fairy Tales, 183
Grosse, Meghan, 143
Güido, Gibran, 15
Gulf Dreams (Pérez), 6

Hames-García, Michael, 15, 16, 62
Harry Potter series (Rowling), 137
Hartinger, Brent, 42
hate crimes: "interrupting hate," 139; violence against queer men, 7, 8
Hate Crimes Prevention Act (2009), 7
hate speech, 169–70
Hate U Give, The (film), 148
Hate U Give, The (Thomas), 10
Heart Has Its Reasons, The (Cart and Jenkins), 3
Heather Has Two Mommies (Newman), 64
Heidenreich, L., 8
Henry Ríos mystery book series, 6
Hermann-Wilmarth, Jill M., 64
Hernández, Ellie D., 15
Herrera, Cristina, 19, 75, 78–79, 99–112, 118, 148, 184–85, 223
heteronormativity: in Latinidad, 5, 25, 26, 31, 36, 46; resistance to, 56–57, 74,

171–72; as social construct, 37; trans men as threat to, 33; white, 75, 117, 121
Hinojosa Rebolledo, Esteban, 164, 171–74
Histories of the Transgender Child (Gill-Peterson), 189
History Is All You Left Me (Silvera), 44, 134
HIV. *See* AIDS crisis
Hoad, Catherine, 151
Hofmann, Stefan G., 213
Hollinger, Veronica, 211
home: as affirmative space, 74–75, 116; foster homes, 46–48
Homecoming Queers (Danielson), 15, 57
homelessness, 32, 46
"homonationalism," 70, 76
Honestly Ben (Konigsberg), 42
hooks, bell, 81
horror tropes, 150–51
Howe, Mark L., 212
How Pop Culture Shapes the Stages of a Woman's Life (Ames and Burcon), 192
Hudson, Renee, 219–20n2
Hunger Games series, 148
Hurley, Natasha, 181
hyperrealism, 10

identity formation: "ambivalent belonging," 59; bisexuality, 42; "coming out," 119–20, 123–24; and disability, 106–11; disidentification, 16, 38, 47, 182, 186–87, 200–201; family responses to queer, 163–76; individuation, 122–23; marginalized groups within Latinx community, 9; queer identity and futurity, 38; and queer kinship, 125–28; role of YA literature, 142; transgender identities, 189–90. *See also* intersectionality; marginalized identities; queer identity
imagination: and future, 211; and memory, 73; power of, 216, 218, 219
"in-between" spaces, 17, 47, 96
Inclinations (Cavarero), 130n5
individualism: contrasted with connection, 57, 125; and self-making, 62, 103, 118
Infinity Reaper (Silvera), 9, 134
Infinity Son (Silvera), 9, 43, 134

Infinity Son series (Silvera), 44
intersectionality, 10, 77, 79–80, 139, 165, 195, 198, 206, 217, 225
Islas, Arturo, 5, 202–3
It Sounds Like This (Meriano), 11
It's Our Prom (So Deal With It) (Peters), 42

Jenkins, Christine, 3, 14
Jiménez, Laura M., 21n14, 43, 217
Jiménez García, Marilisa, 14, 25, 43, 118, 140, 148, 149, 205
JROTC program, 152–53
Juhasz, Alexandra, 199
Juliet Takes a Breath (Rivera), 4, 10, 19, 42, 70, 75–81, 116–29
Just Your Local Bisexual Disaster (Mosqueda), 11

Kennedy, Melanie, 138
Kidd, Kenneth, 12–13, 14
kinship, queer models, 125–28, 129, 163–76. *See also* family structures
Kneen, Bonnie, 42, 52n6
Knott, Lauren M., 212
Kokkola, Lydia, 13
Konigsberg, Bill, 42
Kosciw, Joseph G., 42

La Bestia (The Train of Death), 156–57
Labyrinth Lost (Córdova), 10, 43
La Fountain-Stokes, Lawrence, 16
La Huesita (Santa Muerte), 34–36
Lakelore (McLemore), 9, 11, 95–96, 181
Lalama, Alexander, 18, 25–38
La Llorona (folkloric figure), 20, 180–92
La Llorona (Rodriguez and Stein), 180
Lambda Awards, 21n14, 195
"la naguala" (shapeshifter), 87–88
@lanjerry, 141
La Serenata (film), 18, 56, 57, 62–66
Latinx culture: Chicano nationalism, 5, 15; heteronormative expectations, 6; Latinidad, use of term, 52n2; pan-Latinidad, 29–30; in Silvera's work, 53n13. *See also* Chicanx community
Lebrón, Lolita, 124

Lee, Ariana, 169
Lee, Emery, 11
Lee, Mackenzi, 42
Lemus, Felicia Luna, 57
Lerer, Seth, 182
Lesbiana's Guide to Catholic School, The (Reyes), 11
Lessons in Disability (Stratman), 102, 103–4
Levithan, David, 42
LGBTQIA+ rights/legislation, 69
Life Is Strange 2 (video game), 19–20, 150, 153–59
Lima, Lázaro, 46, 51, 205
Lo, Malinda, 70, 72, 183
Lockhart, E., 137
Lopez, Bianca, 217
Lorde, Audre, 127
Los Angeles: barrios, 28–29; *Cemetery Boys*, 25–38
Love, Heather, 206
Loving in the War Years (Moraga), 5
Low, Low Woods, The (Machado), 224
Loya, Luis, 138, 140, 143
Loza, M. Roxana, 167, 176n3, 177n6, 200
Lugones, María, 15

Maas, Sarah J., 135
Machado, Carmen María, 222, 224–25
Mafi, Tahereh, 135
magical realism, 85–87, 92–93, 181, 193n3
Make Your Home Among Strangers (Crucet), 129
marginalized identities: Latinx people, 25, 27, 32–33, 76, 148; queer people, 70, 76. *See also* erasure; identity formation
Marie, Racquel, 11
Mariposa Club, The (González), 7, 42
Mariposa Gown, The (González), 7
mariposas, symbolism of, 63
Maroh, Jul, 225–26
marriage equality, 7
Martínez, Ernesto Javier, 15, 57, 62–65, 71
Martínez Feliciano, Jorge Gabriel, 62
Martínez-Reyes, Consuelo, 78, 80

masculinity: and heteronormativity, 31, 33–34, 129–30n2; toxic, 47, 59, 76, 78; for trans men, 33, 37
Mason, Derritt, 13, 14, 15, 148, 200
Mathieu, Jennifer, 159n6
Matos, Angel Daniel: on futurities, 17, 70, 174, 182, 210, 218–19; on gaming, 155; on queer identities, 43; on queer Latinx children, 36; on Sáenz, 8, 20, 21n13, 79, 166, 186, 195–207
Matousek, Amanda, 130n4
McCall, Garcia, 184
McGee, Chris, 104
McLemore, Anna-Marie, 4, 9, 11, 19, 20, 43, 85–96, 180–92
McRuer, Robert, 105
media studies, 133–44
Mejia, Tehlor Kay, 90, 181
memory: alteration surgery in *More Happy Than Not*, 10, 209; erasure, 212–14; and imagination, 73; rememory, 225
Meriano, Anna, 11
Merla-Watson, Cathryn Josefina, 27, 38n2, 211
Mesrobian, Carrie, 42
mestizaje, 29–30, 38n2
Meyer, Marissa, 183
Millán, Isabel, 18–19, 64, 70, 71–75
Miller, Jennifer, 70, 73, 80
Mills, Regina Marie, 19–20, 148–59
Minich, Julie Avril, 102, 103
Miranda, Joseph Isaac, 19, 116–29
Mirror Season, The (McLemore), 91–92, 181
Miskec, Jennifer, 104
Miss Meteor (McLemore and Mejia), 90, 181
Mitchell, David, 111–12
Mixquiahuala Letters, The (Castillo), 5
monsters, metaphor of, 27, 155
Montaño, Jesús, 20, 86, 163–76
Moraga, Cherríe, 5, 15, 16, 46, 57, 127–28, 163
More Happy Than Not (Silvera), 4, 9–10, 42, 44, 134, 209–19
Moreman, Shane T., 218

Morrison, Toni, 225
Moruzi, Kristine, 15
Moscote, Celia, 70, 75–80
Mosqueda, Andrea, 11
Moxie (Mathieu), 159n6
multimodal literacies, 144n3
Muñoz, José Esteban: on "Brown common," 125; *Cruising Utopia*, 87, 96, 219; disidentification, 16, 182, 187, 201; on "feeling Brown," 32, 45; on future utopias, 174; futurities, 209, 218; on in-betweenness, 17; influence of, 15; on queer worldmaking, 56–57; on reparative engagement, 198; on symbols of harm, 36

narrative perspectives, first vs. third person, 58, 64
Natov, Roni, 73
Nava, Michael, 6
Nepantla, 47, 96; queer kinship networks, 174–76
Nerds, Goths, Geeks, and Freaks (Boffone and Herrera), 4, 56, 148
Next of Kin (Rodriguez), 57, 123, 163
Niven, Jennifer, 137
nonbinary characters, 9, 11, 71, 224
nonbinary writers, 9, 10
Nuñez, Breena, 222

Obama, Barack, 7
Obejas, Achy, 6
Older, Daniel José, 20–21n4, 129
Olguín, B. V., 27, 211
Once Upon a Time (television series), 183
On Making Sense (Martínez), 57, 62
opacity, lens of, 61, 203–4, 205
Ophelia After All (Marie), 11
Orchard, William, 217
Ortega, Dave, 222
Ortiz, Ricardo L., 219–20n2
Ortiz Taylor, Sheila, 5
Oshiro, Mark, 10
Othering: and disability, 102; and erasure, 76; outsiderness, 4–5

Over the Rainbow (Abate and Kidd), 4, 12–13, 14

Palacio, Monica, 184
paranormal fiction, 10–11
Payne, Matthew, 149
Pearson, Wendy Gay, 211
Pedagogy of the Oppressed (Freire), 136
Peeren, Esther, 30
PEN America banned books report, 69
Pérez, Daniel Enrique, 15, 63, 167
Pérez, Domino Renee, 20, 142, 180–92
Pérez, Emma, 6, 66
Pérez, Gina M., 27, 152–53
Pérez, Héctor H., 66
Pérez-Torres, Rafael, 210
Performing Queer Latinidad (Rivera-Servera), 16
Perrault, Charles, 183
Peters, Julie Anne, 42
Phelps, Elizabeth A., 213
picture books: *Chablita's Heart* (Millán), 70, 71–75; with queer characters, 62–64
Poet X, The (Acevedo), 25
police brutality, 18, 26, 27, 30–31, 154
Ponbe, Sam, 175
popular culture: and disability tropes, 103, 105; fairy tales and women's lives, 183, 192; and queer community, 42
Post-Borderlandia (Cuevas), 171
Postma-Montaño, Regan, 20, 86, 163–76
Prietita and the Ghost Woman (Anzaldúa), 72, 184
"problem novels," 104–5
Puar, Jasbir, 70, 76
Puerto Rico/Puerto Rican culture, 76, 78–79, 118

Queer Anxieties of Young Adult Literature and Culture (Mason), 14, 15
queer identity: fathers and family relationships, 165–67; "queer horizontality," 125. *See also* identity formation

queer kinship networks, 125–28, 129; "Atravesando Nepantla," 163–76
Queer Latinidad (Rodríguez), 15
queer Latinx young adult literature (QLYA): graphic novels/comic books, 222–26; methodology of developing field, 12–18; overview, 5–12; as space of liberation, 17
queerness: definitions and outlines, 12–13; outsiderness, 4–5; queer Latinx theory, 15; repression and stigmatization, 13–14; as taboo, 6. *See also* erasure
queer theory, 5, 15–16
Queer Universes (Pearson et al.), 211
queer young adult (YA) literature: bisexuality, 42–43; clichéd themes, 3; gaps and need for diversity, 41–42, 69; growth of, 41; queer worldmaking, 56–67; scholarship on, 4
Quijano, Augusto, 157

Rae, Addison, 137
Rainbow Boys series (Sanchez), 7, 14, 42
Rainbow High (Sanchez), 7
Rainbow Road (Sanchez), 7
Rain God, The (Islas), 5, 202–3
Ramírez, Catherine S., 211
Reading Chican@ Like a Queer (Soto), 15–16
realism: hyperrealism, 10. *See also* magical realism
Red Riding Hood (film), 183
Representing the Rainbow in Young Adult Literature (Jenkins and Cart), 4, 14–15
Research on Diversity in Youth Literature (journal), 70, 210
Resolutions, The (García), 19, 43, 99–112
respiration, metaphor of, 123–28
Reyes, Erick, 141
Reyes, Sonora, 11
Reynolds, Kimberley, 18
Rhodes, Cristina, 19, 20, 85–96, 101, 167, 198, 206, 209–19
Rice-González, Charles, 4, 42
Riot Grrrl movement, 150–52, 153, 159n6
Rivera, Gabby, 4, 10, 19, 42, 116–17, 222; *Juliet Takes a Breath*, 70, 75–81

Rivera, Lysa, 218
Rivera Montes, Zorimar, 61
Rivera-Servera, Ramón H., 16
Road, Cristy C., 222
Robertson, Norman Campbell, 202
Rodriguez, Emilio, 46
Rodríguez, Juana María, 15, 17, 204
Rodriguez, Patty, 180
Rodríguez, Richard T., 15, 46–47, 57, 123, 163, 166
Rodríguez, Sonia Alejandra, 19, 69–82, 172
Romeo and Juliet (Shakespeare), 85–86
Romo, Richard, 28
Rosario, Vernon, 26
Ruberg, Bonnie, 149, 155
Ruehlicke, Andrea, 137

Sáenz, Benjamin Alire, 4, 5, 7, 8–9, 20, 25; absence of AIDS crisis in series, 195–207; *Aristotle and Dante Discover the Secrets of the Universe*, 164–67, 223
Saint Jude, 34–35
Salcedo, Jacoby, 222
Saldívar, Ramón, 164
Sánchez, Alex, 4–5, 7, 14, 42, 43, 222–23, 225–26
Sanchez, Donaciano, 202
Sanchez, Julissa, 217
Sandoval Sánchez, Alberto, 203
San Filippo, Maria, 47–48
Santa Muerte, 34–36
Schalk, Sami, 211
Schmitz, Rachel M., 217
science fiction, 211–12
Sedgwick, Eve Kosofsky, 198
serenata tradition, 63–65
Sexual Futures, Queer Gestures, and Other Latina Longings (Rodríguez), 15
Sexuality in Literature for Children and Young Adults (Moruzi and Venzo), 15
Shadowshaper (Older), 129
shapeshifters, 87–88
Shepard, Matthew, 7, 8
Side by Side (Jiménez García), 118
Sifuentes-Jáuregui, Ben, 200

Silence = Death slogan, 199, 200–201
Silvera, Adam, 4, 9–10, 19, 42, 43; *They Both Die at the End*, 41–52, 133–44
Smedley, Zack, 42
Smith, Andrew, 42
Snyder, Sharon, 111–12
social media. *See* BookTok; TikTok; Twitter
Sombras en el arcoíris (Brozon), 164, 165, 168–71
Soto, Sandra K., 16
speculative fiction, 9–10, 38n2, 86, 211–12
Stein, Arla, 180
Stockton, Kathryn Bond, 121, 149, 159
Stone, Nic, 10
Stonewall Awards, 21n14, 70, 181
storytelling traditions, 181–82; European vs. Chicanx, 182–83. *See also* fairy tales
Stratman, Jacob, 102, 103–4
Stuelke, Patricia, 205, 206
Summer of the Mariposas (Garcia and McCall), 180, 184
Swimming While Drowning (Rodriguez), 46
symbols and signs: clothing, 152–53; flowers, 92–94, 95, 188; of harm, 36–37; mariposas, 63; of masculinity, 33

Tannert-Smith, Barbara, 104
television, queer characters, 6, 42, 47–48, 52n4
Terrorist Assemblages (Puar), 76
They Both Die at the End, The (Silvera), 9–10, 19, 41–52, 133–44; BookTok, 139–43
This Bridge Called My Back (Moraga), 15, 127
This Is Why They Hate Us (Aceves), 11
Thomas, Aiden, 10–11, 18; *Cemetery Boys*, 25–38
Thomas, Angie, 10
Throw (Degollado), 180
TikTok, 134–44; BookTok, 11; Straight TikTok vs. Queer TikTok, 138
Tommy Stands Alone (Velásquez), 6, 41, 222
Tommy Stands Tall (Velásquez), 6
Toomey, Russell B., 216–17
Torres, Justin, 57, 129
Torres, Vanessa L., 11

toxic masculinity, 47, 59, 76, 78
trans community: Black trans people, 21n5; trans men and masculinity, 33
transformation: childhood as time of, 87; in *Juliet Takes a Breath*, 79–80; queer bodies, 95–96; in *The Weight of Feathers*, 86; whole-body metamorphosis, 87–90; in *Wild Beauty*, 93–95
Translocas (La Fountain-Stokes), 16
transmedia, 144n3
Transmovimientos (Hernández et al.), 15
transphobia, 7, 11, 12, 21nn5–6, 31, 35, 139, 225
Trites, Roberta Seelinger, 13–14, 104–5, 111, 186–87
Trujillo, Carla, 15
Trujillo, Josh, 222
Trump era, 157, 159
Tulloch, Rowan, 151
Turning Pointe, The (Torres), 11
Twitter, 133–34
Tyler Johnson Was Here (Coles), 10

Vanderhoef, Jeff, 149
Velásquez, Gloria, 6, 222
Velez, Ivan, 222
Venzo, Paul, 15
video games, 19–20, 148–59; "walking simulators," 149–50
Villa, Raúl, 28
Villareal, Alberto, 175
Villasante, Alexandra, 209, 214–15
violence: antiqueer, 36; and coming-of-age narratives, 176n4; familial, 170; against queer men, 7, 8

"walking simulators," 149–50
Wargo, Jon Michael, 13, 17, 36, 70, 137, 139, 174, 198, 210
Wayward Witch (Córdova), 10
We Came All the Way from Cuba So You Could Dress Like This? (Obejas), 6
Weight of Feathers, The (McLemore), 85–86, 181
We the Animals (film), 18, 56, 57–62
We the Animals (Torres), 57, 61–62, 129

We Were Liars (Lockhart), 137
What If It's Us (Silvera and Albertalli), 44, 134
When the Moon Was Ours (McLemore), 9, 20, 86, 88–89, 92–93, 180–92
white supremacy, 8, 14, 18
Wickham, Anastasia, 104
Wild Beauty (McLemore), 43, 86, 93–95, 181
Will & Grace (television program), 6
With Her Machete in Her Hand (Esquibel), 15, 72
writing process: as activism, 51; as healing, 72; and self-making, 57

Yo Soy Joaquin/I Am Joaquin (Gonzales), 66
You Brought Me the Ocean (Sanchez), 225–26
Young, Helen, 151

Zagar, Jeremiah, 57
Zamora, Lois Parkinson, 86
Zepeda, Monica, 11
Zimonja, Karla, 151, 160n9

Printed in the United States
by Baker & Taylor Publisher Services